Riding the Wind with Liezi

列子

SUNY series in Chinese Philosophy and Culture
Roger T. Ames, editor

Riding the Wind with Liezi

列子

New Perspectives on the Daoist Classic

Edited by
Ronnie Littlejohn
and
Jeffrey Dippmann

SUNY PRESS

Published by State University of New York Press, Albany

Printed in the United States of America

For information, contact State University of New York Press, Albany, NY
www.sunypress.edu

Production by Ryan Morris
Marketing by Anne M. Valentine

Library of Congress Cataloging-in-Publication Data
Riding the wind with Liezi : new perspectives on the Daoist classic / edited by
Ronnie Littlejohn and Jeffrey Dippmann.
p. cm. — (SUNY series in Chinese philosophy and culture)
Includes bibliographical references.
ISBN 978-1-4384-3456-8 (paperback : alk. paper)
ISBN 978-1-4384-3455-1 (hardcover : alk. paper) 1. Liezi, 4th cent. B.C. Liezi.
I. Littlejohn, Ronnie, 1949– II. Dippmann, Jeffrey Walter. III. Title:
New perspectives on the Daoist classic.
BL1900.L485R53 2011
299.5'1482—dc22

2010031922

10 9 8 7 6 5 4 3 2 1

Contents

Applying the Teachings of the Liezi

Acknowledgments

As co-editors, we would like to express our thanks and deep gratitude to each of this volume's contributors. Without their patience and enthusiastic support of this project, it would have never seen fruition. We wish to thank Roger Ames in particular for his steadfast encouragement and wise counsel throughout the entire process, from conception to publication. In addition, we need to express our appreciation for the community of friends and scholars that we have come to cherish through the Asian Studies Development Program, and the Association of Regional Centers. Both organizations owe their inception to the work of Roger, Peter Hershock, and Betty Buck, and their members have been stalwart supporters and in some cases contributors to this anthology.

I want to express my deep gratitude to Jeff Dippmann for his friendship and deep commitment to our project in this book, and to the many contributors who allowed us to bring their new work on *Liezi* into the ongoing conversation about Daoism. As always, my thanks and affection goes out to my family and colleagues who inspire me to follow the Dao.

I would like to personally thank Ronnie Littlejohn for his unwavering friendship and support throughout this process, and can never fully express my gratitude for all that he did to ensure the success of this volume. Most importantly, my thanks to my loving wife Cheri, and children Angela, Brooks, David, and Jennifer, whose unfailing support, encouragement and advice made this volume possible.

列子
Introduction

Roger T. Ames

The *Liezi* as a text seems almost as elusive as Liezi the historical person. The *Liezi* is associated with perhaps the most mystical of all the Daoist adepts who surfaces here and there in the philosophical literature only to ride elsewhere on the winds. What *Liezi* was originally as a text we do not know, but as it has been received, it is a compendium of hyperbolic anecdotes, seemingly paradoxical aphorisms, and curious parables, an anthology that ranges as far and as wide as the winds blow, that loses its reader in a wild world of unfathomable change and indeterminacy, and that quite literally makes a great deal out of nothing. Like most of the Daoist texts, the *Liezi* is normative, recommending a way of being in this world that presumably enables the willing adept to make the most of the human experience.

This present volume is a long-overdue collection of seminal essays on this most curious *Liezi*, one of the most understudied texts in the classical Chinese corpus. Rather than being read for what it is, *Liezi* has often been disrespected if not dismissed in the historical scholarship because of what it is not. In sum, then, this present volume contests this unfortunate situation. It begins from the recognition that most if not all of the classical Chinese philosophical texts are suspicious in their origins and as such, are other than what they purport to be. Setting aside the problem of "authenticity" as an only marginally relevant question, this set of essays provides a multidimensional argument for the historical, literary, and philosophical importance of this document by an assembly of some of our finest interpreters of the classical Chinese literature. These scholars certainly embrace the now seemingly incontrovertible evidence against the traditional pre-Qin dating of this text, but on other more compelling grounds, they also insist on reevaluating and indeed reinstating its philosophical and historical worth.

It is entirely appropriate that the opening section of this anthology—a critical discussion of the *Liezi* as a text—begin with a series of essays that engage and make use of Angus Graham's the "Date and Composition of the *Lieh-Tzu* [*Liezi*]." Although not included in this volume, Graham's essay is seminal, and is appropriately rehearsed here to remind us of the ground on which these new essays are constructed. Graham's essay opens by reporting on the ambivalence that Western and Japanese sinologists have had to the unwavering opinion of their Chinese counterparts that the *Liezi* is a spurious document (*weishu* 僞書) dating from the Wei-Jin period in the late fourth century CE. Indeed, it was this groundbreaking essay of Graham's that effectively turned the tide on this resistance, and brought world sinology into firm agreement that the present *Liezi* far from being that eight-chapter text listed in a Han dynasty bibliography is in fact a later and a most deliberate forgery.

Graham's essay is comprehensive. He provides a list of passages from the *Liezi* that overlap with other Han and pre-Han texts that in sum run to approximately one quarter of the entire document. Loading the charge of his arguments by invoking various forms of grammatical evidence and textual devices, Graham demonstrates persuasively that by and large, this portion of the *Leizi* as we have it today was compiled by copying directly from earlier sources. Having thus retained the grammatical features of these original documents, this borrowed portion of the text has all the markings of an earlier age. As argued further in the essay by Ronnie Littlejohn below, what complicates the picture somewhat is that where *Liezi* copies from the *Zhuangzi* as its major source, it is a different, fuller, and perhaps better redaction of the *Zhuangzi* than we have available to us today. Again, another interesting observation that Graham makes with respect to the origins of this text is that the compilers of the *Liezi* seem to have scoured the early corpus for any reference to the person Liezi, and to have included all of these passages herein regardless of their length, importance, or overall consistency.

Having explained the nature and the origins of the copied portions of the *Liezi*, Graham then turns to a detailed linguistic analysis of the remaining three quarters of the text, applying the best of our current understanding of the evolution of classical Chinese grammatical patterns and usages. Demonstrating that the language of this substantial portion of the *Liezi* is largely homogeneous, this philological evidence can then be added to other anachronistic historical and literary allusions to claim fairly that this larger portion of the text is of a fourth-century Wei-Jin period vintage. Such then are Graham's conclusions.

Tim Barrett in his contribution to this anthology provides us with a history of how the *Liezi* has been read across the centuries. "Reading the *Liezi*: The First Thousand Years" carries us back to the earlier days of the *Liezi* when its readers would be confronted with a very different, much more complex experience. Each passage of this syncretic work would certainly invoke in a literate reader intricate allusions to other familiar works on their library shelves. But further, assumed by its reader to be a transmitted original in the tradition of the *Laozi* and *Zhuangzi*, the lines of the *Liezi* themselves became increasingly honeycombed by a persistent yet always evolving commentarial tradition that sought to authorize the fluid intellectual, social, and political machinations of the times. Barrett locates the widespread readings of this increasingly nested Daoist text within the changing material, commentarial, and intellectual culture of early and middle China. He registers the contributions made by an invested company of literati and bibliographers who each in his own unique way sought to perpetuate the aggregating legacy of a living *Liezi*. Indeed, it is this much "appreciated" *Liezi* that has been bequeathed to us today for our own further interrogation and enjoyment.

In "The *Liezi*'s Use of the Lost *Zhuangzi*," Ronnie Littlejohn continues Barrett's narrative in rehearsing the complex textual history of the *Liezi*, and in so doing, brings new light to the notion of textual "overlap" by focusing on a possible relationship between the received *Liezi* and the lost passages from a much longer *Zhuangzi*. This no longer extant, fifty-two chapter version of the *Zhuangzi* was edited into its shorter, received form by Guo Xiang (d. 312). Taking chapter 2 of the *Liezi* as his case in point, Littlejohn provides the reader with one sample of the nine passages that overlap between the *Liezi* and the existing *Zhuangzi*, showing the remarkable degree of correspondence between these two texts. Building on this evidence, the sleuthing Littlejohn is able to demonstrate persuasively that beyond the identifiable *Liezi* "overlap" we are able to piece together an additional substantial portion of text that probably belongs to the unexpurgated *Zhuangzi*. What distinguishes this "recovered" text and what might well have been Guo Xiang's rationale in deleting it from his edited thirty-three chapter version of the *Zhuangzi* is the persistent theme of extraordinary powers owned by the Daoist masters. Reflexively, having discovered that Guo Xiang in his editorial work has "rationalized" this seminal Daoist source in some discernible way, Littlejohn on this basis encourages a speculative reassessment of our own tradition. That is, we might be prompted to reconsider the possibility of rehabilitating lost "embarrassing" dimensions of some of our early Greek philosophers. Littlejohn's detective work is not only enabling in achieving a more nuanced reading of the *Liezi* text itself, but further underscores the indelible worth of a document that has often been deprecated as a "spurious" work.

In the next essay, May Sim asks the question "Is the *Liezi* an Encheiridion?"—that is, is it a manual on how to live the good life? Using both Epictetus and the *Liezi*, Sim finds some compelling similarities between the Stoics and the *Liezi*'s Daoism on how to think about living well. Both of them insist that there are large aspects of the human experience over which we exercise little or no control, and yet at the same time, neither of them recommends passivity or withdrawal. On Sim's reading, both *Liezi* and Stoicism assume that the conditions of our lives are predetermined and that there is no way for us to change the world around us. Where they differ is that Stoicism promises us freedom, happiness, and tranquility if we comport ourselves according to the ordering of the world as it has been decreed by the gods—an ordering that is recommended to us as the best of all worlds by virtue of its origins in the best judgments of the gods. For the Stoics, the light of reason illumines a way for us because it is consonant with the rational order of the universe. *Liezi* on the other hand offers no such succor in following the indeterminate primordial simplicity, or *dao*, which is itself a mixture of perceptible order and inescapable chaos. Indeed, the *dao* is itself the alternation between joy and sorrow, life and death, and our best path is to achieve a kind of genuine knowledge of the process by resisting distinctions such as outer and inner, self and world, pleasure and pain. Indeed the sage through a comprehensive knowledge of the primordial indeterminate "nothing" is able to know everything and to achieve a balance and harmony—a virtuosic posture of *wuwei*—that allows for productive transactions with everything that constitutes the world of experience. Although there are commonalities between *Liezi*'s Daoism and Stoicism, the differences are substantial and reflect fundamentally different ways of living in the world. While Stoicism provides us with Epictetus's *Encheiridion*, the vagaries and paradoxes of Daoism will not accommodate such a rationalization of the good life.

John Berthrong thinks through what "process" might mean cosmologically in his essay, "Torches of Chaos and Doubt: Themes of Process and Transformations in the *Liezi* 列子." He explores the signature themes of generativity, transformation, growth, and the spontaneous emergence of novelty in the early Daoist cosmology that is much in evidence in the *Liezi*. Locating the *Liezi* historically as it is being transported on the road to the south in the troubled times of early-fourth-century Wei-Jin China, he argues that the actual survival and subsequent influence of this eclectic text is an object lesson in its own message: that is, the pursuit of harmony amid chaos, and the achievement of a productive spontaneity in the midst of ceaseless flux. Building upon the insights of our best sinologists, Berthrong searches the *Liezi* itself to make explicit the particular features of the Daoist process cosmology, summoning persistent Zhuangzian expressions of ceaseless change as made explicit in the vocabulary of "generativity" (*sheng* 生), "transformation" (*hua* 化), "reform" (*gai* 改), "propensity" (*shi* 勢), "alternations of shape" (*bian* 變), "primal change"(*yi* 易), "spontaneity" (*ziran* 自然), and implicated in the very notion of *qi* 氣 itself. Berthrong allows the text to speak for itself in his explication of a montage of passages that are dedicated to the theme of process, a sensibility that is sedimented into an extraordinary range of its images and metaphors such as water, the echo, the mirror, the infinite, and so on. In thus making these grounding cosmological assumptions explicit, Berthrong is able to provide the reader with the interpretive context necessary to take the *Liezi* on its own terms.

In Thomas Michael's contribution to this volume, he explores the intricacies of early Chinese cosmology and thus follows Berthrong in attempting to provide a broad context for a nuanced reading of the *Liezi*. Beginning from the Western philosophical and religious narrative, Michael surveys the importance of the notions of "God" and "Truth" as foundational concepts that have had a defining force on setting both the cultural boundary of the Western narrative and its frontier, too. In so doing, "God" and "Truth" have provided both "closure" and "challenge" to the evolving human experience. By way of contrast, in early China, it was the protean notion of *dao* as first consolidated in the seminal works of Confucianism and Daoism—the *Analects* and the *Daodejing* respectively—that became the foundational concept for the growth of Chinese culture. The reference to *dao* in these early works ranges from cultural to cosmogonic significance—from *dao* as a specific way of thinking and living in the world to *dao* as a primordial source of all that is. In the absence of any strict sense of transcendence and the dualism such transcendence entails, the early Han sources were able to negotiate the gap between these two different meanings of *dao* and establish them on a "this-worldly" continuum. Although we must not elide the significant differences between the notions of *dao* and *God*, we can still allow that *dao* served the early Daoist tradition as both closure and challenge, as both a specific image of the divine source of things, and as something bottomless and ineffable that challenges the limits of human thought. Although it has been resolved that the *Liezi* is a work of a much later vintage, Michael argues persuasively that broadly speaking, and particularly in its various allusions to "*tai* 太" cosmogony and the cosmogonic *dao*, this composite text is a more genuine expression of ideas found in the seminal Daoist texts than the interpretations offered by the later commentators such as Wang Bi, Heshanggong, and Guo Xiang.

P. J. Ivanhoe in his essay explores a quality of "unselfconsciousness" in thought and conduct as a hard-won achievement characteristic of classical Chinese thinkers broadly, but particularly in evidence in the Daoist anecdotes of the *Liezi*. Beginning by identifying three modalities of unselfconsciousness that facilitate knowing, doing, and being—that is, that assist in our understanding, in our actions, and in our state of mind—Ivanhoe then turns to reconstruct the seemingly persistent value of overcoming a preoccupation with oneself. In the process, he makes a distinction between two senses of unselfconsciousness: a modest and limited *everyday* sense that makes daily life easier, and an achieved *religious* unselfconsciousness that we might aspire to—an ultimate ideal of selflessness that is the result of being able to identify oneself utterly with the patterns of the cosmos. From a careful analysis of passages from the *Liezi* and stories about the person Liezi in the *Zhuangzi*, Ivanhoe is able to provide examples of these three felicitous modes of unselfconsciousness, and then to show how there is a demystifying continuum to be found between the everyday sense of developing unselfconsciousness, and the demanding yet elusive religious sense of unselfconsciousness as an ultimate goal. To the extent that unselfconsciousness is ever achieved, it is this religious sense as an ultimate ideal that suffuses all of one's knowing, one's actions, and one's dispositions as a fully consummate way of life. It is, however, the ideal that the religious sense shares with the more prosaic sense of unselfconsciousness that allows for an appreciation of its basic value.

In "Reading the *Zhuangzi* in *Liezi*: Redefining *Xian*ship," Jeffrey Dippmann challenges the conventional wisdom that would site the *Liezi* as an elite, philosophical text fundamentally impatient with the religious upheaval of fourth century China. Dippmann argues vigorously for a continuity between the anecdotes of the *Liezi* and the magico-religious practices of sectarian Daoism. He claims that not only does the *Liezi* seem to accept the cultivation of miraculous powers and the concomitant pursuit of immortality associated with the shamanistic tradition, but it also attempts to read the appropriated portions of the *Zhuangzi* as fundamentally sympathetic to its own religious aspirations after "*xian*ship" or immortality. This claim raises an interesting question that is not lost on Dippmann, and that would bring the two editors of this volume—Dippmann and Littlejohn—into dialogue. Recalling that Guo Xiang's principle of expurgation in editing the *Zhuangzi* seems to have been the editing out of those passages that would ascribe magical powers to the Daoist masters, are we in fact given access to an original *Zhuangzi* that was itself sympathetic to such religious Daoist practices (Littlejohn's thesis)? Or alternatively, does the *Liezi* "reread" the appropriated *Zhuangzi* passages to make them consistent with the shamanistic practices of sectarian Daoism (Dippmann's position)? In either case, the *Liezi* does seem to at least endorse if not even advocate a practicable Daoism that would resist the contention that it is antagonistic to the religious dimensions of this tradition.

Livia Kohn's essay, "Body and Identity," is the first foray in the final and more pragmatic section of this volume entitled

"Applying the Teachings of the *Liezi*." Kohn begins by registering the resonances between the holistic and integrative assumptions of traditional Chinese medicine and the Daoist understanding of the lived body—itself a concentration of vital *qi*-energies—as the locus of personal growth and spiritual transformation. Because the body lies at both the beginning and at the end of the process of recovering our primordial state, somatic practices and a nuanced bodily regimen are integral to the Daoist aspirations to attain pure spirituality and personal longevity. An analysis of the *Liezi* as a seminal Daoist text provides insights into the Daoist conception of the body and its role in a complex range of cultivation practices. Kohn uses the language of the contrasting *adaptive* and the *transformative* functions of the body to explain the more passive and the more active roles that the body must play in the *Liezi*'s account of the ultimate accommodation sought between the outer and the inner landscapes. Not only do Daoist practitioners seek to become one with *dao*, but they also seek to have access to and a guiding hand in what emerges from its creative core.

Daoist philosophy is generally assumed to be a kind of naturalism in which the cosmic patterns and natural order are taken as models for human action, and in which artificial and contrived activity is dismissed as an obstruction to the consummate human experience. However, in "I, Robot: Self as Machine in the *Liezi*," Jeffrey L. Richey explores two strange tales from the *Liezi* that seem to celebrate artifice and contrivance. The first is an anecdote sited in the Zhou court of King Mu who is historically renowned for his Daoist associations. A humanoid figure entertains and then awes the King and his entourage. The second story describes a machine-like person whose actions are wholly lacking in any degree of self-awareness. With respect to the first anecdote, by first identifying the allusions that this story of an automaton might be making to the Chinese domestic and Buddhist corpus, Richey then speculates on its many possible implications without advancing any one in particular, leaving it up to his readers to make their own best choice. The second story is repeated from *The Book of the Yellow Emperor* that describes the superlative human being in terms that associate the conduct of this figure with cyborgs. Richey finds some points of comparison between the restorative function of a cyborg and the various strategies for personal cultivation offered by the early Chinese corpus. Perhaps the most intriguing speculation that these stories bring to mind is the resistance Daoist philosophy has to allowing human beings any special status in their interactions with the rest of the myriad things. Recalling the essay of P. J. Ivanhoe above, these texts are uniformly suspicious of those deliberate and self-conscious qualities that ostensibly set the human being apart from other things.

In "Dancing with Yinyang: The Art of Emergence," Robin R. Wang rehearses an anecdote from the *Liezi* that offers a distinction between the diagnosis for an illness available from three different kinds of doctors—the "common doctor" (*zhongyi* 眾醫) who focuses on the environment alone, the "good doctor" (*liangyi* 良醫) who focuses only on the medical history of the patient, and the "divine doctor" (*shenyi* 神醫) who prescribes the cultivation of the life force itself. In exploring the vocabulary of this life force, Wang tries to bring some nuance and sophistication to our understanding of the familiar and yet still opaque vocabulary of *yinyang*: the oscillating and rhythmic movement of an autogenerative *qi* 氣, its inexhaustible process of generation and transformation (*hua* 化), the calibrational and proportional (*zhi* 質) aspects of *qi*, the emerging patterns of its interaction (*jiao* 交) and the quality of its responsiveness (*ganying* 感應). Using recent advances in biology as her inspiration, Wang argues that although a now familiar "correlative" vocabulary respects the transformational nature of the *qi* process, the emergent and consummatory character of *qi* requires that we move from a binary to a trinary way of describing Chinese cosmology, and from a correlative to a trinary model in our thinking about it. Indeed, we need to understand the trinary nature of *qi* in order to appreciate the prescription of the "divine doctor" (*shenyi*): that is, to abjure medication and simply cultivate your life force.

In "How to Fish like a Daoist," Erin M. Cline uses a careful comparison of an anecdote from the *Liezi* with the Butcher Ding story in the *Zhuangzi* to develop a more complex and sophisticated understanding of a major theme in Daoist philosophy, the notion of "effortless action" (*wuwei* 無爲). It is this modality of activity that enables the Daoist fisherman Zhan He to comport himself effortlessly and unselfconsciously, and in so doing, to accord spontaneously with the natural circumstances as they unfold—that is, to follow the rhythms of nature in returning to the unadulterated *dao* 道. A persistent cosmological claim found in the *Liezi* is that all creatures are part of the same whole, and that skill in living in the world emerges from a cultivated respect for an inclusive, symbiotic relationship with nature. It is this sense of the oneness of nature with the human experience that distinguishes the Daoist from the anthropocentric Confucians. In comparing the fisherman Zhan He story with the *Zhuangzi*'s Butcher Ding, Cline remarks on how both of these exemplars describe in detail the long process of cultivating their *wuwei* state of mind. Beyond the more obvious commonalities here, however, an additional comparison with the *Daodejing* brings into focus a contrast between the supple, flexible quality of the natural objects out of which the fisherman's gear has been shaped, and the sharp, penetrating character of the butcher's chopper. This difference between the *Daodejing* and the *Zhuangzi* is magnified in the repeated association that the *Daodejing* makes between *wuwei* and effective social and political leadership (*de* 德), an association not to be found in a *Zhuangzi* text that seems oblivious to political responsibility as a desired outcome of an achieved *wuwei* relationality.

In the closing essay of this volume, David Jones illustrates the Daoist theme of "returning" by using the *Liezi* to reverse the gravity of the human experience. Rather than celebrating the putatively numinous and abstract, the *Liezi* rehabilitates the body and locates the human life within the complexity of our much maligned and all too often denigrated physical experience. In "When Butterflies Change into Birds: Life and Death in the *Liezi*," Jones argues that the *Liezi* has a unique contribution to make to some of the major themes of the classical Daoist literature—in particular, an appreciation of the emergent and evolutionary nature of change, and of the inseparability of life and death. While these themes are certainly present in the other Daoist texts, the virtue of the *Liezi* is the accessibility and consistency of its accounts of them. The *Liezi* offers us straightforward and explicit counsel on the most profound of life's vagaries.

Jones cites at length and analyzes in detail the *Liezi* passage that provides a vivid account of the organic and interdependent nature of species transformation in the living world where the life of one creature emerges from the death of another. In this spontaneous, autogenerative process there is no guiding hand or grand teleology to lead the way, and no special value ascribed to the human form. Being human is no more than just one among many of *qi*'s diverse phases. Perhaps the most compelling wisdom of this *Liezi* text is captured in the Daoist notion of returning: that is, to go down and to go back. In the *Liezi* we have an exhortation to abandon our arrogance and superiority both as individuals and as a species, to cultivate of an unselfconscious humility in how we live our lives, and to return to nature by comporting ourselves as one modest aspect in an organic whole.

With this substantial collection of essays, a new opportunity emerges to re-engage the *Liezi* and to find overlooked dimensions of Daoist philosophy. Perhaps the most important contribution of this anthology is a reasoned argument that puts any lingering doubts about this text into proper context, and in so doing, that reasserts the proper place of the *Liezi* in the Daoist canons.

The Liezi Text

列子

Reading the *Liezi*

The First Thousand Years

T. H. Barrett

Whatever its origins, the *Liezi* is undeniably a book that can speak to us today, as the essays collected in this volume will testify in their different ways. Yet equally we can be quite sure that the way in which we read it today—especially if we read it as translated into a language other than Classical Chinese—is nothing like the way in which it was read throughout most of its existence. This is not just a matter of the meaning of the text itself. Let us assume for sake of argument that its meaning can and has been translated perfectly, by A. C. Graham or by whichever translator is our particular favourite. Our reading experience will still be quite radically unlike that of most of our predecessors, for one simple reason. We can concentrate on the *Liezi* itself and read it "like a book." Paradoxically, most of our predecessors never had that option, since for them thoughts of other books would have obtruded constantly, pushing them to make linkages that we can remain blissfully ignorant of for as long as we like. And these interruptions would have troubled not only the erudite reader, the virtuoso who like Graham could point to the overlaps between the text of the *Liezi* and more than a score of other early works.[1] For from the start the *Liezi* was scarcely ever read without the commentary of Zhang Zhan, the man who introduced it to a wider readership in the late fourth century from its supposed preservation within the resources of his family. And Zhang himself finishes his introduction to the *Liezi* after drawing attention to its parallels with Buddhist sources in general with a short list of more specific Chinese overlaps—some of them now invisible to us because of the disappearance of the works to which he refers—besides pointing to a fair few more in the course of his commentary, which is further expanded by citations from commentaries or other works on these related texts. Again, the list of such references, which by no means coincides with those given by Graham, involves the reader in the consideration of something like a couple of dozen other titles.[2]

As it happens, Zhang does not simply cite other books when the overlapping of text between the *Liezi* and some other work triggers the need for comment; he quotes both *Zhuangzi* and *Laozi* without such prompting on occasion, and also such later individuals as the Wei period writer Xiahou Xuan (209–254).[3] It is, however, the commentary he cites on the overlapping materials that offers the most intriguing prospects for research. At one point, for example, Zhang quotes lost commentary from Xiang Xiu on a lost passage of the *Zhuangzi*.[4] Xiang's commentary is listed in our sources as having covered less of the *Zhuangzi* than that of his more prominent successor Guo Xiang, the earliest substantially surviving commentator.[5] But if the current state of Guo Xiang's commentary represents its original extent, this fragment of material points to a clear difference in textual judgement between them. Conversely, probably only a thorough textual comparison between Guo as quoted by Zhang and the surviving text of his work would be able to show us if what we now have is not the totality of his commentary.[6]

What is striking, then, about Zhang's commentary is its bibliographical richness. Though Zhang was by no means the first Chinese scholar to make a point of displaying his erudition in writing, he is certainly the earliest—or one of the earliest—surviving commentators to cite other named texts and authors explicitly on such a scale, setting a trend that was soon to be taken up with a vengeance by yet more assiduous workers.[7] Why did this development take place? One can readily appreciate that Zhang Zhan wished to stress the opulence of his family library, if only to support his claims about the origins of the *Liezi*—though his documentation of its ties with other works does expose him to the analysis by Graham and others of the work's composition out of a variety of separate sources. But to this may we not add another, more purely technological reason? By this stage, as research has shown, paper was coming into its own as a writing material, and one of its great advantages over wooden slips for the majority who could not afford silk was the rapidity and smoothness with which a text could be unrolled for more convenient consultation. This feature was indeed already remarked upon in the late third century.[8] Once the bulk of surviving literature had been transferred to this format, allusion or citation from memory could be replaced where necessary by direct textual comparison, linking text and text more firmly and more readily than had been the case before.

The *Liezi,* moreover, does not simply emerge into the light of day with this extra textual baggage strapped to it. The new technology also ensured that it could readily be transmitted in this way. Only in the Ming, when the intellectual environment encouraged the direct confrontation of reader and text, did the *Liezi* briefly appear in editions without any commentary attached, and although otherwise from the Song period Zhang's work was sometimes removed so that another commentary could be substituted, for the most part the knowledge packaged in his commentary was cumulated with later work—a phenomenon that can certainly be already observed in the mid-eighth century. The commentary of Lu Chongxuan, our earliest after that of Zhang Zhan, survives in the Taoist Canon as cumulated together with both Zhang's work and two later commentaries of Song date.[9] It is more easily consulted in reproductions of its Qing edition, where the editor, Qin Enfu (1760–1843) has disentangled it from its fellows and prints it alone, together with his own observations. This, however, results in a somewhat artificial creation, since Lu refers directly to Zhang Zhan's commentary in several places, suggesting that he was adding his own remarks to a manuscript with those of Zhang already present. This even includes one place where, as Qin points out, the text given for Zhang's remarks has subsequently disappeared from all other editions.[10]

Lu's second reference to Zhang is in fact highly antagonistic, which is not surprising, since the function of his commentary was a rather different one, as a glance at the background to his work makes clear. As Qin first noted, Lu appears in the *Xin Tang shu* listed as the younger brother (evidently very much younger brother) of Lu Cangyong, a writer and statesman who had died in 713 and who is now chiefly remembered for having tried to persuade the greatest Taoist leader of his day to pursue his life as a hermit as close to the capital as possible.[11] But Lu Chongxuan's official title, and even more precisely the title whereby he refers to the emperor, places the composition of his work late in the reign of Xuanzong, specifically in the period 739–742. In 741 the emperor launched upon a number of measures designed to establish an alternative Taoist curriculum for the imperial examinations, and the *Liezi* is mentioned more than once as having been involved in these measures.[12] What was clearly required for the text, if it was to become a part of Xuanzong's ideological schemes for educating his bureaucrats, was a commentary rereading the fourth-century thinking of Zhang Zhan so that his outlook was made compatible with the much more Buddhism-influenced, religious Taoist outlook of the Tang ruling house—in short, something like the seventh-century sub-commentary of Cheng Xuanying on the *Zhuangzi,* which was plainly intended to mitigate the less religious outlook of the indispensable Guo Xiang.[13]

It is this that Lu provides. Despite his personal name, "Twofold Mystery," his commentary does not clearly align itself with the trend of Taoist thought associated with that term, in which Buddhist philosophical influences are to the fore.[14] But he does respond to Zhang Zhan's mention of Buddhist parallels to discuss in a general way, without specific references, a couple of passages in which he feels that the text shows a Chinese justification for Buddhist beliefs. The first is a story from the sixth chapter in which a possible alternative life for the Duke of Qi is envisaged very much in passing—if the world were different, and men lived for ever, he would be a peasant now, because his ancestors would never have vacated their positions.[15] This Lu declares to be an unambiguous account of reincarnation, a doctrine that had become part of medieval Taoism.[16] The second passage, from the final chapter, challenges the notion that animal life has been provided for our benefit.[17] This allows Lu to argue for a Chinese sagely justification for vegetarianism, again a feature of Buddhism that had won widespread acceptance.[18]

Given that Zhang Zhan had already carried out most of the work of intertextual linkage, Lu's citations from and allusions to other specific texts fall within a much narrower range, and clearly reflect his intellectual preoccupations. By my rough count, Lu makes thirty-two explicit references to other works, including thirteen from *Zhuangzi*, eight from the *Daode jing,* eight from the *Book of Changes,* and two from the *Analects.* The predominance of the first three, the "Three Mysteries," reflects their continued status since the Liang dynasty.[19] The *Book of Changes,* with the *Analects,* was also to remain a staple source of allusion for all examination candidates throughout the Tang.[20] This work was evidently memorized with its officially accepted commentary, for Qin Enfu points out that one citation is not from the text itself, but from the commentary of Wang Bi.[21] Memorization of the *Changes* and *Analects* for examination purposes probably explains the tacit allusions to these sources that also occur in Lu's commentary. But even more revealing is Qin's note on the one remaining explicit citation and Lu's only excursion from philosophy into philology, which would appear to be to the *Huainanzi.* But in fact he shows that Lu is reproducing the *Huainanzi* only as cited in Xu Shen's famous dictionary of the second century CE, the *Shuowen jiezi.*[22]

This introduces a new consideration into the history of reading. Already we have seen in Lu's work something that was already a possibility in Zhang's day—namely, that related texts were called to mind not in isolation, but in the company of the commentary in which they had become embedded. Now it appears that reading could be accompanied by the consultation of ready reference works, in which texts appeared only in the form of quotations in the context of other similarly classified materials. As is well known, the following century was to see improvements on the scroll as a medium for ready reference or public recitation with the appearance of new formats for the book, an innovation similar to the appearance of the codex in the West, making consultation of dictionaries and the like even easier.[23] There are indications too in at least one surviving commentary from the early ninth century that its author was expanding his erudition by means of an encyclopedia.[24] This makes the next surviving commentary on the *Liezi* a work of exceptional interest, since it was started sometime around 800 but ended much later, in the eleventh century, when the spread of printing had begun to change ways of dealing with text even more radically, as researchers have not failed to observe.[25] Since the work in question has a complicated history in itself, and some of the published information about it is mistaken, we need to say a little about its own composition before turning to the question of how it reads the *Liezi.*[26]

The *Liezi shiwen* by Yin Jingshun is indubitably a Tang text in origin: its circulation in the late Tang is attested by a reference to Yin and his work in the *Youyang Zazu* of Duan Chengshi

(803–863).[27] A comparison with the surviving text shows a certain degree of difference between this citation and what we now have, though we cannot be sure how freely Duan was quoting, and his text too has undergone some corruption: one character of Yin's name is accidentally repeated, an error already present in the version of this passage that was copied, apparently in slightly edited form, into the *Taiping Guangji* in the late 970s.[28] In any case, Yin Jingshun's commentary only survived into the Song, as far as we know, in a single manuscript found at a Taoist institution on the Tiantai Mountains, originally copied out by a famous Taoist priest named Xu Lingfu, or, as he styled himself, Moxizi. Now Xu's links with the Tiantai area are well known.[29] But according to Yin's eleventh century editor, he had signed himself on this manuscript Moxizi of Hengshan.[30] In editing another text by Xu, a commentary on the Wenzi, Wang Liqi has recently pointed out that in the preface to this commentary Xu says he moved to Hengshan in 804 and took eight years over his work; another of Xu's compositions puts the date of his subsequent move to Tiantai in 815.[31]

Yin must therefore have compiled his commentary before the latter date at the latest, if not at some date impossible to determine even earlier, and the citation in his work of another commentary dated to 819, which misled the Qing scholar Ren Dachun (1738–1837) into dating it later, must be due to Yin's Song editor.[32] In fact, though Ren must be congratulated on rescuing Yin's work from obscurity and publishing it once more, a comparison of his edition with modern reprints of the Taoist Canon reveals that the copy from a printing of that canon that he used as the basis for his work was in itself defective, missing the last couple of pages.[33] Even if we base ourselves on the current Taoist Canon edition, there are indications that it, too, suffered some textual loss between Southern Song times and its printing in the Ming.[34] As far as I am aware, modern scholarship has so far corrected just one error in the Taoist canon text, and Yin's commentary has never been properly edited in modern times.[35] Outside Taoist circles, moreover, the absorption of Yin's text into Zhang's commentary caused the obliteration of his work during the early Southern Song, when his observations are already cited under Zhang's name.[36]

On the other hand, Yin's Song editor was a Taoist with a peerless reputation as a scholar who seems to have made even the learned bureaucrats who thronged the court feel threatened.[37] Chen

Jingyuan (1025–1094) is chiefly known for his highly regarded textual work on the *Zhuangzi* and the *Daode jing*, but there is no reason to suppose that he approached the task of editing Yin's work with any less critical a spirit.[38] The Taoist libraries of the Tiantai Mountains were furthermore an excellent source during this period for valuable manuscripts.[39] It is also somewhat arbitrary to blame Chen for the occasional mistake in the *Liezi shiwen,* since there is no reason to suppose that Yin was infallible.[40] All in all, there seems no reason to doubt Chen's own assessment, in his preface of 1069, that he had come across a Tang manuscript that had lost about 40 to 50 per cent of its content due to damage, and that he had used it together with a manuscript he found later elsewhere copied by Xu Lingfu of Lu Chongxuan's commentary to check the printed editions of the *Liezi* published by the Directorate of Education, after which he attempted to restore Yin's text.

This, however, presents something of a puzzle to the modern reader: Which portions of the *Liezi shiwen* are from the Tang, and which portions are from the Song? We cannot assume from Chen's account that he topped up the missing parts to make up for the loss he records: his contribution may have been much smaller, or possibly even much larger. The chances are that the valuable citations the text contains—a quotation from Xiang Xiu, for example, not found in Zhang Zhan—are of Tang date, whether taken directly from the works concerned or indirectly, but how can we be sure?[41] In about a half-dozen cases Chen clearly marks editorial additions to the text, but such marking—in the text as we now have it, at least—does not seem to be invariably present. Where information with a clearly labeled Song date is added to the end of a note, perhaps Chen was relying on the common sense of the reader to distinguish his addition from the existing information given by Yin. If so, then since the passage in question ending this way earlier mentions a Tang era that ended in 756, we can feel fairly safe in assuming that Yin lived in the late eighth century, if not the early ninth.[42] A minute check, too, on the administrative geography mentioned in his commentary might further pin down the date more precisely, since shifts in official nomenclature often define usage to within a narrow period. It is regrettable that the mention of the commentary on the *Xunzi* that caused Ren Dachun to date the text to after 819 is marked neither as an editorial addition nor as a passage of explicitly Song date, though the total entry in question is internally marked as structured into different parts, so perhaps its status as an addition is at least implied.[43] Again, closer study might identify some criteria for distinguishing the two layers.

As far as concerns one important aspect of the reading of the *Liezi,* however, the transition from Tang to Song is quite clearly highlighted by this commentary as we now have it. Yin plainly lives in a world of manuscripts. Even if he did not possess a copy of every book he cites, he must have had at least three copies of the *Liezi* in front of him, since in one place he compares three different textual readings.[44] His method of referring to these manuscripts, however, is exactly that shown by Tang copies of the work he takes as his model, the *Jingdian shiwen* of Lu Deming (c. 560-c. 630).[45] Each manuscript was, after all, *sui generis,* not usefully reducible to collective categories, so identification being more or less beside the point, Yin simply states throughout his commentary "a manuscript says" or "manuscripts say." Chen, by contrast, is dealing with printed copies as representatives or exemplars of identifiable editions, serried ranks of identical volumes. In both his preface and in the editorial additions he signals to Yin's text, textual variants are precisely attributed to "the edition of the Directorate of Education" or the like.[46] This practice conforms not only to his usage in other publications, but to general usage in Song times wherever several different editions of "modern," printed books are contrasted with one another.[47]

The overall outcome of this process was not simply that the *Liezi* became involved in yet more books through the merging of Yin's commentary with that of Zhang Zhan—though that was of course true from the start, in that Yin was clearly commenting on Zhang's work as well as the original text, as is shown by his commentary on Zhang's preface, and on other material in the body of Zhang's work.[48] Yin's reference to several copies of *Liezi,* and Chen's references to whole editions, should also remind us that the *Liezi* was also becoming involved throughout the Tang-Song transition with more and more readers. And these readers increasingly started to communicate the results of their reading in yet more books. Though no genre of philosophical criticism grew up at this time in the way that poetry criticism did, anyone listing the *Liezi* for whatever purpose in some larger booklist soon had plenty of reader's reviews to append to the title. Admittedly, to speak of reviews may in some ways be putting too modern a gloss on the practice, and reading perhaps still remained rather different from what we might expect today. Even during the tenth century what we take to be "modern" reading—that is, silent reading—was still apparently regarded as somewhat out of the ordinary.[49] But looking to European norms may in any case be misleading as a measure of the extent to which people had come to feel at ease with reading, however that process was carried out.[50] Well before the tenth century, after all, Duan Chengshi turns out to be jotting down not simply gossip (a longstanding tradition) or exotic tales that he had heard, but also things that he had read, and this trend manifests itself yet more clearly in the jottings and collected reading notes of writers of the Song dynasty.

One good source for assessing the reading of the *Liezi* during this period, beyond the bounds of formally composed commentaries—which of course continued to emerge throughout the Song—is the bibliography of an encyclopedia compiled close to a thousand years after the *Liezi* first emerged in the fourth century. The *Wenxian tongkao* of Ma Duanlin (1254–1324/5) is so vast an achievement that it has rarely been given its due.[51] Its bibliographical section alone fills two stout volumes in a modern reprint. And in that reprint one may find, appended to Ma's listing of the *Liezi* in Zhang Zhan's version, half a dozen notices culled from other sources concerning that work.[52] The first, from a famous private library catalogue of the twelfth century, the *Junzhai dushu zhi*, originally compiled by its owner, Chao Gongwu, provides some basic bibliographical information, plus some rather hostile comments from a "Confucian" perspective.[53] The last is a notice by Gao Sisun, the late-twelfth-century editor of an anthology of information about ancient philosophers, the *Zi lue*.[54] Gao addresses the apparent Buddhist influences on the *Liezi*, affirming that these were quite possible in pre-imperial China, but he concludes: " Even so, what is suspect and strange about this book does not lie in this issue [of Buddhism]."

A glance at the intervening essays shows what the problem is that prompts Gao to conclude in this way. The earliest is from the age of manuscripts, from the great prose writer Liu Zongyuan (773–819), who was by this point accepted as a model of prose style for all aspiring authors, making his works widely available in printed editions.[55] Liu is frankly puzzled by the book's implied chronology of pre-imperial history, which seems to him inconsistent, and so concludes that the text has been subjected to later interpolations on a considerable scale, though it contains enough of its original material to be commendable to the discriminating reader, as much for style as content. Style is also very much to the fore in the next excerpt chosen by Ma, from the brush of Ye Mengde (1077–1148): we may find the *Liezi* somewhat uneven, but we have to take account of its aim in trying to reach a wider audience in later and more degenerate times, something that inevitably corrupts style—just look at the way in which Zen masters have taken the message of the Buddha down market. Ye's observation here concerns the *yulu* or "Recorded Sayings" genre, which by his day was being printed in quantity, though doubtless that is not all his insight involves.[56]

Ma's remaining two quotations also focus on matters of literary style rather than anything approaching philosophy or the like. The first is from the *Rongzhai suibi,* the *Miscellaneous Jottings* of Hong Mai (1123–1202), who considers the excellence of the *Liezi's* narrative style to be beyond the abilities of a later age.[57] Finally, the *Recorded Sayings* of the great neo-Confucian master Zhu Xi (1130–1200) are quoted to similar effect: the *Liezi* has some unevenness about it, as do some other early Chinese texts, but Liu Zongyuan was right about the good bits.[58] Ma's selection, however, turns out to be far from comprehensive, even for the authors excerpted. Chao Gongwu and Gao Sisun are constrained by the formats they use from too discursive an approach, but the other Song period figures turn out to be positively garrulous on the subject of the *Liezi* when one looks elsewhere in their writings.[59] Hong Mai, for example, discusses elsewhere both the question of Buddhism in the *Liezi* and the existence of parallels (not overlaps) between the *Liezi* and both Buddhist and pre-imperial sources.[60] And one does not have to read very much farther into the jottings of Song scholars to find yet more references to *Liezi,* or yet more intriguingly, to its commentaries.[61]

How might we summarize the reader reaction to the *Liezi* as it had developed over its first millennium? There is certainly a degree of suspicion expressed about the book, from Liu Zongyuan onward, and this feeds into a continuous stream of debate—citing figures such as Liu and Gao Sisun—that stretches in an unbroken line into the postimperial period of Chinese scholarship. A good example of this may be found in Huang Yunmei's *Gujin weishu kao buzheng,* which expands on the early Qing period work of Yao Jiheng—who starts from these two figures—and ends up with the modern scholarship of Ma Xulun and others.[62] At the same time the persistent praise for the style of the *Liezi*—or at least the style of the *Liezi* at its best—convey a more nuanced message, so the whole verdict on the *Liezi's* reputation might be paraphrased as "This book seems a little suspect, but it is still well worth reading!" Note in particular that those like Zhu Xi who might be expected to find the contents philosophically inimical have the most to say on style over content, no doubt wishing to defend the pleasure of reading something that their principles might have found problematic.

And who are we, in any case, to criticize? If in the opening portion of this chapter I have laid some stress on the underlying technology supporting reading, this is not because of any belief in technological determinism. It is simply that the underlying technological differences between the Western experience and that of China are so banal that they are often overlooked, though now some on the Western side at least are trying to probe some aspects of the consequences.[63] Hypothetically, however, until the introduction of paper China was probably in a worse position than Europe, with its papyrus scrolls, in terms of ease of reading. But thereafter the move in Western Europe in particular to the more durable but intractable parchment yielded the advantage, and Chinese reading got seriously under way. Half a millennium of paper manuscripts followed by half a millennium of print then created a situation in China without parallel elsewhere. Something of a similar sense of ready connectedness with the literature of the past may have lingered in Byzantium. But Byzantium withered and died, and Europe had to learn again about antiquity in the Renaissance.

Meanwhile, in China the constant tradition of widespread reading meant that past literature was subjected to uninterrupted scrutiny and reflection in a way that still seems—to me, at least—quite staggering. Even a Tang writer, such as the poet Du Fu, has undergone within the Chinese tradition a period of sustained reading and rereading that makes the reputation of a Dante or a Shakespeare look like a snap judgement.[64] True, the Bible has been read and reread, and incessantly commented on, in Christendom. But it has never been treated as just a book, a book among other books. Yet that has been precisely the position of the *Liezi,* which, to repeat, from its very first appearance has been involved in comparison and so in critical evaluation—and, as its readership grew, casual, even everyday discussion. After our journey through a millennium of reading, we are now in a position to come back to where we started, and to consider the individual reader and the text of the *Liezi* once more.

Reader, do you remember the day that you saw a familiar-looking volume in someone else's hands, and realized that you were not the only person in the world who enjoyed reading Nietzsche, or P. G. Wodehouse, or whoever your favorite author happened to be? Similar or analogous experiences must be very common—I can tell you that as an educator in Asian Studies, prone to the gloomy notion that I have been spending my life trying to persuade people to show an interest in things they find blankly exotic, there was a day when glancing around a subway car, I saw that everyone in sight was reading something about Asia—about a holiday in Thailand, or Tibetan Buddhism, or Chinese cooking, or poverty in Indonesia, or Japanese martial arts. Now that the tradition of reading out loud to a group has become almost extinct in adult life, our books tend to foster the illusion that they are speaking to us as individuals. And maybe Ye Mengde was right—maybe the *Liezi* was written with you in mind, someone unimpressed by rhetoric, but quick to pick up on the subtleties built into an imaginary dialogue. An eye to posterity is, after all, an important element in Chinese writing from quite early on.[65]

But the notion that the *Liezi* was written for you alone, no matter how strong the subjective experience, is of course an illusion. From the beginning the *Liezi* has kept company with a convivial throng of other books, and other people. At the moment they may be invisible to you—and maybe for a while longer, since it certainly forms no part of the plan of the foregoing desultory and incomplete remarks to point the way to a whole book on this topic. But they are certainly there, generations of men and women, not only Chinese, even if predominantly so—and maybe you should get to know them. After all, if you like the *Liezi,* and so do they, I think you may find something in common with them.

Notes

1. See the (incomplete) list of overlaps provided on pp. 225–28 of A. C. Graham, "The Date and Composition of *Lieh-tzu*", as reprinted in his *Studies in Chinese Philosophy and Philosophical Literature* (Albany:

SUNY Press, 1990), 216–82; for one overlap not included, see p. 36 of T. H. Barrett, "Taoist and Buddhist Mysteries in the Interpretation of the *Tao-te ching*," *Journal of the Royal Asiatic Society* 1 (1982): 35–43, though I am less confident now that the text concerned could be as late as I then thought.

2. Kitahara Mineki, *Resshi Chô Tan chu sakuin* (Kita Kyûshû: Kita Kyûshû Chûgoku shoten, 1988), appends a list of books and shorter pieces quoted by Zhang, but this includes cross-references to the chapters of the *Liezi* and excludes works cited by author, not title; pp. 36 and 48 do, however, provide a means of judging the number of works explicitly cited.
3. *Chongxu zhide zhenjing*, 1.1b7, 4.5a6, and 4.2b13, in the Northern Song edition of the *Liezi*. For Xiahou Xuan, see Richard B. Mather, *Shih-shuo Hsin-yü* (Ann Arbor: Center for Chinese Studies, University of Michigan, 2002), 558.
4. *Chongxu zhide zhenjing*, 1.1b7.
5. See Wu Chengshi, *Jingdian shiwen xulu shuzheng* (Beijing: Zhonghua shuju, 1984), 164–65.
6. Some textual scholars, including Ma Xulun and A. C. Graham, would seem to envisage some quite radical modifications as having taken place to Guo Xiang's text after its composition, though their hypotheses do not involve loss of text. See *A Companion to Angus C. Graham's Chuang Tzu*, ed. Harold D. Roth (Honolulu: University of Hawaii Press, 2003), 51.
7. In the fifth century, for example, the commentary of Pei Songzhi on the *Sanguo zhi* is reckoned to cite more than two hundred different works. Earlier, Zheng Xuan (127–200) cites forty-five different sources on the *Li ji* or *Book of Rites*, but this was a substantial work already at the heart of the scholarly tradition.
8. Note on this point the rhapsody by Fu Xuan (234–294), cited in Tsuen-hsuin Tsien, *Written on Bamboo and Silk: The Beginnings of Chinese Books and Inscriptions* (Chicago: University of Chicago Press, 2004), 151.
9. Harvard-Yenching Index number 732, in modern reproductions of the Ming canon.
10. Note Qin Enfu, ed., *Laozi zhu* (*Liezi jicheng* ed.), 4.8a7; cf. 7.6b9, 8.16a3.
11. *Xin Tang shu caixiang shixi biao jijiao*, ed. Zhao Zhao (Beijing: Zhonghua shuju, 1998), 506; Alan J. Berkowitz, *Patterns of Disengagement: The Practice and Portrayal of Reclusion in Early Medieval China* (Stanford: Stanford University Press, 2000), 138.
12. For a brief summary, see T. H. Barrett, *Taoism under the T'ang: Religion and Empire during the Golden Age of Chinese History* (London: Wellsweep, 1996), 65. A reference to having "twice received the emperor's instruction" in Lu's preface (2a2) might allow a yet more precise date for this work within the overall pattern of events.
13. On this work one may read the monograph by Shiyi Yu, *Reading the Chuang-tzu in the T'ang Dynasty: The Commentary of Ch'eng Hsüan-*

ying (fl. 631–652) (New York: Peter Lang Publishing, 2000) as an adequate introduction to the issues.

14. For a description of this trend, coupled with a strong warning not to construe it as an organised "school," see Robert H. Sharf, *Coming to Terms with Chinese Buddhism: A Reading of the Treasure Store Treatise* (Honolulu: University of Hawaii Press, 2002), 52–71.
15. A. C. Graham, *The Book of Lieh-tzu* (London: John Murray, 1960), 133.
16. Lu, *Liezi zhu*, 6.10a10-10b1.
17. Graham, *Book of Lieh-tzu*, 179.
18. Lu, *Liezi zhu*, 8.14a7-9.
19. Yu, *Reading the Zhuangzi*, 22–23, 30–31.
20. Note Robert des Rotours, *Le Traité des Examens* (Paris: Leroux, 1932), 291.
21. Lu, *Liezi zhu*, 4.12a9; cf. Richard John Lynn, *The Classic of Changes* (New York: Columbia University Press, 1994), 130, and David McMullen, *State and Scholars in T'ang China* (Cambridge: Cambridge university Press, 1988), 74–75, for Wang's status at this time.
22. Lu, *Liezi zhu*, 8.10a1-2.
23. A similar, but more complex, process: see Jean-Pierre Drège, "The Dunhuang and Central Asian manuscripts and the history of books," in *British Library Occasional Papers 10: Chinese Studies*, ed. Frances Wood (London: the British Library, 1988), 171–75; Liu Guojun and Zheng Rusi, *The Story of Chinese Books* (Beijing: Foreign Languages Press, 1985), 64–65.
24. See my observation on p. 170, at n.12, of T. H. Barrett, "On the Transmission of the *Shen Tzu* and of the *Yan—sheng yao-chi*", *Journal of the Royal Asiatic Society* (1980) 2: 168–76. I now consider the arguments against the unitary authorship of the commentary in question to be unsound.
25. Susan Cherniak, "Book Culture and Textual Transmission in Sung China", *Harvard Journal of Asiatic Studies* 54, no. 1 (1994): 5–125.
26. As explained below, the *terminus post quem* that I originally accepted for its date of composition, 819, turns out to be less than sound, so p. 302 of my entry concerning the *Liezi* in *Early Chinese Texts: A Bibliographical Guide*, ed. Michael Loewe (Berkeley: Society for the Study of Early China, 1993), 298–308, stands in need of correction.
27. For a recent summary of scholarship on this text and its author, see Carrie E. Reed, *Chinese Chronicles of the Strange* (New York: Peter Lang, 2000), 1–30.
28. Compare Duan Chengshi, *Youyang zazu, xu*, 4 (Beijing: Zhonghua shuju, 1981), 239–40; Li Fang, *Taiping Guangji* 228 (Beijing: Zhonghua shuju, 1961), 1751–12; Yin Jingshun, *Chongxu zhide zhenjing* 1.10a, in the edition of the Taoist Canon, Harvard-Yenching Index number 733.
29. See for example my remarks in *Poems of Hanshan,* trans. Peter Hobson (Walnut Creek, CA: Altamira, 2003), 126–28, where Xu is accidentally assigned to the "early eighth century," rather than ninth.
30. Yin, *Chongxu zhide zhenjing*, preface, 1b.
31. Wang Liqi, *Wenzi shuyi* (Beijing: Zhonghua shuju, 2000), preface, 2, and also Xu's preface, 2 and n. 16 on p. 5.

32. Yin, *Chongxu zhide zhenjing*, 2.7b.
33. Compare Ren Dachun, *Liezi shiwen,* 2.18a, in the *Liezi jicheng* reprint, with Yin, *Chongxu zhide zhenjing,* 2.14b-2.16b.
34. Loewe, *Early Chinese Texts*, 303.
35. Ma Tailai, "Xindiao guo", *Dalu zazhi* 39, no. 1–2 (July, 1969): 23, and cf. Yin, *Chongxu zhide zhenjing*, 2.7a.
36. Note e.g., Hong Mai, *Rongzhai suibi,* series 4, 1 (Shanghai: Shanghai guji chubanshe, 1978), 618 and cf. Yin, *Chongxu zhide zhenjing,* 2.8b.
37. Piet van der Loon, *Taoist Books in the Libraries of the Sung Period* (London: Ithaca Press, 1984), 10–11.
38. See the survey of his achievements in Judith M. Boltz, *A Survey of Taoist Literature: Tenth to Seventeenth Centuries* (Berkeley: Institute of East Asian Studies, University of California, 1987), 203–95.
39. See Chen Guofu, *Daozang yuanliu kao* (Beijing: Zhomghua shuju, 1963), 127, 129, 131.
40. Yang Bojun, *Liezi jishi* (Beijing; Zhonghua shuju, 1979), 105.
41. Yin, *Chongxu zhide zhenjing*, 1.11a.
42. Ibid., 1.1a.
43. Ibid., 2.7b.
44. Ibid., 2.13a.
45. On Lu Deming and his work, see Paul Thompson, *The Shen Tzu Fragments* (Oxford: Oxford University Press, 1979), 56–61, and for the feature in question, any reproduction of the Dunhuang manuscript Pelliot 3315.
46. Yin, *Zhide zhenjing shiwen,* 1.5b, 2.15b, and preface, 2a.
47. For example, in the edition of the *Collected Works of Han Yu* prepared by Zhu Xi.
48. E.g., Yin, *Zhide zhenjing shiwen,* 1.10b, identifies one of the early *Zhuangzi* commentators used by Zhang—and by Yin himself.
49. This we may deduce from a story from Dunhuang, transcribed in a manuscript, S. 2073, dated 972: cf. Arthur Waley, *Ballads and Stories from Tun-huang* (London: George Allen and Unwin, 1960), 111.
50. For the Western experience, see Alberto Manguel, *A History of Reading* (London: Flamingo, 1997), 41–53.
51. For one exception, see Hok-lam Chan, """Comprehensiveness" (*T'ung*) and "Change" (*Pien*) in Ma Tuan-lin's Historical Thought," in Hok-lam Chan and Wm. Theodore de Bary, eds., *Yüan Thought: Chinese Thought and Religion under the Mongols* (New York: Columbia University Press, 1982), 27–87.
52. Ma Duanlin, *Wenxian tongkao: jingji kao* 38 (Shanghai: Huadong shifan daxue chubanshe, 1985), 895–98.
53. For the somewhat complex history of this work, see van der Loon, *Taoist Books,* pp. 25–27.
54. For a brief description, see Y. Hervouet, ed., *A Sung Bibliography/Bibliogaphie des Song* (Hong Kong: Chinese University Press, 1978), 215.
55. For a study of Liu within the context of the development of prose style, see Yu-shih Chen, *Images and ideas in Chinese Classical Prose: Studies of Four Masters* (Stanford: Stanford University Press, 1988), 71–107. Liu's piece on *Liezi* may be found in the fourth fascicle of editions of his *Collected Works.*

56. I have not so far traced the source of Ma's extract from Ye, and some of his voluminous writings have been lost since the fourteenth century. For some preliminary remarks on the impact of Zen colloquial literature in publishing at this time, see T. H. Barrett, "Buddhist Scholarship in East Asia: A Brief Study of the Contribution of Buddhism to Chinese Literature," in Lakshman S. Perera et al., eds., *Buddhism for the New Millennium* (London: World Buddhist Foundation, 2000), 184–92.
57. Ma is quoting in edited form from Hong, *Rongzhai suibi* 12, p.362. For Hong's writings, see the useful discussion in Valerie Hansen, *Changing Gods in Medieval China, 1126–1276* (Princeton; Princeton University Press, 1990), 17–23, and n.b. note 20 on p. 18.
58. The quotation is evidently from a version of Zhu's *Recorded Sayings* not quite like that which survives, or else it has been somewhat edited, since it does not correspond to anything in the section of his *Classified Sayings* that deals with the *Liezi:* cf. Li Jingde, ed., *Zhuzi yulei* 125 (Beijing: Zhonghua shuju, 19), 2991–92. We know, however, that earlier collections once existed, and for some reason Li's collection does not include all the material once in circulation: cf. Hervouet, *Sung Bibliography*, p. 225.
59. For Zhu Xi, see the preceding note; Ye Mengde has a number of mentions of the *Liezi* in his *Bishu luhua,* which I have consulted in the *Bai hai* (Taibei: Xinxing shuju, 1968) reprint of the Zhenlutang edition: cf. Ye, *Bishu luhua,* pp. 1.22b-24a, 2.16b.
60. Hong, *Rongzhai suibi,* series 4, 1, 622–23 and 14, 777; cf. n. 36, above, also.
61. For sake of example, in the late twelfth century Wu Zeng, *Nenggaizhai manlu* 9 (Shanghai: Shanghai guji chubanshe, 1979), 273, appeals to the phonological commentary on the *Zhuangzi* and *Liezi* to establish the pronunciation of a place name—on this source, see Hervouet, *Sung Bibliography,* pp. 290-91.
62. Huang, *Gujin weishu kao buzheng* (Jinan: Qilu shushe, 1980), 244–52.
63. H. Gregory Snyder, *Teachers and Texts in the Ancient World: Philosophers, Jews and Christians* (London and New York: Routledge, 2000), asks some basic questions about how knowledge was transmitted in late Western antiquity: we have no such comparable study for China.
64. The matter of Du Fu's reputation has at least been explicitly addressed by Eva Shan Chou, *Reconsidering Tu Fu: Literary greatness and cultural context* (Cambridge: Cambridge University Press, 1995).
65. As has been very eloquently pointed out by Stephen Owen, *Remembrances: The Experience of the Past in Classical Chinese Literature* (Cambridge: Harvard University Press, 1986).

列子

The *Liezi*'s Use of the Lost *Zhuangzi*

Ronnie Littlejohn

Introduction

Among the many intriguing mysteries in the study of Daoism is what was contained in the lost *Zhuangzi* 莊子. The *Zhuangzi* is one of the two foundational texts of classical Daoism. The received text of this work was edited by a scholar official named Guo Xiang 郭象 (d. 312 CE) and it contains thirty-three chapters. Most of these, like the *Daodejing* 道德經, contain many component text pieces put together by an editor as one might place beads on a string. However, unlike the case of the *Daodejing*, we know that there was a much larger and older *Zhuangzi*. This "lost *Zhuangzi*" consisted of fifty-two chapters and it is the document with which Guo Xiang was working. The lost *Zhuangzi* is the work mentioned in Imperial bibliographies dating from about 110 CE, but it was undoubtedly older than these compilations themselves, even if we do not know by how much (Watson, 13).

What the contents of the lost *Zhuangzi* were, whether it contained materials that differed in significant ways from those passages preserved by Guo Xiang, and what characterized the passages he chose to eliminate have long been questions thought to be unanswerable. Livia Knaul (Kohn) holds that Guo Xiang may have reduced the lost *Zhuangzi* to thirty-three chapters in part because he felt the discarded materials contained "superstitious" ideas and practices to which he and other educated intellectuals objected (Knaul, 54–55). The evidence for this claim has been sketchy because it has long been believed that we do not have any material that can be assigned with confidence to the lost *Zhuangzi.*

In this chapter, I argue that the contents of the lost *Zhuangzi* have not vanished entirely because some of its passages are preserved for us in the second chapter of the *Liezi* 列子 (hereafter *LZ*). I take note of the passages in the second chapter that are also in the received *Zhuangzi,* and I call attention to those that were ascribed to a *Zhuangzi* by early commentators, although they are not in our received text. Relying on the work of A. C. Graham (1990b) devoted to the grammar and style of the text blocks of chapter 2 and his emphasis on the quoting pattern of the editor, I hold that it is defensible to conclude that all of the text beads in the chapter except the last one are derived from a *Zhuangzi* source shared by Guo Xiang and the *LZ* editor. I hold that this source was probably the lost *Zhuangzi.* Upon this basis, I make some concluding observations about the implications of finding that chapter 2 may be traceable to the lost *Zhuangzi.*

The *Liezi* Editor's Copying of the Source *Zhuangzi*

If the modern scholarly consensus resting largely on Graham's careful analysis of the date and composition of the text is correct, the received version of the *LZ* is to be dated to the early part of the fourth century CE. The preface of Zhang Zhan 張湛 (fl. 370) tells us the history of the formation of the received text, and there is no external evidence that the present book existed before Zhang Zhan and no Han writers quote the *Liezi* (Graham 1990b, 221). Zhang wrote,

> My late father (Zhang Zhan's grandfather), Liu Zhengyu, and Fu Yinggen were all maternal nephews of the Wang family. When they were young they played together in the maternal family's house. My father's maternal uncle was Wang Zizhou and his elder first paternal cousins Wang Zhengzong and Wang Fusu (Wang Bi), all liked to collect books. They had collectively secured Wang Chongxuan's library, which totaled almost ten thousand *juan* (text beads somewhat resembling chapters). . . . When they reached their maturity, having met the disorders of the Yongjia period (307–312 CE), my father, along with Fu Yinggen, escaped south in order to avoid the disaster. The carts were heavy and loaded to their capacity. Moreover, because the

> bandits were numerous and the road in front still long, my father said to Fu Yinggen: "Now it is unlikely that we will be able to preserve all that we are carrying, so let's merely select whatever items we estimate the world will want and each of us preserve and copy these works so that they will not be lost." Fu Yinggen therefore only saved his grandfather's Xuan's and his father Xian's collected works. Upon arriving south of the Yangzi there was only a part of these works left. Of the *Liezi* there was only the "Yangzhu" and "Explaining Conjunctions" chapters and the report [of Liu Xiang], in three *juan*. At the time of the disorder, Liu Zhengyu became the governor of Yangzhou and came across the river to our side. Afterwards my father obtained four *juan* from Liu's home, and subsequently also sought out six *juan* from Zhao Jizi, Yang Bi's son-in-law. By collating and comparing what was and was not in the various texts, only then was he able to compile the complete edition (of the *Leizi*).[1] (Wang, 178)

It is clear that the *LZ* is a text assembled from many other works. The *LZ* commentary of Lu Chongxuan 盧重玄 (c. 740 CE), our earliest after that of Zhang Zhan, survives in the Daoist Canon as *DZ* 732, along with portions of Huizong's 徽宗 commentary (1118 CE) and that of Fan Zhixu 范致虛 (1119 CE) (Schipper and Verellen, 683). Lu calls attention to a number of parallels and allusions in *LZ* to other texts, including thirteen to the *Zhuangzi*. Having done an even more in-depth analysis of the *LZ* source materials than these earlier commentators, Graham called attention to an extensive list of passages and parallels shared by *LZ* and other texts, concluding, in fact, that about one-fourth of the *LZ* is found in other sources (1990b, 225–28). T. H. Barrett has identified even a few more passages than Graham.

With respect to comparing the *LZ* and *Zhuangzi*, Graham observes that the relationship between these texts is very complex, and he offers evidence that *LZ* Ch. 2 has extensive direct connections to the received *Zhuangzi*. In fact, as we can see in the passage I have selected below, some *LZ* passages are virtually identical to Guo Xiang's *Zhuangzi*, strongly suggesting that the long-held assumptions of Lu, Huizong, and Fan were correct: the editor of *LZ* is copying from a *Zhuangzi* text, not relying on memory or paraphrase. For ease of reference in displaying this pattern, and for the study of other passages in *LZ* Ch. 2, I will refer to the text blocks by following the convention of giving the chapter by number, the text bead within the chapter by an alphabetical letter, and the page number from Graham's English translation of the work (e.g., *LZ* 2a, 33–35).

Identifying the Source *Zhuangzi* for *LZ* Ch. 2 Text Blocks

LZ 2d, 37	*Zhuangzi* 19b, 198
列子問關尹曰: "至人潛行不空,蹈火不熱,行乎萬物之上而不慄。請問何以至于此? "關尹曰: "是純氣之守也,非智巧果敢之列。 姬! 魚語女。凡有貌像聲色者,皆物也。物與物何以相遠也? 夫奚足以至乎先? 是色而已。則物之造乎不形,而止乎無所 化。夫得是而窮之者,焉得為 正焉? 彼將處乎不深之度,而藏乎無端之紀,游乎萬物之所終 始。壹其性,養其氣,含其德,以通乎物之所造。夫若是 者,其天守全,其神無郤,物奚自入焉? 夫醉者之墜于車也,雖疾不死。骨節與人同,而犯害與人異,其神全也。乘亦弗知也,墜亦弗知也。死生驚懼,不入乎其胸,是故遻物而不慴。彼得全 于酒,而猶若是,而況得全于天乎? 聖人藏于天,故物莫之能傷也.	子列子問關尹曰: "至人潛 行不窒,蹈火不熱,行乎萬物之上而不慄。請問何以至於此? "關尹曰: "是純氣之守也,非知巧果敢之列。 居! 吾 語女。凡有貌象聲色者,皆物也,物與物何以相遠? 夫奚足以至乎先? 是色而已。則物之造乎不形,而止乎無所 化,夫得是而窮之者,物焉得而止焉! 彼將處乎不淫之度,而藏乎無端之紀,遊乎萬物之所終 始,壹其性,養其氣,合其德,以通乎物之所造。夫若是 者,其天守全,其神無郤,物奚自入焉! 夫醉者之墜車,雖疾 不死。骨節與人同,而犯害與人異,其神全也,乘亦不知也,墜 亦不知也,死生驚懼不入乎其 胷中,是故遻物而不慴。彼得全於酒而猶若是,而況得全於天 乎! 聖人藏於天,故莫之能傷.
Graham translation	**Watson translation**
Lieh Tzu asked Kuan-yin: "The highest man can walk underwater and does not suffocate, treads fire and does not burn, walks above the myriad things and does not tremble. May I ask how he achieves this?" "It is by holding fast to his purest energies; it has nothing to do with skill and daring. Come, let me tell you. Whatever has features, likeness, sound, colour, is a thing. How could one thing put a distance between itself and other things? How can it deserve to get ahead of them? It is mere form and colour. But one who can grasp and	Master Lieh Tzu said to the Barrier Keeper Yin, "The Perfect Man can walk under water without choking, can tread on fire without being burned, and can travel above the ten thousand things without being frightened. May I ask how he manages this?" The Barrier Keeper Yin replied, "This is because he guards the pure breath—it has nothing to do with wisdom, skill, determination, or courage. Sit down and I will tell you about it. All that have faces, forms, voices, colors—these are all mere things. How could one thing and another thing be far removed

fathom the Unshaped from which things are created, the Changeless by which they are brought to a stop—how can other things succeed in stopping him? He will cling to his degree and not exceed it, hide far back along the skein without beginnings, and roam where the myriad things end and begin; he will unify his nature, tend his energies, maintain the virtue inside him, until he penetrates to the place where things are created. If you can be like this, the Heaven inside you will keep its integrity, the spirit inside you will have no flaws; where can other things find a way in? When a drunken man is thrown from a cart, swiftly though he falls it does not kill him. His bones and joints are the same as another man's, yet he is not harmed as another man would be, because of the integrity of his spirit. He rides without knowing it, falls without knowing it; life and death, astonishment and fear, find no entry into his breast, and so he does not shrink from hitting things. If this is true even of a man who gets his integrity from wine, how much more is it true of those who get it from Heaven! The sage hides himself in Heaven, therefore no thing can harm him." (Graham 1990a, 2d, 37–38)	from each other? And how could any one of them be worth considering as a predecessor? They are forms, colors—nothing more. But things have their creation in what has no form, and their conclusion in what has no change. If a man can get hold of this and exhaust it fully, then how can things stand in his way? He may rest within the bounds that know no excess, hide within the borders that know no source, wander where the ten thousand things have their end and beginning, unify his nature, nourish his breath, unite his virtue, and thereby communicate with that which creates all things. A man like this guards what belongs to Heaven and keeps it whole. His spirit has no flaw, so how can things enter in and get at him? When a drunken man falls from a carriage, though the carriage may be going very fast, he won't be killed. He has bones and joints the same as other men, and yet he is not injured as they would be, because his spirit is whole. He didn't know he was riding, and he doesn't know he has fallen out. Life and death, alarm and terror do not enter his breast, and so he can bang against things without fear of injury. If he can keep himself whole like this by means of wine, how much more can he keep himself whole by means of Heaven! The sage hides himself in Heaven—hence there is nothing that can do him harm." (Watson 19b, 198–99)

Using grammatical study, Graham is able to associate two passages, which I label in the table below as 2k and 2l, with a style of writing very unique to the *Zhuangzi* as we know it in its received form, but which do not appear in that version. Moreover, 2k is assigned specifically to *Zhuangzi* by an early commentator. Graham also shows that the text bead labeled 2j begins by following the received *Zhuangzi* in the quoting pattern of the ten "identical passages" mentioned above, and then it is interrupted by a number of lines not found in the received text. And yet, 2j in its entirety is attributed to *Zhuangzi* by the *Taiping Yulan* 太平御覽. These literary critical findings suggest it is more likely that both *LZ* and Guo Xiang were working from a common source than that the *LZ* editor was copying from our received *Zhuangzi*. That common text was probably the lost *Zhuangzi* of fifty-two chapters. To summarize: we may reasonably conclude that *LZ* chapter 2 is likely copied in large measure from the lost *Zhuangzi* because: (1) ten text beads (2d, e, h, i, j, m, n, o, p, and t) are virtually identical to known *Zhuangzi* passages; (2) grammatical study shows that two additional passages make use of a structure unique to the known *Zhuangzi*, but do not belong to it; and (3) while one other passage contains lengthy strands of received *Zhuangzi* text it is interrupted with material not in the received text and yet it is attributed in its entirety to *Zhuangzi* by an early commentary.

A related kind of evidence for my claim that the *LZ* editor is following the lost *Zhuangzi* in a pattern of direct quoting is the interesting fact that the received *Zhuangzi* often mentions Liezi, but the *LZ* never once mentions Zhuangzi or specifically cites the *Zhuangzi*, although it does often name others of its sources (e.g., *The Book of the Yellow Emperor* 黃帝書 Graham 1990a, 1e, 22). A possible explanation for the editor's not citing the *Zhuangzi* is that the sort of extensive copying as is being done in chapter 2 is a very different use of his source material than when he is taking isolated passages from other works in order to make a point. Putting all of this together we can allow Graham to express our conclusion in this manner: "The editor of *Lieh-tzu* evidently knew the full text [of *Zhuangzi*] . . ." (Graham 1990b, 235).

A Breakdown of the *Zhuangzi* Materials in *Liezi* Ch. 2

LZ text bead Graham pagination	*Zhuangzi* text bead Watson pagination	Comments
2a, 33–35	Reminiscent of 11d, 118–20 may be in lost *Zhuangzi*	After the Yellow Emperor had ruled for years (difference in number), he built a hut and retired in spiritual retreat for three months, then returned to rule with the dao and greatness.
2b, 35	Reminiscent of 1f, 33 may be in lost *Zhuangzi*	In the Gushe mountains there lives a divine man (*shenren* 神人).
2c, 35–36	Reminiscent of 1c, 32 may be in lost *Zhuangzi*	Liezi came riding on the wind.
2d, 37–38	19b, 198	Liezi asks Barrier Keeper Yin how the highest man (*zhenren* 真人) can do his feats.
2e, 38–39	21i, 230–31	Bohun Wuren's test of Lie Yukou's (Liezi's) commensurate skill in archery. Belongs to skillfulness text set in *LZ* and *Zhuangzi.*
2f, 39–42	lost *Zhuangzi* ?	Shang-qiu Kai's skillfulness as a divine man is based on his "forgetfulness." Belongs to skillfulness text set in *LZ* and *Zhuangzi.*
2g, 42–43	lost *Zhuangzi* ?	Liang Yang's skillfulness in training tigers and birds. Belongs to skillfulness text set in *LZ* and the "lost" *Zhuangzi.*
2h, 43–44	19d, 200	Confucius teaching Yan Hui about the ferryman in the gulf of Shangshen who handled his boat with commensurate skill. Belongs to skillfulness text set in *LZ* and *Zhuangzi.*
2i, 44	19j, 204–205	Confucius at Lu-liang waterfall questioning the diver with commensurate skill. Belongs to skillfulness text set in *LZ* and *Zhuangzi.* The *LZ* passage has some text not included in the received *Zhuangzi.*
2j, 44–45	19c, 199	Confucius and the hunchback cicada-catching man. Belongs to skillfulness text set in *LZ* and *Zhuangzi.*

LZ text bead Graham pagination (continued)	*Zhuangzi* text bead Watson pagination *(continued)*	Comments *(continued)*
2k, 45–46	lost *Zhuangzi*	Seagull loving man learns to do nothing (i.e., *wu-wei*) Graham notes this text bead is attributed to *Zhuangzi* (must be the lost *Zhuangzi*) by an early commentator who presumably has the lost version. Graham ties it to the received *Zhuangzi's* unique style of pronoun usage.
2l, 46–47	lost *Zhuangzi*	The man who lives in stone and walks through fire. Graham assigns this to the lost *Zhuangzi* based on its relationship to 2k in pronoun usage (232).
2m, 47–49	7e, 94–97	Huzi (Master Hu), his disciple Liezi, and the village shaman.
2n, 49–50	32a, 353–54	Liezi receives Bohun Wuren's instruction about not seeking profit or fame.
2o, 51–52	27g, 307–308	The unteachable Yang Chu.
2p, 52	20j, 220	Yang Chu and the innkeeper with two concubines.
2q, 52–53	lost *Zhuangzi* ?	There is a Way by which one will always conquer and one by which one will never conquer.
2r, 53–55	lost *Zhuangzi* ?	Powers of the sages, like those of the *zhenren* may be used to conquer.
2s, 55–56	Reminiscent of 2k, 41 may be in lost *Zhuangzi*	The "three in the morning" monkey-keeper story given a different point in *LZ*. Here it is used as an example of the *zhenren's* power to read the thoughts of animals.
2t, 56	19i, 204	Ji Shengzi the game cock trainer for King Xuan, but which is also used to make the same point as 2s, much more so than the point the account has in the received *Zhuangzi.*
2u, 56–57	lost *Zhuangzi* ?	Hui Ang promises King Kang of Song a way by which one will always conquer. In this way, the passage continues the stream begun in 2q.
2v, 57		Editorial addition to 2u, not to be considered as connected with *Zhuangzi.*

What we see by means of the table above is that while 2a, 2b, and 2c are not identical with the received *Zhuangzi*, they are clearly related to well-known passages in that text. We might think that they are only allusions to the received text, rather than passages copied from the lost *Zhuangzi* were it not for the quoting pattern in which the *LZ* editor is known to be dealing with his source material (i.e., 2d, e, h, i, j, m, n, o, p, and t). As I have shown above, in those ten places where we can compare *LZ* chapter 2 with the known *Zhuangzi*, the editor seems to be copying directly from his source and this explains why so many text blocks in *LZ* chapter 2 are identical to those in the received text which was little more than an editor's cribbing of the lost *Zhuangzi*. I believe this copying does not begin with 2d, but includes 2a, 2b, and 2c as well. These text beads are strongly reminiscent of the received *Zhuangzi* in phraseology, terms, themes, and sentiments. However, since this *Zhuangzi* is lost, I cannot offer a knock down proof for my claim. But maybe some indirect reasoning will support it.

If the editor is copying from his source in 2d, 2e, 2h, 2i, 2m, 2n, 2o, and 2p, and if Graham is correct in adding 2k, 2l, and 2j as texts that derive from the *Zhuangzi* source text, then we have an extended sequence of 2d, 2e, 2h, 2i, 2j, 2k, 2l, 2m, 2n, 2o, and 2p. This in itself suggests a great deal of momentum for the position that 2a, 2b, and 2c are also copied from the source *Zhuangzi*.

But before we go back to comment on 2a, 2b, and 2c, let's consider 2f and 2g. It seems that because of the identical textual correspondence with the received *Zhuangzi* in all the passages surrounding 2f and 2g, it is more likely that the editor is copying a source he has in common with Guo Xiang, than that the editor might insert 2f and 2g from some other source and break away from his copying pattern. Additionally, 2f and 2g are passages meant to teach about *wu-wei* 無為 through the skillfulness troupe just as are the text beads preceding and following them (2e, 2h, 2i, 2j, 2k), suggesting that their placement in *LZ* may follow the way they are set in the source *Zhuangzi*, rather than the received text. On this view, 2f and 2g are likely from the same source as the ten copied passages and they are probably direct quotes as well.

On this reading, then, we can extend our connections of passages tied to the lost *Zhuangzi* in the chapter from 2d to 2p, but this still does not get us back to 2a, 2b, and 2c. In this connection, consider that the chapter concludes with a series of passages 2q, 2r, 2s, 2t and 2u devoted to the powers of the Daoist master with

2t being the only bead in which we can see the use of text identical to that of the received *Zhuangzi*. Nonetheless, it seems that 2s is likely to have a *Zhuangzi* source home because of its close tie to the "three in the morning" monkey-keeper tale so familiar from the received *Zhuangzi's* second chapter. In this, I hold that 2s is recapitulating the pattern we also see in 2a, 2b, and 2c. Although we cannot trace these four texts blocks (2a, 2b, 2c, 2s) to identical passages in the received *Zhuangzi*, there can be no doubt that they do contain close similarities in phraseology, terms, themes, and sentiments with that text. Furthermore, we know that the received *Zhuangzi* often contains more than one version of a passage (e.g., compare 4a, 54–58 and 6g, 90–91) with unmistakable connections but differences between the passages on the point being made or various details of the accounts. It is quite possible that the lost *Zhuangzi* had more than one version of the "three in the morning" text bead and that the *LZ* editor copied the one which made the point he desired. I conclude that the same argument can be made for assigning 2a, 2b, and 2c as direct quotes from the lost *Zhuangzi*.

This leaves only the three text beads 2q, 2r, and 2u to account for. By their association with 2t and 2s in theme they too are likely to have come from the same source, given all the other literary critical factors we have noted. So, this is the line of reasoning we might apply to offer the defensible, but by no means certain conclusion, that the entirety of *LZ* chapter 2 (excluding 2v) may be thought to be derived from the lost *Zhuangzi*.

What we want to know next is whether there is any philosophical significance to this finding. Does it make any real difference to our understanding of and appreciation for the formation of the *LZ*? Does it shed any new light on our understanding of the picture the *LZ* gives us of Daoism or Daoist masters? Does it contribute in any way to the project of comparative philosophy?

Interpreting *Liezi*'s Use of the Lost *Zhuangzi*

Let's consider first whether the positon that chapter 2 of *LZ* is derived from the lost *Zhuangzi* throws any light on the formation of the *LZ* text. We might arrive at some interesting interpretive suggestions about the formation of the *LZ* if we could demonstrate that the material in *LZ* chapter 2 which appears identical to that found in the received *Zhuangzi* was always taken from the same strata of the received text. If this proved true, we might be able to make inferences about the lineage traditions associated with the *LZ* editor and his family, since we believe that the text strata of the received *Zhuangzi* are traceable to lineage vines of the pre-Qin period. However, setting out on the trail of such a goal is rather wrongheaded. It may very well be the case that the lost *Zhuangzi* of fifty-two chapters was not in the same order Guo Xiang used in making what has become the received text. Moreover, even if we accept the questionable assumption that the order was the same, when we follow the most recent construction of the received text's literary strata, it is clear from the chart below that there is no decided strata preference being exercised by the *LZ* editor.[2]

Comparison of LZ Ch. 2 Text Beads with Their Received *Zhuangzi* Counterparts Arranged by Strata of the Received Text

LZ text bead Graham pagination	*Zhuangzi* text bead Watson pagination	*Zhuangzi* strata in received text
2a, 33–35	Reminiscent of 11d, 118–20 may be in lost *Zhuangzi*	
2b, 35	Reminiscent of 1f, 33 may be in lost *Zhuangzi*	
2c, 35–36	Reminiscent of 1c, 32 may be in lost *Zhuangzi*	
2d, 37–38	19b, 198	Zhuangzi Disciples
2e, 38–39	21i, 230–31	Zhuangzi Disciples
2f, 39–42	lost *Zhuangzi* ?	
2g, 42–43	lost *Zhuangzi* ?	
2h, 43–44	19d, 200	Zhuangzi Disciples
2i, 44	19j, 204–205	Zhuangzi Disciples
2j, 44–45	19c, 199	Zhuangzi Disciples
2k, 45–46	lost *Zhuangzi*	
2l, 46–47	lost *Zhuangzi*	
2m, 47–49	7e, 94–97	Inner Chapters
2n, 49–50	32a, 353–54	Zhuangzi Disciples

LZ text bead Graham pagination *(continued)*	*Zhuangzi* text bead Watson pagination *(continued)*	Zhuangzi strata in received text *(continued)*
2o, 51–52	27g, 307–308	Zhuangzi Disciples
2p, 52	20j, 220	Zhuangzi Disciples
2q, 52–53	lost *Zhuangzi* ?	
2r, 53–55	lost *Zhuangzi* ?	
2s, 55–56	Reminiscent of 2k, 41 may be in lost *Zhuangzi*	Inner Chapters
2t, 56	19i, 204	Zhuangzi Disciples
2u, 56–57	lost *Zhuangzi* ?	
2v, 57		

Missing the mark on finding out something about what lineage traditions might be associated with the *LZ* editor is not a great loss. In fact, I think that there might be more interesting insights we can gain about the picture the *LZ* gives us of Daoism and masters of the *dao* by paying attention especially to the passages we have labeled as belonging to the lost *Zhuangzi*.

Shifting the focus a bit, we may explore briefly whether the recognition of chapter 2 as having its source in the lost *Zhuangzi* throws any light on our understanding of the picture *LZ* gives of Daoism and Daoist masters. Perhaps the significance of finding that *LZ* chapter 2 makes use of the lost *Zhuangzi* lies, in part at least, in how this material helps us construct an understanding of the masters of the *dao* who originated the teachings of the *Daodejing* and *Zhuangzi*. As is well known, the date of the *Liezi* was long debated in Chinese philosophical history. Many scholars took it to be a pre-Qin work. Other Chinese scholars had their doubts about considering the work to be of such antiquity. In the modern period, Graham seems to have demonstrated without serious question that the text is not much older than the fourth century CE. For many interpreters this single fact has made the *LZ* of less interest. However, if the *LZ* contains textual materials that date to the pre-Qin period, as would be the case with materials from the lost *Zhuangzi*, then we have arrived at a finding that the *LZ* may yet be giving us a very early snapshot of Daoist belief and practice.

So, while the editing of *LZ* is the fourth century CE, at least one of its sources likely contained material from the classical period of Daoist formation.

Additionally, descriptions of masters of the *dao* that we see embedded in the editor's choice of lost *Zhuangzi* material may indeed lend support to Knaul's (Kohn's) claim the Guo Xiang discarded materials containing "superstitious" ideas to which he and other educated intellectuals objected. The snapshot portrayal of masters of the *dao* to which I refer may be seen when we isolate the following set of lost *Zhuangzi* passages.

2f, 39–42	lost *Zhuangzi*	Shang-qiu Kai's skillfulness as a divine man based on his "forgetfulness." Belongs to skillfulness text set in *LZ* and *Zhuangzi*.
2g, 42–43	lost *Zhuangzi* ?	Liang Yang's skillfulness in training tigers and birds. Belongs to skillfulness text set in *LZ* and *Zhuangzi*.
2l, 46–47	lost *Zhuangzi*	The man who lives in stone and walks through fire. Graham assigns this to the lost *Zhuangzi* based on its relationship to 2k in pronoun usage (232).
2q, 52–53	lost *Zhuangzi*	There is a Way by which one will always conquer and one by which one will never conquer.
2r, 53–55	lost *Zhuangzi*	Powers of the sages, like those of the *zhenren* may be used to conquer.
2s, 55–56	Reminiscent of 2k, 41 may be in lost *Zhuangzi*	The "three in the morning" monkey-keeper story given a different point in *LZ*. Here it is used as an example of the power to read the thoughts of animals.
2u, 56–57	lost *Zhuangzi*	Hui Ang promises King Kang of Song a way by which one will always conquer. In this way, the passage continues the stream begun in 2q.

One thing that seems clear from the passages above is that they all give a good deal of attention to the powers of the Daoist master and they strain credulity in ways that Guo Xiang may have thought to be so obviously offensive to scholarly intellectuals as to be discardable.

In the case of Shang-qiu Kai (2f, 39–42), the men of Zihua bully him and play tricks on him. They get him to jump off a cliff, but instead of falling to his death, he flies like a bird and lands safely. They lie to him telling him that there is a great pearl at the bottom of a deep lake and badger him into diving in, but he surfaces actually holding such a pearl. In the end they get him to walk through the burning Fan family storehouse to recover fine materials, but he emerges unburned and heroic. In each case, the bullies intend to humiliate Shang-qiu, but he always comes out on top. In the final analysis, they hail him as a Divine Man *shen ren* 神人. He protests that he does not know by what power he does these things, only that he has forgotten which things can harm and which can benefit him. Clearly, this story is available in the tradition for more than merely the etiological explanation for why the retainers of Zihua would not bully simple-looking persons. It is a narrative expansion of the teachings that the *zhenren* 真人(perfected person) cannot be harmed by fire or drowning (e.g., Watson, 2r, 46).

The account of Shang-qiu Kai is not the only passage about the powers of the master of the *dao* to be selected from the lost *Zhuangzi* by the editor of the *LZ*. In fact, it is only a little less dramatic than is the account of the man who "lived in stone and went through fire" in text bead 2l, a passage that Graham insists belongs to the lost *Zhuangzi* based on its grammatical similarities to the known received *Zhuangzi* passages.

There is further evidence of the *LZ* editor's extreme interest in selecting from the lost *Zhuangzi* those passages having to do with the powers of the masters of the *dao*. For example, while it might appear at first that 2q, 2r, 2s, and 2u are included in order to offer teachings about rulership, this is actually only a tangential concern of these text beads. They are principally occupied with showing, as did 2f and 2l, the powers of the Daoist master. Text bead 2q follows closely the teachings of the *Daodejing*, and even the Huang-Lao strata of the received *Zhuangzi*, in teaching that there is a time to be strong and a time to be weak, that the softness that becomes hardness at the proper time is the force that cannot be defeated and the "way by which one will always conquer." Whereas, the overreliance on force and hardness is as surely the "way by which one will never conquer," text bead 2r moves into another realm. It reports that the "way by which one will always conquer" is related to the ability to command the animals and the ghosts *gui* 鬼 by the use of ritual dance and music (cf. with *Zhuangzi* 14c, 156–58; 23a, 248–54).

> Even now, in the country of Chieh in the East, there are many people who understand the speech of domestic animals; this is a discovery possible even to our own limited knowledge. The divine sages of the most ancient times knew the habits of all the myriad things, and interpreted the cries of all the different species; they called them together for meetings and gave them instructions, as though they were human beings. So the fact that the sages would meet the spirits and goblins (鬼神魑魅) first, next summon the human beings of the eight quarters, and finally assemble the birds and beasts and insects, implies that there are no great differences in mind and intelligence between living species. The divine sages knew that this was the case, and therefore in teaching they left out none of them.

The manner in which the *LZ* editor is taking material from the lost *Zhuangzi* in order to show "the way one will always conquer" is reflected as well in 2s which seems to be an allusion to the "three in the morning" story of the monkeys in the received text. However, the version of the story as taken from the lost *Zhuangzi* actually carries a very different moral.[3] In *LZ*, the point of the story is not so much that the monkeys did not know how to regard all things as equal as in the received text, but that the keeper has the power of the *zhenren* to read the minds of the monkeys!

In 2u, Master Hui Ang visited the court of King Kang of Song but encountered a very hostile reaction from the monarch. However, he offered to teach the king a way to always conquer. This language ties 2u to the text beads on which we have been commenting. In fact, what Hui Ang offered specifically was "a way to make anyone, however brave and strong, miss when he stabs or strikes at you. . ." (Graham 1990a, 56). He promises the king a way to ensure that the will of any man will be diverted from harming the king, and that all men will have only thoughts of loving and benefiting the king. Unfortunately, when the king exclaims that this is just the kind of thing he is interested in being taught the passage comes to an end.[4] It seems likely that we may be able to credit the picture we get from these lost *Zhuangzi* passages as reliably informative about what was *believed to be true* of masters of the *dao* in the pre-Qin period, even though the *LZ* itself is surely no pre-Qin text. If this is correct, the *LZ* makes a significant contribution to our understanding of the masters to whom the classical texts of *Daodejing* and *Zhuangzi* are traceable. In taking this position, we do not commit ourselves to some new eccentric or bizarrely skewed portrait of the masters of the *dao*. In fact, in the received version, we see already that the masters of the *dao* were believed to be able to

> transform the shape and substantiality of their five phase instantiations (Watson, 7e, 94–97);
> heal illness and prevent disease (Watson, 1f, 33);
> use rituals to direct and acquire numinal power (Watson, 14c, 156–58; 23a, 248–54);
> bind ghost spirits (Watson, 19h, 203–204);
> write talismans addressed to the numinal powers of the universe (Watson, 18d, 193–94);
> alter their consciousness (Watson, 2b, 37; 7c, 91–92; 13f, 152; 21d, 225–26);
> gain understanding through dreams (Watson, 2u, 47; 4d, 64; 14d, 158–59; 18d, 193; 21h, 230; 26f, 298);
> communicate with the *shen* in the stars and use calendrics (Watson, 6a, 82; 13c, 149–50); and
> sit in solitude and stillness to gain oneness with *dao* (Watson, 21d, 225–26).

What we have displayed in isolating the *LZ* editor's choice of material to copy from the lost *Zhuangzi* is his fascination with the powers of the Daoist master. The accounts preserved here, but apparently rejected by Guo Xiang, take the masters' abilities quite literally. While the *LZ* itself almost certainly does not date into the formative period of the pre-Qin Daoism, it may contain lost *Zhuangzi* textual materials that do reach back into that period and to the traditions of the earliest masters.

We may raise one final question. If *LZ* chapter 2 is derived from the lost *Zhuangzi*, then what implications would follow for comparative philosphy? Based on chapter 2's portrayal, we can now think more fruitfully of the Western analogues to the early masters of the *dao* during the classical period. In doing so, we recognize immediately that the best comparisons are certainly not Socrates, Plato, or Aristotle. We should look elsewhere in the Greek philosophical heritage. In Greek tradition, Epimenides of Knossos (Crete), who is perhaps as much a shadowy figure as is Laozi, was nonetheless said to be a philosopher-diviner-healer-poet who Plutarch (c. 46–120 CE) tells us lived in a Cretan cave for fifty-seven years. He was credited in Plutarch's *Life of Solon* with knowledge of rituals that saved the Athenian state and purified its rulers from corruption. Instead of being called a "master, as he might have been addressed in China, he was known in Greek as an 'Iatromantis'. This word means 'healer-prophet'" (Kingsley 2003, 33). Iatromantis figures in ancient Greece included Parmenides (c. 550–450 BCE) as well. The arts of healing, divination, and ritual with which Epimenides and Parmenides were associated are traceable in large measure to their practice of lying down in an enclosed space, usually a cave, and entering into a state that was neither sleeping nor waking; but an altered form of consciousness produced by stillness. This explains why they were also called by the title "Pholarchos." "Pholeos" is a lair or den, usually a cave where an animal seeks shelter. "Pholarchos" means "lord of the lair" or "lord of the den" (Kingsley 1999, 78). According to Strabo's (c. 63 BCE-24 CE) massive seventeen-volume work entitled *Geography,* there was a cave in the region of Caria, South of Phocea in which Pholarchos lived and on the basis of the dreams and visions they had while lying in the cave, they would utter philosophical aphorisms not unlike those found in the *Daodejing*, practice ritual, and prescribe treatments for the sick (*Strabonis Geographica* 14.4.4.).

Needless to say, the received histories of Parmenides' philosophy say virtually nothing about these aspects of his work and life. They present him only as a logician and abstract thinker, and they tend to be embarrassed by the fact that his only known surviving work is a poem of some 150 lines. In this poem, he makes the striking claim that wisdom and understanding are not gained by going into the light, but by unknowing and entering ignorance, by unlearning and emptying oneself of distinctions and doctrines in ways that are very suggestive of comparison to the teachings of the classical Lao-Zhuang tradition. In this state, Parmenides taught that there is no realization of a dogma or set of propositional truths, only subtlety and awareness, with the emerging power of spontaneous action like that of a child ("kouros") (Kingsley 1999, 70). Here we are reminded of the *Daodejing's* question, "Can you become an infant?" (*DDJ* 10, 55). The one who enables another in finding this experience is a nurturer of the "kouros" or a "kourotrophos," an analogue that may fit the master-adept interactions we see so clearly in the *Zhuangzi*.

Likewise, Parmenides' younger contemporary Empedocles (c. 490–430 BCE) is studied primarily for his contributions to Greek process cosmology and atomism. However, Empedocles' hagiographies also represent him as having great powers, similar to those we find reported of Daoist masters in the *Zhuangzi* in both its received and lost forms (i.e., as the lost *Zhuangzi* is made somewhat visible in *LZ* chapter 2). Included among these powers was a type of spontaneous action quite apart from any sense of behaving by a set of moral or political discriminations, a sense of the evenness of life's changes and experiences comparable it seems to *Zhuangzi's* teaching to make all things equal, and the overcoming of death and transformation to immortality. Empedocles is referred to as one who is divine, *daimon* in Greek, what the Daoists would call a *zhenren* or *xian* 仙 (Kingsley 2003, 318–19, 358).

Once again, we see from this excursion into the *LZ* text how the *LZ* offers fertile ground both for the study of Chinese Daoism itself and for comparative philosophy as well, proving itself to be a major Daoist text worthy of ongoing study.

Notes

1. My parenthesis.
2. Contemporary scholars, such as A. C. Graham (1986), Liu Xiaogan (1994), and Harold Roth (1991), have all suggested revised models for understanding the structure of the text of the *Zhuangzi*, but each of these has its detractors. In my most recent work, *Daoism: An Introduction*, I offer a construction of the textual strata of *Zhuangzi* adapting critical studies by Liu and Roth especially: Inner chapters (1–7); *Daode* chapters (8–10e, 29); Huang-Lao chapters (11; 12a, 126–28; b, 128–29; 13a, 142–48; 14a, 154–55; c, 156–58; e, 161–62; f, 163–64; g, 163–65; h, 165–66; chaper 15; chapter 16; 18a; 19a, 22a); Zhuangzi Disciples chapters (17–28 and 32); and the World chapter (33).
3. We should not hastily conclude that 2s is simply an example of the editor's having taken the "three in the morning" passage from the received text and given it a new moral. As is mentioned in the body of this chapter, there are many examples in the received text of told and retold passages with different points (e.g., in 4a, 54–58 Kongzi recommends to Yan Hui that he practice fasting of the heart-mind, in 6g, 90–91, it is Yan Hui who teaches Kongzi).
4. There really can be little doubt that the addition of the final text bead in this chapter is from the editor and not from the source he copied throughout the rest of the chapter. It begins, "The teaching of Confucius and Mo-tzu is what I have in mind . . ." (Graham 1990a, 57).

References

Barrett, T.H. 1982. "Taoist and Buddhist Mysteries in the Interpretation of the *Tao-te ching.*" *Journal of the Royal Asiatic Society* 1: 35–43.

Graham, A. C., trans. 1990a. *The Book of Lieh-tzu.* New York: Columbia University Press.

———. 1990b. "The Date and Composition of *Lieh-tzu*" in *Studies in Chinese Philosophy and Philosophical Literature.* Albany: State University of New York Press, 216–82.

Knaul (Kohn), Livia. 1982. "Lost Chuang-tzu Passages." *Journal of Chinese Religions* 10: 53–79.

Littlejohn, Ronnie. 2009. *Daoism: An Introduction.* London: I. B. Tauris.

Roth, Harold. 1991. "Who Compiled the Chuang-tzu?" In *Chinese Texts and Philosophical Contexts*, ed. Henry Rosemont Jr., 79–128. La Salle: Open Court.

Schipper, Kristofer, and Franciscus Verellen, eds. 2004. *The Taoist Canon: A Historical Companion to the Daozang.* 2 vols. plus index. Chicago: University of Chicago Press.

Watson, Burton, trans. 1968. *The Complete Works of Chuang-tzu.* New York: Columbia University Press.

Yang Bojun. 1965. *Liezi jishi* [Collected Commentaries on the *Liezi*]. Hong Kong: Taiping Book Co.

列子

Is the *Liezi* an Encheiridion?

May Sim

On the face of it, there seem to be numerous similarities between Liezi's Daoism and Epictetus's Stoicism.[1] Both thinkers advocate a certain way of living. For Epictetus, the proper way to live is one that accords with nature; for Liezi, the proper way to live is one that accords with the *dao*. Both Epictetus's nature and Liezi's *dao* dictate the way things are regardless of human beings' desires and preferences, respectively.

Epictetus's view of nature is that external things such as our bodies, possessions, reputations, or public offices are not up to us to change, whereas internal things such as our desires, emotions,[2] thoughts, and attitudes are up to us to change. He says, "Some things are up to us and some are not up to us. Our opinions are up to us, and our impulses, desires, aversions—in short, whatever is our own doing. Our bodies are not up to us, nor are our possessions, our reputations, or our public offices, or, that is, whatever is not our own doing. The things that are up to us are by nature free, unhindered, and unimpeded; the things that are not up to us are weak, enslaved, hindered, not our own" (11).[3] Accordingly, Epictetus holds that we will live well if we try to change only the things that are up to us and not the things that are not up to us.[4] He says, "If you think that things naturally enslaved are free or that things not your own are your own, you will be thwarted, miserable, and upset, and will blame both gods and men" (11). On the other hand, if you think that the things that are naturally free are free, and if you do not think that things that are enslaved are free, Epictetus says, "you will not do a single thing unwillingly, you will have no enemies, and no one will harm you because you will not be harmed at all" (11).

In a similar vein, Liezi seems to maintain that things in the world are independent of our control. He says, "Long life and short, failure and success, high rank and low, wealth and poverty, come about of themselves" (122).[5] Again, Liezi has Master Dong Guo say to Ximenzi (who has always been successful and honored) and Beigongzi (who has always been a failure and dishonored): "Your success is not due to wisdom, nor is his failure due to foolishness. Both are from heaven and not from man. . . . Neither of you perceives the principle that things must be as they are" (123). Since things must be as they are, Liezi maintains that human wisdom is impotent to change them. He quotes the following to illustrate the Way of heaven and how man is powerless:

> Inscrutably, in endless sequence,
> They come to pass of themselves by the Way of Heaven.
> Indifferently, the unbroken circle
> Turns of itself by the Way of Heaven.
> Heaven and earth cannot offend against this,
> The wisdom of sages cannot defy this, . . .
> Being of themselves as they are
> Silently brings them about,
> Gives them serenity, gives them peace,
> Escorts them as they go and welcomes them as they come.
> (127–28)

Epictetus and Liezi seem to share the same view about man's life and death, success and failure, wealth and poverty. These things are dictated by Epictetus's nature and Liezi's Way, respectively, such that they are beyond human control.

According to these two thinkers' respective views of nature and the *dao*, both hold that we are to train ourselves to be indifferent to such things that do not depend on us. For instance, Epictetus wants us to look at the death of a loved one in the same way as we would look at the death of someone else's loved one. Just as we would say that death is "the lot of a human being" when we are faced with the death of someone else's loved one, Epictetus wants us to adopt that same attitude with respect to our own loved one

(26). Similarly, Liezi tells us about a man who did not grieve when his son died. He replied as follows when his wife asked him why he did not grieve: "I used to have no son . . . and when I had no son I did not grieve. Now that he is dead, it is the same as it was before when I had no son. Why should I grieve over him?" (133).

More elaborately, both Liezi (29) and Epictetus (11) use the language of a loan or a temporary gift, as opposed to a possession, to describe our loved ones. Such a metaphor enables them to portray the impermanence of relationships, and stress that the giver or lender determines when relationships begin and end. Consequently, the proper way to regard our loved ones is to return them when the giver asks for the gift back, and to expect such a return.

Despite the fact that both Liezi and Epictetus maintain that the way things are in the world is independent of our control, neither of them advocates a life of withdrawal from the world. Both maintain that we are to respond to this external world. In fact, both Liezi and Epictetus would tell us that the proper way to act is determined by the role that one has and the circumstances within which one finds oneself. For instance, Epictetus says, "Appropriate actions are in general measured by relationships. He is a father: that entails taking care of him, yielding to him in everything, putting up with him when he abuses you or strikes you" (30). One's role as a son determines his duties, which are beyond his power to change. Even when the circumstance he encounters is one of abuse, what is appropriate from him is to control his attitudes, thoughts, and emotions because being external, this circumstance is beyond his control. Epictetus advises one in such an abusive situation as follows: "Do not consider his action, but instead consider what you can do to bring your own faculty of choice into accord with nature" (30). According to Epictetus, what one can do in such a situation is to choose not to think of oneself as harmed, and no harm can befall one. Generalizing, Epictetus says, "In this way, then, you will discover the appropriate actions to expect from a neighbour, from a citizen, from a general, if you are in the habit of looking at relationships" (30). In fact, one's roles and circumstances are the opportunities for one to be virtuous for Epictetus: "If you see a beautiful boy or woman, you will find the capacity of self-control for that. If hardship comes to you, you will find endurance. If it is abuse, you will find patience" (10).[6] In short, Epictetus maintains that attunement to the nature of things occurs when an agent always acts to bring his subjective thoughts and feelings into accord with the external situation. He violates the nature of things when he tries to change the situation itself.

Like Epictetus, Liezi proposes that one act according to one's role and circumstance rather than act counter to them. This is apparent in his story of Duke Huan of Qi (685–643 BC), who appointed as his chief minister his enemy Guan Zhong. Because Duke Huan wanted to rule the empire, and Guan Zhong was the most capable person to help him achieve this goal, Duke Huan appointed him in spite of his initial wish to kill him (124–25). Liezi's account of Duke Huan's action is similar to Epictetus's account of the son's action because both agents are acting according to their respective roles, and both are acting in ways to fulfill their proper goals. One could easily imagine that a son or a duke in these respective circumstances might have a strong subjective impulse to act otherwise were each not a Stoic or a Daoist. But Epictetus's Stoic son continues being a filial son and Liezi's Daoist duke continues being a powerful ruler.

Just as the son portrayed by Epictetus does not have a choice in his role as a son, neither does the duke portrayed by Liezi have a choice in his role as a duke. Epictetus further emphasizes our lack of choice with respect to our roles and how long we remain in these roles by comparing us to actors in a play. He says, "Remember that you are an actor in a play, which is as the playwright wants it to be: short if he wants it short, long if he wants it long. If he wants you to play a beggar, play even this part skillfully, or a cripple, or a public official, or a private citizen. What is yours is to play the assigned part well. But to choose it belongs to someone else." Similarly, Liezi also speaks of the different roles people play, which roles are determined for them. This is apparent in his descriptions of four men who exemplify diverse, contrasting characters and behaviors in their dealings with the world; each believing that his is the right response. Here are three out of five sets of different characters and attitudes Liezi mentions:

> Four men, Tricky and Simple, Tactless and Fawning, went about together in the world, each following his own bent. To the end of their lives they never discussed their methods, for each was assured of the subtlety of his own skill.
>
> Four men, Underhand and Frank, Tongue-tied and Brow-beater, went about together in the world, each following his own bent. To

> the end of their lives they never explained themselves to each other, for each was convinced that his talents would win him success.
>
> Four men, Cheeky and Stolid, Daring and Timid, went about together in the world, each following his own bent. To the end of their lives they never pointed out each other's faults, for each of them supposed that his conduct was irreproachable. (131)

For Liezi, each of these men assumes that his attitude and way of behaving is the correct one and each doesn't think that he needs to explain or justify his way to another. Liezi claims that despite their differences, all of these men "traveled on the Way in the direction destined for them" (131).

From the foregoing comparisons, Liezi's Daoism seems quite similar to Epictetus's Stoicism. They seem to acknowledge that the world is a certain way because of a certain metaphysics. This metaphysical determinant is nature for Epictetus and the Way or *Dao* for Liezi. Both authors seem to maintain that things in the world are beyond human control so that human beings should adopt a certain attitude to the world and its happenings. Yet, both seem to agree that action rather than withdrawal from the world is called for from these human beings. They also seem to agree that the appropriate actions are to be determined by one's roles and circumstances, both of which are beyond one's control.

On closer scrutiny however, Liezi's Daoism and Epictetus's Stoicism are quite different. They differ with respect to their views of the metaphysical nature of the world, how one is to attain the proper attitude toward the world's events, the relation of the self to the world, and the morality of actions and our knowledge of principles.

Let me begin with their respective views concerning the metaphysical nature of the world. In contrast to Liezi, Epictetus has very little to tell us about the metaphysical nature of the world. Inferring from what he says, the world for Epictetus is by nature divided into external things that are not up to us to change and internal things that are up to us to change. Epictetus also tells us that this arrangement of the way things are is the product of the gods' best judgment. He says,

> The most important aspect of piety toward the gods is certainly both to have correct beliefs about them, as beings that arrange

> the universe well and justly, and to set yourself to obey them and acquiesce in everything that happens and to follow it willingly, as something brought to completion by the best judgment. (31)

The gods are not only the creators of Epictetus's universe, but because they have the best judgment, the universe is ordered in the best and most just way. This means that what is good or bad is entirely up to us. The greatest goods for human beings are freedom, happiness and tranquility for Epictetus (1, 12). These goods are attainable as long as we adhere to the gods' ordering of the universe into things that are up to us and things that are not up to us. Simply put, we will always be free, happy, and tranquil if we do not seek to have things happen as we want, "but instead want them to happen as they do happen" (8). In brief, Epictetus's worldview is one where the world is ordered in the best way and human beings can fulfill their freedom and happiness by adhering to their nature and to the nature of a divinely ordered universe.

Liezi's world, unlike Epictetus's, neither issues from a definite creator or group of creators to whom we owe piety, nor is it inhabited by humans who aim to attain freedom, happiness, or tranquility. In contrast to the pursuit of an individual's own freedom, happiness, and tranquility, Liezi's sage seems to have a certain function just as heaven and earth have their proper functions. He says:

> It is the office of heaven to beget and to shelter,
> The office of earth to shape and to support,
> The office of the sage to teach and reform,
> The office of each thing to perform its function. (19)

Liezi does not say that carrying out our human function will lead to our own tranquility and happiness.[9] Liezi's Daoist world is not Epictetus's Stoic world that is set up in such a way that one's good or bad, happiness or unhappiness is entirely up to the individual. Liezi says,

> What heaven does not know
> How can man discern?
> Blessings do not come from heaven,
> Nor calamities from the sins of men. (128)

So the world for Liezi, unlike the world for Epictetus, is not created in the best way for human beings where they can attain their own happiness and tranquility as long as they accord with the nature of things. Each individual's happiness does not depend on his own actions. For Liezi, everything that happens to one is already destined: "When we say that a thing is destined, how can there be anyone who directs it?" (122). Even though Epictetus and Liezi would agree that there is no way to change the external world, they would disagree about the individual's desire and ability to attain his own tranquility and happiness. Whereas Epictetus maintains that it is entirely up to the individual to achieve his good or bad, happiness or unhappiness by adhering to nature, Liezi denies that the individual can achieve his own happiness and tranquility by such an accord. Liezi says, "There is no point in trying to accord with the will of heaven, and measuring the benefit or harm of what we do" (130).

This is because the Way already dictates that some of us will succeed while others will fail, and some of us will be wealthy while others will be poor. There is no sense in trying to pursue one of these alternatives as the goal or as one's happiness because all of these are equal as manifestations of the Way. Thus, the individual should not want to pursue his own happiness for Liezi since the individual's happiness is not what the Way prescribes. As Angus C. Graham puts Liezi's view: "In thought we distinguish alternatives, joy and sorrow, life and death, liking and dislike, and we mistake the principles which guide us to the preferred alternative for the Way itself. But the alternation of joy and sorrow, life and death, is itself the Way, and we run counter to it when we strive to perpetuate joy and life."[10] Epictetus, on the other hand, would urge us to ignore the external changes but try to pursue our own happiness. Regardless of whether one is rich, or poor, or abused, for Epictetus, one can always attain happiness by accepting these external conditions and valuing one's own virtues.

Instead of a god or several gods who created the universe in the best order as in Epictetus's Stoicism, Liezi's Daoist source is an intangible simple (19) that is unborn, unchanging (18), boundless, shapeless (19); a Nothing (22) that begets something when it stirs.[12] In other words, the Nothing that characterizes Liezi's Daoist source is not an absolute nothing, but rather, it is a source, which begets something when it stirs. Liezi says, "When Nothing stirs, it begets not nothing but something" (22). Liezi adds that this primal simplicity does nothing, knows nothing and "is capable of nothing; yet there is nothing which it does not know, nothing of which it is incapable" (20). What could Liezi mean by these seemingly paradoxical assertions? I propose that we try to understand these claims by distinguishing between the source or first cause of all things and the proximate causes of particular things for Liezi. Whereas Liezi's primal simplicity is the former, that is, the cause of all things, it is not the latter, that is, the proximate cause of particular things.[13] Primal simplicity for Liezi "preceded the appearance of the breath," which breath needs to begin, take shape, become substance, and eventually separate to create the myriad things (19). This primal simplicity is said to do nothing (in particular), know nothing (in particular), and to be capable of nothing (in particular) for it is apparent that it is not the proximate cause of any particular thing for Liezi. The proximate causes for Liezi seem to be heaven and earth, after the creation of heaven and earth themselves by the separation of breath into the pure and light, which formed the heaven, and the separation of breath into the muddy and heavy, which formed the earth (19). More elaborately, for Liezi, the shapeless simple issues in breath, which breath alters and then unites. The unity of breath is also the beginning of shape that forms heaven and earth, which in turn give rise to the myriad things. Thus, heaven and earth, rather than the primal simplicity, are the proximate causes of the myriad things. However, to the extent that the primal simplicity is the source or cause of everything, for instance, breath, shape, substance, heaven and earth, Liezi can also claim that it knows everything and is capable of everything (20). Due to the primal simplicity's boundlessness, shapelessness and priority over everything else that issues from it, Liezi says, "will the Way end? At bottom it has had no beginning. Will there ever be no more of it? At bottom it does not exist" (22–23). Since the primal simplicity is the source, it does not have a beginning. Nor will it end since it does not exist as any particular thing.

Liezi's source of everything, the primal simplicity or nothing, is quite different from Epictetus's gods in that the latter are determinate whereas the former is indeterminate, not being any particular thing. Moreover, Liezi's source seems to be altered in the process of generating heaven, earth, and the myriad things. He says, "The Simple had no shape nor bounds, the Simple altered and became one, and from one altered to sevenfold, from sevenfold to ninefold. Becoming ninefold is the last of the alterations of the breath. Then it reverted to unity; unity is the beginning of the alterations of shape" (19). Such alterations are most assuredly absent in Epictetus's gods who are characterized as having the best judgment. While Epictetus's gods created the universe in the best order according to their best judgment, Liezi's source cannot be said to create anything in the best order since it cannot be said to create any particular thing; it being said to do nothing (in particular). In fact, Liezi seems to attribute "confusion"—where the myriad things have not been separated from one another—to one of the stages of the generation of heaven, earth, man, and the myriad things from the simple (19).[14] Only subsequently, through the agencies of heaven and earth do the myriad things and order come to be. In contrast to Epictetus's account of creation where the gods created the best ordered universe without any confusion or stage of confusion, Liezi's account of creation has its source create in such a way that confusion is a part of the process.

Another difference between Liezi's Way of Nothing as the source of everything and Epictetus's gods who created the universe, is the place of rationality in each. Due to the gods' rationality or best judgment which resulted in a universe that is in the best order, man can access the rational order of the universe through reason for Epictetus. For example, Epictetus says, "It is possible to learn the will of nature from the things in which we do not differ from each other" (26). He uses the example of someone else's favorite cup breaking and someone else's loved one dying to show that we can apply our reasoning, which downplays the gravity of these events in someone else's life, to our own situations that are similar in order to understand the real nature of things and deal with them in a way that will lead to our happiness. Because the Stoic way of life is accessible through reason, Epictetus is also able to provide an account of it in his Handbook.

In contrast to Epictetus, knowledge of the Way for Liezi does not seem to be attainable by reason. No general principles can be reached by comparing one's life with another, nor by using reason because Liezi's Way, though governing everything in the world, manifests itself differently in different people and circumstances.[15] Before discussing in detail Liezi's skepticism about using reason to access the Way, let me elaborate on the Nothing and what Liezi thinks is knowledge. Liezi's Nothing is said to know nothing and to be capable of nothing. On the other hand, Liezi's Nothing is also said to know everything and to be capable of everything. It is plausible to interpret these characteristics of Liezi's Nothing in a less paradoxical way by distinguishing between two kinds of knowledge and two kinds of skill. One kind of knowledge and skill is genuine while the other kind of knowledge and skill is conventional. The former is accessible to the sage while the latter is accessible to the ordinary person. Liezi prizes the genuine and puts down the conventional. He says, "What common knowledge knows is shallow" (46, see also top of 167). Criticizing the man who took three years to make a jade mulberry leaf, Liezi says, "If heaven and earth grew things so slowly . . . there would not be many things with leaves." Liezi's remark here betrays his skepticism about conventional skill. Even though such skill may be prized by society, it cannot measure up to the power of the Way in the world, and to one's knowledge of and practice according to it. Concluding, he says, "Therefore the sage trusts the transforming process of the Way, and puts no trust in cunning and skill" (161).

In contrast to conventional skill, genuine knowledge for Liezi manifests itself in the highest man's ability to walk under water without suffocating. Liezi says, "It is by holding fast to his purest energies; it has nothing to do with skill and daring" (37). Liezi compares this purest energy to the energy in infancy which is totally concentrated. Combined with the oneness of the infant's inclinations, Liezi praises this stage for its harmony and virtue (23). Such a concentration of pure energy that seems to be common to the sage and the infant, is akin to the pure energy or breath that issues from the Nothing when it stirred, prior to its becoming the heaven, the earth, and the myriad things (18–19).[16]

Beyond infancy, Liezi maintains that to attain genuine knowledge and skill takes years of discipline and training. Achievement of the Way requires concentration of pure energy, or breath, which is frequently associated with what speech cannot communicate. This is apt since it is so close to the Nothing, which precedes the myriad things, and hence precedes the distinctions upon which speech relies. Thus, Liezi says, "The utmost in speech is to be rid of speech, the utmost doing is doing Nothing" (46, see also top of 167). Again, when Liezi's disciples asked him to share what his master, Huzi, told him, Liezi replied: " What did Huzi ever say?"

(17). Since genuine knowledge cannot be communicated by speech for Liezi, there is also not a handbook for the Daoist Way.

Instead of using reason to find the right Way, then, Liezi seems quite skeptical about using reason in general. This can be seen in Liezi's use of Confucius as a character in his text to criticize two elderly persons who were singing joyfully in spite of their proximity to death. One of them is a ninety-year-old man named Rong Qiqi who professes to have many joys. He is joyful to be a human rather than anything else, joyful to be a man rather than a woman, joyful to have lived to ninety rather than to have died when he was younger. Asserting that "poverty is the norm and death is the end" for all men, Rong is unconcerned by his approaching death (24). Liezi's Confucius responded to Rong by saying that he is one who knows how to console himself.

The other elderly man whom Liezi portrayed as evoking a similar attitude from Confucius was Lin Lei, who was nearly a hundred. Lin Lei expresses his reasons for being happy as follows: he did not bother to learn when he was young, never strove to make his mark when he grew up, and he had no wife and sons at his old age. Additionally, he is not afraid of death because he does not know if he might not be reborn elsewhere. Lin Lei speculates that death might be as good as life; it might even be a delusion to crave life for death might be better than life. Confucius is portrayed as saying that Lin Lei is a man "who has found it, yet not found all of it" (25). Liezi seems to be against those who use reason to console themselves or to persuade themselves that they are better off than they are. To rationalize in these ways about life and death is to remain caught up with the negativity of death itself. Such reasoning does not provide us with the proper knowledge of the Nothing, nor does it provide us with knowledge of the proper way to live. For Liezi then, genuine wisdom is not attainable by reasoning. In contrast, Epictetus's view of the knowledgeable man is one who could reason in such a way that he wants things in the world to occur just as they do (8) for "(w)hat upsets people is not things themselves but their judgments [or reasons] about the things" (5). If Epictetus is a firm believer in the power of reason to lead a life that accords with nature, Liezi is a skeptic about the power of reason to lead a life that accords with the Way.

Thus far, we have seen that Epictetus's understanding of the metaphysical nature of the world differs quite radically from Liezi's understanding. Epictetus talks about the gods creating the universe, whereas Liezi talks about the Nothing as the source of everything. Whilst Epictetus's gods created the best-ordered universe from their best judgments, Liezi's Nothing or source is not the direct or the proximate cause of everything in the universe. Rather, Liezi's primal simplicity issues in breath that changes to create the myriad things.[17] More elaborately, the changes in breath result in heaven and earth and subsequently, the myriad things. Unlike Epictetus's best-ordered universe from the gods, Liezi's primal simplicity undergoes chaos at certain stages of creation prior to the final outcome. Epictetus's gods are determinate and unchanging beings whereas Liezi's source is indeterminate and is subject to change. Even though both thinkers admit that what occurs in the world is beyond man's power to change, Epictetus thinks that man's control of those things that are internal and by nature free, enables him to achieve the life of happiness and tranquility, while Liezi denies that man can and ought to defy destiny and attain happiness and tranquility by himself. Whereas Epictetus maintains that there is a way to understand the nature of the world by reason, Liezi eschews reason as a way of understanding the Way of Nothing. The Stoic way of life can be communicated by speech while Liezi's Daoist Way cannot be communicated by speech. Hence, there is a handbook for the former and not for the latter.

The differences between these two thinkers' ways of dealing with the world stem partly from their attitudes toward a distinction between what is inside the individual and what is outside him and partly from the difference between their respective views of control. Let me begin with the former point. Whereas Epictetus sharply distinguishes between what is inside and what is outside the individual, Liezi does not maintain such a sharp distinction between what is inside and what is outside the individual. Liezi goes so far as to claim that the sage does not distinguish between himself and anything else in the world. While describing what happened to him after studying with his Master, Old Shang, for nine years, Liezi says that

> he thought without restraint whatever came into his mind and said without restraint whatever came into his mouth without knowing whether the right and wrong, benefit and harm, were his own or another's. Only then, when he had come to the end of everything

> inside him and outside him, his eyes became like his ears, his ears like his nose, his nose like his mouth; everything was the same. His mind concentrated and his body relaxed, bones and flesh fused completely, he did not notice what his body leaned against and his feet trod, what his mind thought and his words contained. (81)

Liezi adds, "If you can only be like this, none of the principles of things will be hidden from you" (81).

The main point of this passage is that after years of studying with his Master, Liezi no longer makes any distinctions—either physically or mentally. There is no difference between what is inside of him and what is outside of him.[18] The lack of distinction between what is inside and outside one manifests itself in knowledge. More elaborately, when Liezi mentioned that his mind concentrated, one is reminded of his talk of the concentration of the purest energy or breath in my earlier discussion of genuine knowledge for him. Like the pure energy or breath that issues from the Nothing when it is stirred, which pure energy is prior to the becoming of heaven, earth, and the myriad things, Liezi's concentration of his mind or pure energy returns him to a harmonious state that is prior to distinctions. Such a state is much closer to the Nothing than to the world of myriad things, which are distinct from each other.[19] Just as the Nothing is the source of everything, including genuine knowledge, Liezi's being in such a state of concentrated energy enables him to be knowledgeable about the Nothing as the source of all things. This results in his knowledge of everything.

Another instance of how for Liezi, genuine knowledge is the transcendence of what common knowledge takes to be inside and outside the individual, so that knowledge is a state where everything is the same and there are no distinctions between him and the rest of the world, is the following. Prior to Liezi's enlightenment by his master, Huzi, Liezi liked to travel because he enjoyed contemplating the ever changing things. But Huzi informs Liezi that while he contemplates the ever-changing things in outward travel, he actually neglects inward contemplation, which will reveal that he himself is never the same too. As tempting as it is to think that there is an outward as opposed to an inward distinction here, we will see that Huzi's point is really that the two states are exactly alike. Drawing a parallel between travel and contemplation, Huzi says, "How perfect is travel! In perfect travel we do not know where we are going, in perfect contemplation we do not know what we are looking at. To travel over all things without exception, contemplate all things without exception, this is what I call travel and contemplation" (82). This comparison of the all-inclusiveness of travel with contemplation accords with Liezi's view that ultimate knowledge is the knowledge of Nothing, which, as the source of everything, is prior to all distinctions. How can one contemplate all things and yet not know what he is contemplating for Huzi? This is possible if one is contemplating Nothing, the source of all things which source is prior to all distinctions. Hence, one who contemplates this nothing does not know what he is contemplating; yet he knows everything by knowing the source.

Not only do Epictetus and Liezi differ in their views about a distinction between what is inside and outside the individual, they also differ in their views about knowledge. Whereas Liezi's view of knowledge is that it is of Nothing and hence is devoid of all distinctions, knowledge, for Epictetus, is the philosopher's knowledge of nature, where things are divided into those that are outside the individual and those that are inside the individual. Put otherwise, knowledge, for Epictetus, is the philosopher's knowledge of clear distinctions of things in the universe, while Liezi eschews any distinctions whatsoever.

Having considered the two thinkers' respective views toward the distinction between what is inside and outside the individual, and how that distinction or lack thereof leads to knowledge for each, let us now consider their respective views toward control when dealing with events in the world. The state of sagehood without distinctions that Liezi described above is not a state where one attempts to control the outside world. Not controlling the external world is also a state with which Epictetus agrees. However, Liezi and Epictetus part company when Epictetus encourages the stoic to control his own thoughts and emotions so that his inside would harmonize with the events of the external world. Because there is nothing internal in Liezi's concentration of pure energy, it does not make sense to speak of controlling one's inner world for him. Liezi's pure energy is akin to that which issues from the Nothing prior to distinctions. Hence, Liezi's pure energy is neither internal nor external. As such, there is also nothing internal to control.

Even though there is not an inside that one is to control for Liezi, he would agree with Epictetus that one ought to harmonize with the "outside" world. Whereas Epictetus recommends the use of reason or judgment to determine what is inside and outside one, controlling what is within oneself to harmonize with the outside world, Liezi would recommend the overcoming of reason or judgment for such a harmony. More elaborately, recall the same passage about Liezi's discipleship under Old Shang for nine years, cited earlier. This same passage appeared earlier in the text with a different ending. There, Liezi says, "I did not notice what my body leaned against and my feet trod, I drifted with the wind East or West, like a leaf from a tree or a dry husk, and never knew whether it was the wind that rode me or I that rode the wind" (37). A. C. Graham points out that the different conclusions correspond to the different themes of the chapters: knowledge on the one hand, and power on the other (81). Having discussed the issue of knowledge earlier, let me turn now to the power to harmonize with heaven, earth and the myriad things.

Repeatedly, Liezi stresses that man's power to harmonize with the things around him is not accomplished by bodily or mental effort, use of his senses, or knowledge. As he puts it,

> The man who successfully accords with the way uses neither eyes nor ears, neither effort nor mind. If wishing to accord with the way, you seek it by means of sight and hearing, body and knowledge, you will not hit on it. (91)

In this context, it is important to note that the knowledge about which Liezi speaks is not the genuine knowledge of nothing, but rather, common or conventional knowledge. Liezi is saying that neither such conventional knowledge nor reliance on the regular bodily senses will enable one to act according to the Way. This is because reliance on such means can distance one from the things around us. Not only can one be distracted by one's thoughts that sight is different from hearing, and both of these are different from the mind, but one can also be distracted by how one's bodily and mental faculties are different from the thing about which one is acting. One cannot harmonize with what is around if one is caught up in such distractions, for Liezi. This is especially true for Liezi given that his ideal is a state where everything is the same so that there are no distinctions between him and the world. Instead of Epictetus's emphasis on the Stoic's use of reason to preserve his character and integrity in the face of a changing world or realm of appearances, Liezi's Daoist Way has the individual lose himself entirely, not use his mind or bodily senses, so that he fuses with the thing and becomes one with it. Liezi quotes Guan-yin saying the following with approval:

> If nothing within you stays rigid, outward things will disclose themselves. Moving, be like water. Still, be like a mirror. Respond like an echo. (90)

Despite the fact that Liezi eschews the use of bodily senses and mental efforts in according with the Way, it does not mean that anyone who is untrained can accord with the Way by simply ignoring or relinquishing such faculties. Rather, it is more like how Liezi spent nine years with his master, Old Shang, before he was rid of the distinctions in his bodily senses, his thoughts, and his words. He ultimately reaches a state of concentration where he is the same as the things upon which he acts.[20] What does this sameness with the things mean? Liezi offers numerous examples of such a unity of the actor and the thing or situation upon which he acts. Most of these examples involve the agent's attaining a kind of flexibility so that he is completely adapted to the situation. Contrary to our common understanding of action where one exerts power upon the external world, or contrary to the Stoic understanding of action where one exerts power upon one's self, Liezi's Way consists in what the Daoists call non-action (*wu-wei*), or acting by not acting. It is precisely such a way of non-action or weakening of oneself in the face of the other that gives one the power to harmonize with the things around and succeed in according with the Way. Let us look at some of Liezi's examples of how the Daoist adapts himself to and harmonizes with his surrounding.

Liezi tells us that "Equalising the give and the pull is the ultimate principle of dealing with the world" (105). He illustrates this principle with examples of fishing and archery. In both cases, the equipment used for fishing and archery are made of the weakest of materials. For instance, the fishing equipment consists of a line made from a single strand of silk thread from a cocoon and a rod made of pygmy bamboo. The hook is made from "a beard of wheat" and the bait is "a split grain of rice" (105). The archery equipment, by the same token, consists of a weak bow and an arrow attached to a thin line. Despite the weakness of their equipment, the fisherman was able to catch a fish the size of a cart amid the currents of water seven hundred feet deep, and the archer was able to shoot down two black cranes on the edge of a dark cloud, respectively. Liezi attributes these men's successes to their ability to equalize the give and the pull so that they are not pulling too hard nor giving too much. Such equalization of the give and pull prevents the equipment from breaking in spite of the strength of the surrounding forces of water and wind, respectively. It also enables both men to harmonize so well with the environment that they can approach their prey without startling them.[21] Liezi reports the account by the fisherman, Zhan He, of how he fished after taking five years to learn the principle of equalizing the give and pull as follows:

> When I overlook the river holding my rod, there are no distracting thoughts in my mind. I contemplate nothing but the fish. When I cast the line and sink the hook, my hand does not pull too hard nor give too easily, so that nothing can disturb it. When the fish see the bait on my hook, it is like sinking dust or gathered foam, and they swallow it without suspecting. This is how I am able to use weak things to control strong ones, light things to bring in heavy ones. (106)

Zhan He's description of how he fishes in this passage reveals the Daoist Way of *wu-wei*, or acting by not acting. Surely *wu-wei* or not acting does not mean that the Daoist does nothing at all.[22] Rather, it means that he does not overact or exert his power or strength over the fish. Such overaction would only startle the fish and send it fleeing. Instead of exerting strength, *wu-wei* is a way of negating strength, as seen in the weakness of the fishing equipment and bait, as well as the required balancing act in dealing with the flimsy equipment and the changes in the environment, that is, the water current. Balancing and harmonizing oneself with the environment is the way of *wu-wei*; not battling and trying to overpower it. Nor would one simply ignore the environment and retreat into one's own inner thoughts for Liezi. Rather, the Daoist's mind is completely focused on the fish so that he is at one with it. For a human to be at one with the fish, weakness is called for. Weaknesses in dealing with the equipment, environment, and thoughts are accomplishments that will take years of training for the Daoist.

Several differences arise when we compare Liezi's Way of acting through *wu-wei* with the Stoic way of action. First, whereas Epictetus believes that one should only attempt to change or control one's inner thoughts, desires, and emotions, and not attempt to change or control those things outside of one, for example, one's public office or reputation, Liezi believes that his Daoist Way of *wu-wei* is applicable to changing or "controlling" the external world. This is evident when Liezi has Zhan He recommend his Daoist Way of *wu-wei* to the king of Chu at the end of his description of fishing. He says, "If your majesty is really able to rule his state in the same way, he can turn the empire within the span of his hand; what can give you trouble?" (106).[23]

Second, change for Epictetus takes place by strengthening one's internal self. Such strengthening is achieved by holding fast to a set of fixed virtues, such as piety toward the gods, guarding one's integrity, and character. Change for Liezi, on the other hand, comes in the form of weakening one's inner, distracting thoughts, and focusing on becoming one with the external task, such as being one with the fish and its environment, or being one with the cranes and their environment. More elaborately, as we have seen earlier, change for Epictetus entails the radical separation of what is internal to man and what is external to him, whereas change for Liezi entails a radical unification of what is internal (if there is such a thing) to man with what is external to him. While Epictetus concentrates on what is inside man when change is called for, Liezi concentrates on what is outside man when change is called for. This difference between the two with respect to focusing on what is inside or outside of one in change also accounts for whether the object of change is one's internal state or the external world.

Finally, these two thinkers also differ in their views of the good. Both thinkers aspire to a goal that is good, the goal being nature for Epictetus and the Way for Liezi. But the makeup of this goal or good is quite different for each. Epictetus would maintain that nature is something that is fixed for all times whereas Liezi would refuse to make the same claim about the Way. As we have seen, Epictetus's nature is that external things such as our bodies, possessions, reputations, or public offices are not up to us to change, whereas internal things such as our desires, emotions, thoughts, and attitudes are up to us to change. So one who attempts to change the latter, changeable things, will be free and will also lead a good life. Unlike Epictetus's absolute view about nature, Liezi is relativistic about the Way. Even though the Way governs everything in this world, it manifests itself differently in different people and situations.[24] That different people could follow the Way and yet behave radically differently has been touched on in my earlier discussion of three examples illustrating the different characters and attitudes of four men. For example, recall the four men, Tricky, Simple, Tactless, and Fawning, and how they are all said to have traveled the Way for Liezi. That the Way can manifest itself in completely different or opposite actions or states is further evident when Liezi sums up the completely different endings of two families' sons who followed the exact same professions and actions. Whereas the sons in the first family succeeded, the sons in the second family met with utter failure when they pursued the same actions as those in the first family in an attempt to be as successful as they. Liezi has the father, Mr. Shi of Lu, from the first family that succeeded conclude as follows when he was approached by the father and sons of the second family:

> [N]owhere is there a principle which is right in all circumstances, or an action that is wrong in all circumstances. The method we used yesterday we may discard today and use again in the future; there are no fixed right and wrong to decide whether we use it or not. (163, see also p. 72)

Unlike Epictetus's absolute certainty about the morality of certain actions as well as one's ability to know their principles through reason, Liezi eschews such certitude about moral actions along with one's ability to know their principles through reason.

In conclusion, despite several apparent similarities between Epictetus's Stoicism and Liezi's Daoism, on closer examination, their differences are quite numerous and substantial. Perhaps this is to be expected given their different views of the metaphysical nature of the world, along with their different approaches regarding how man is to relate himself to the world.

Notes

1. Earle J. Coleman, "Aesthetic Commonalities in the Ethics of Daoism and Stoicism," *Journal of Chinese Philosophy* 29, no. 3 (September 2002): 385–95, compares Daoism to Stoicism in general. In spite of Coleman's recognition of a major difference between the Daoists and Stoics with regard to the latter's elevation of reason and the former's deprecation

of reason and reliance on intuition instead, his essay focuses primarily on the similarities between these two traditions. I will show that there are substantial differences between these two schools of thought by comparing the Stoicism of Epictetus to the Daoism of Liezi.

2. For the Stoics, emotions can be controlled by reason because they result from voluntary judgments. Steven K. Strange, "The Stoics on the Voluntariness of the Passions," in *Stoicism: Traditions and Transformations*, ed. Steven K. Strange and Jack Zupko (Cambridge: Cambridge University Press, 2004), 32–51, puts it as follows: "[T]he emotion is a movement of the soul necessarily consequent upon an evaluative judgment and occurs in one and the same *hêgemonikon* or controlling part of the soul as the judgment, and there is full continuity between a particular occurrence of a type of evaluative judgment (that a certain future available object is good or appropriate, say) and the particular resulting motion (that I pursue it on that occasion). The cause (the particular act of judgment) and effect (the particular pursuit of the object) are always present together, and there are no grounds for separating them" (42–43).

   See also Lawrence C. Becker, "Stoic Emotion," in *Stoicism: Traditions and Transformations*, op cit, 250–75, who argues for the necessity of the emotions to our practical deliberations (265), and for how the Stoic's concern for virtue in his rationality entails caring for both physical and psychological or emotional health, among caring for life, liberty, and material resources for agency, except that these concerns are subordinated to the excellence of his rationality (272).

   See Martha Nussbaum's "Duties of Justice, Duties of Material Aid: Cicero's Problematic Legacy," in *Stoicism: Traditions and Transformations*, op. cit., 214–49, for her criticism of Stoicism's separation between duties of justice and duties of material aid, which separation is based upon the radical separation between the mental life from the external world of material things and activities, so that a Stoic can be quite happy regardless of being enslaved, tortured, raped or poor (226 and 228). Accordingly, Nussbaum would not be entirely sympathetic with Becker's reading of Stoicism, which gives a place, albeit a subordinate place to the material goods.

3. Unless stated otherwise, all parenthetical references from Epictetus refer to chapters from *The Encheiridion*, translated by N. P. White (Indianapolis: Hackett, 1983).

4. Following A. A. Long, "The Socratic Imprint on Epictetus' Philosophy," in *Stoicism: Traditions and Transformations*, 10–31, Epictetus believes that human beings "are innately motivated to seek their own happiness and to prefer right to wrong" (19). Such preconceptions (*prolepseis*) about seeking happiness and the good are common to all human beings; errors occur in their applications, e.g., when someone thinks that an act is courageous or just when it is not (20). Long continues by saying that Epictetus's task is "to show how people's particular value judgments are typically in conflict with their ethical preconceptions, and thus people fail to achieve the happiness and correct behavior they naturally want" (21).

5. Unless stated otherwise, all parenthetical references from Liezi refer to the page numbers from *The Book of Lieh-Tzu*, trans. Angus C. Graham (New York: Columbia University Press Morningside Edition, 1990).
6. Virtuous acts in such circumstances are the sources of one's happiness. As A. A. Long, "The Socratic Imprint on Epictetus' Philosophy," in *Stoicism: Traditions and Transformations*, op. cit., puts it, "The Stoics' hardest and most notorious thesis was that genuine and complete happiness requires nothing except moral virtue" (11).
7. A. A. Long, "The Socratic Imprint on Epictetus' Philosophy," op. cit., maintains that Epictetus is disinterested in the physical makeup of the world. Long says, "Like Plato's Socrates, [Epictetus] professes no interest in speculation about he exact details of the physical world" (28).
8. Steven K. Strange, "The Stoics on the Voluntariness of the Passions," confirms that the Stoics think that "the world is so providentially arranged that all irresistible (cataleptic) impressions are, in fact, true. . . . Because all cataleptic or irresistible impressions are in fact true, nature never leads us completely astray. In the case of noncataleptic impressions, it is wholly up to us to assent or not" (48).
9. The term *tranquility* is ambiguous when applied to both Daoists and Stoics. If by "tranquility" one means being at "peace" with the external world so that one is not trying to change it, then it is applicable to both Daoists and Stoics since neither of them seeks to change the course of what is happening around them. However, if "tranquility" refers to the Stoic's state of mind where he desires only those things that are up to him, i.e., those things in his mind (such as the virtues) that are completely separate and distinct from things outside of him, then it is not applicable to the Daoist. This is because the Daoist does not seek to preserve or pursue anything that is completely distinct from the external world that surrounds him. Since the Daoist aspires to a state of vacuity or a state of desirelessness so that he is at one with the external world, he would not share in the Stoic's "tranquil" state of desiring something that is entirely up to him, e.g., the virtues, and being at peace or tranquil with what he desires. Nor would the Stoic aspire to the Daoist's state of desirelessness. See A. A. Long, "The Socratic Imprint on Epictetus' Philosophy," (11) and when he says that Epictetus "takes it to be self-evident that people want their desires to be fulfilled. . . . The problem here . . . is not in wanting a desire to be fulfilled; human beings naturally seek the fulfillment of their desires. Accordingly, the remedy for frustration is to focus one's desires exclusively within the mental domain, where success can be assured" (27–28). See also Steven K. Strange's "The Stoics on the Voluntariness of the Passions," op. cit., where he says, "*Boulêsis* for the Stoics is defined as reasonable desire or pursuit (*eulogos orexis*), reasonable because it is desire that aims at what is in fact good and is not merely apparently so" (33–34). Since Stoicism is not a philosophy that aspires to desirelessness or vacuity, Coleman, "Aesthetic Commonalities in the Ethics of Daoism and Stoicism," op. cit. (especially 387), is mistaken in asserting that freedom for Epictetus is gained by eliminating desires, not by satisfying them. Accordingly, he is also mistaken in claiming that the Daoists and Stoics are similar on the issue of wanting to eliminate desires.

10. *The Book of Lieh-Tzu*, trans. A. C. Graham (New York: Columbia University Press Morningside Edition, 1990), Introduction, 3.
11. Another way of putting this contrast between the Stoic worldview and the Daoist one is by focusing on how the former is teleological whilst the latter is not. Zhu Bokun, "Daoist Patterns of Thought and the Tradition of Chinese Metaphysics," *Contemporary Chinese Thought* 29, no. 3 (Spring 1998): 13–71, points out that Laozi challenges the traditional view that the natural world is decreed by heaven, saying that "heaven and earth are not benevolent," and they do not give rise to themselves, but rather, they imitate the Way, which in turn proceeds by *wu-wei*, or spontaneity—i.e., nonpurposive activity. As Bokun puts it,

> Thus the way takes as its rule "what is so of itself." This means the Way—as the supreme principle of the universe—is inaction which is so of itself. Heaven and earth take the way as their rule, which means that the changes in the natural world are also spontaneous and are lacking in purposive activity. . . . This theory of spontaneous inactivity rejects human intentionality, feelings, desires, and comparable psychological aspects. (24)

Thus, the Daoist view of the creation of the world and man's role in it is nonteleological, unlike the Stoic view. See also Xiao Jiefu, "A Sketch of the Daoist Character," *Contemporary Chinese Thought* 30, no. 1 (Fall 1998): 58–74, where he says, "Daoism exerts its strength in the study of the principle of "naturally being so without purposive action" (69).
12. Loreta Poškaitė, "The Problem of Identity and Difference in Classical Chinese Philosophy," *Dialogue and Universalism*, no. 1–2 (2003): 177–97, puts it as follows: "The main characteristic of *Dao* is the absence of characteristics. It is colorless, shapeless, scentless, empty, limitless, bottomless, nameless, that is impersonal and substantiveless . . ." (190).
13. Tang Yi, "Taoism as a Living Philosophy," *Journal of Chinese Philosophy* 12 (1983): 397–417, explains that both Zhuangzi and Laozi distinguish the specific principles that cause the myriad things from the *Dao* as the origin of all things:

> For [Laozi] the reason why [*Dao*] is unnameable is simply that he believes it to be the origin of the cosmos and as such it is not cognizable through the senses. . . . [Zhuangzi] puts this view in a more direct statement: "The myriad things have specific principles, whereas [*Dao*] is not confined to any; therefore it is not nameable." Wang Pi interprets [Laozi] in the same light. [*Dao*], unlike the specific principles, is not "tied up with" any of the limited objects, and thus is styled the Great for lack of a name. (402)

Similarly, Zhu Bokun, "Daoist Patterns of Thought and the Tradition of Chinese Metaphysics," tells us that the Way is the "principle of metaphysics" for Daoists. He says, "The significance of this principle is that the thing which serves as the origin should be universal and eternal in character and it is not some given concrete or individual thing. Laozi simply called it nonbeing" (48).

14. Compare this confusion in Liezi's source to Laozi's account of the Way when he says, "There is a thing confused yet perfect, which arose before Heaven and Earth" (*Daodejing*, Philip J. Ivanhoe, trans., 25). Bokun, "Daoist Patterns of Thought and the Tradition of Chinese Metaphysics," explains the inchoateness of the Way as follows: "According to this way of speaking, the "Way" considered in terms of an inchoately formed thing, is a substance without shape or form that transcends sensibility, but this is not to say it is an empty nothing" (47).
15. For example, see note 23 and my discussion at the beginning of this article regarding the different characters and attitudes of four men who all accord with the Way.
16. It will be interesting to compare the power of Liezi's Nothing to the incipience of the Confucian *zhong* in the *Zhongyong*. For a detailed account of the latter, see my "Harmony and the Mean in the *Nicomachean Ethics* and the *Zhongyong*," *Dao: A Journal of Comparative Philosophy* 3, no. 2 (2004): 253–80.
17. Tu Youguang's assertion about Daoism in "Daoism Stresses Individual Objects," *Contemporary Chinese Thought* 30, no. 1 (1998): 45–57, is relevant here. Tu says, "the Way is essential *qi*. This interpretation of the Way is present in all schools of Daoism" (46).
18. To attain such a state where one no longer makes distinctions entails a sharpening of the Daoist's mind so that he can be attuned to the manifestations of the *Dao*. Such a state also requires that the Daoist not be hindered by his personal desires. As Tang Yi, "Taoism as a Living Philosophy," op. cit., puts it in the case of the sage's cultivation of the "ultimate virtue" which will allow him to observe the *Dao* in Laozi's *Daodejing* 10:

    > In cultivating this virtue it is necessary for the sage to sharpen his mind's eye to the utmost, in order to observe the subtle workings of [*Dao*] without being handicapped by any petty desires. Elsewhere he refers to desirelessness (1), ultimate vacuity and true tranquility (16) as the correct state of mind for the observations of the manifestations of [*Dao*]. (404)

19. As Loreta Poškaitė, "The Problem of Identity and Difference in Classical Chinese Philosophy," op. cit., puts it, "In Daoism the way of identity begins with the equalization of a human being with all other things, and ends with the extension of human identity into non-being, emptiness, in which the boundaries between identity and difference disappear" (197).
20. Loreta Poškaitė, "The Problem of Identity and Difference in Classical Chinese Philosophy," op. cit., explains such a Daoist state when she says,

    > For Daoists, the center of the bodily and spiritual energy is the heart-mind (*xin*), which thus becomes the manifestative center of universal identity ("this"). It is not, however, definable by any characteristics (by goodness or compassion, for example, as in Confucianism) because of its emptiness (as an ideal condition). It means absolute receptivity, which makes one's free communication with others (the identification of the

object and subject, human and things) possible, in the same way as a window or a mirror. That is why Zhuangzi (Laozi and Mencius too) suggests purifying one's heart, clearing it from doubt, making it calm in order to make it bright and limpid). (195)

21. The principle of equilibrium and harmony in *wu-wei* is also applicable to traditional Chinese medicine. Tang Yi, "Taoism as a Living Philosophy," puts it as follows:

> Health in the human body is viewed as a dynamic equilibrium between the negative force *yin* and the positive force *yang*. Tip the balance, and you have disease and even death. The business it is of medicine, as well as the hygienics, to prevent this and failing that, to help recover, the balance by harmonizing *yin* and *yang*. . . . Although this theory is somewhat touched by the dynamic philosophy of the *Yin Yang* school, its tone is undoubtedly [Daoistic], the implication being that it is the natural course of nonaction that keeps the balance of yin and yang. (401)

22. Compare this with Tang Yi's, "Taoism as a Living Philosophy," op. cit., account of *wu-wei* in Laozi's politics. He says:

> In so far as [Laozi's] politics is concerned, Non-action does not mean no action or no government, but governing wisely, without overtaxation, without cunning knowledge, without unnecessary property . . . without expansion and aggressive war . . . so that the people can be happy in the development of their natural propensities. (410)

23. One might, at this point, recall my earlier discussion regarding Liezi's view that things in the world, such as the length of one's life, success or failure, rank and wealth, are not up to us but are the results of the Way of heaven. If this is the case, then how can I assert that Liezi's Way of *wu-wei* is applicable to changing and controlling the external world like the act of ruling? A plausible response is this. The Way is indeed ultimately responsible for all these aspects of our lives, i.e., longevity, success, rank, and wealth. People who possess genuine knowledge of the Way, however, are also those who have spent years perfecting the Way of *wu-wei*. Hence, they are able to let the Way work through them and in their particular situations. In these cases, they are also working with destiny and hence accomplishing what is destined for them. *Wu-wei* then, need not be inconsistent with destiny. Compare this practicality of the Way with Laozi's account in the *Daodejing*, Philip J. Ivanhoe, trans. (Indianapolis: Hackett, 2002) when he says, "Hold fast to the *Dao* of old, in order to control what is here today" (14).
24. This point about the Way is expressed quite well by Xia Jiefu, "A Sketch of the Daoist Character." Xia explains the *Zhuangzi* as follows:

> The lively fables of "the frog in the well," "the Earl of the River," and "the Overlord of the Sea" show that "from the point of view of the Way, there is no distinction of noble and common applicable to things; from the point of view of things, each thing considers itself valuable and other things mean." (71)

Interpretive Essays

列子

Torches of Chaos and Doubt

Themes of Process and Transformations in the Liezi 列子

John H. Berthrong

Background of the *Liezi* Text

The aim of this chapter is to examine the interrelated traits of process, flux, change, generation, spontaneity, or transformation found in the text of the *Liezi* 列子 (hereafter *LZ*).[1] Succinctly, what role does the trait of process play, broadly defined as the principle of transformation or the generation of something new or fresh, in the philosophical vision of the *LZ* text? It will come as no surprise for any attentive reader of this famous text that protean transformation plays an important role in the work—Daoists always, for instance, love to talk about the wonders of transformative change, if for no other ironic reason than to taunt their stodgy Confucian cousins. One of the best definitions of classics for any cumulative philosophical or religious tradition is that they are works with an astounding surplus of meaning and that they also can survive translation from one culture to another. In the case of the *Liezi* one of the surplus areas has to do with notions of generativity, transformation, growth, and process. Zhuangzi wrote, "The torch of chaos and doubt—that is what the sage steers by. So he does not use things but relegates all to the constant. That is what it means to use clarity" (Watson 1968, 42). The irony here is that the constant is change or spontaneity, *ziran* 自然 itself; this is hardly the kind of constant norms or moral precepts so dear to the mind-hearts of Confucians or Legalists.

The *LZ* is one of those books recognized by critical traditional Chinese textual scholars as a prime exemplar of *weishu* 偽書 or spurious texts. Nor is such a label surprising; there are many such texts extant. It always helped the reputation of any classical text to be attached to the authority of an ancient worthy, and so there was continually the temptation to attribute a work to an earlier, famous author. Moreover, modern scholarship has tended to confirm the early Chinese doubts about the authenticity of the received text of the *LZ* (Graham 1986a). Once the seed of doubt is planted, it is plain to see, as generations of commentators have noticed, that great chunks of the present *LZ* text were ingested and then digested whole from the *Zhuangzi*. However, as we shall note, the problem of the provenance of the received text of the *LZ* is not a fundamental problem for our purposes.

In fact, the question of the provenance and dating of the text is one of the reasons for my interest in it. If the modern scholarly consensus is correct, the received version of the *LZ* is to be dated to the early part of the fourth century CE. This is a period that marks the end of classical period of Chinese thought in a decisive way and is known traditionally as the Wei-Jin period, after two of the dynasties from the era. Of course, scholars also plausibly argue that the real end of the classical period comes somewhere in the Han dynasty. What they are trying to describe is the clear differentiation in cultural sensibility found in the works of the last decades of the Zhou and the early days of the Han and the kinds of writing preserved after the fall of the Han and before the rise of Buddhism. The third and fourth centuries C.E. are typically categorized as the age of the flourishing of *xuanxue* 玄學 "Obscure Learning" [often called Neo-Daoism as well] and the arrival and "conquest" of China by the Buddha dharma (Wagner 2000; 2003; Zücher 1959; Ziporyn 2003).

Any reasonable elucidation of what is encompassed by these taxonomic claims about Xuanxue discourse and Buddhism would demand an elaborate study of the historical development of Chinese thought during the classical and postclassical periods.[2] Such a presentation, though useful, would deflect us from our search for the motifs and metaphors of process in the *Liezi* and must therefore be wistfully abandoned. Suffice it to note that the received *LZ* text probably represents quite well the eclectic intellectual currents of the Wei-Jin period. In fact, the text's combination of older Zhou and Warring

States sources and newer eclectic material makes it a good place to rummage for motifs and traits of process sensibilities in one of the great transition periods of Chinese intellectual history.

The Acerbic Cosmos of the *Liezi*

Any choice of a text to examine for process themes in "philosophical" Daoism is arbitrary; in fact, the whole notion of some special school or tradition we can meaningfully call "philosophical Daoism" is now highly disputed.[3] H. G. Creel once told his University of Chicago seminar on Zhuangzi that he considered Zhuangzi one of the greatest of all philosophers. Furthermore, Creel went on to say that as far as artistic flair went, only Plato could equal Zhuangzi's astounding incantations of words and images. The Daoists are not only stellar philosophic raconteurs; some of them were pure magicians of words and images, and working in the Zhuangzi tradition, whoever edited the final version of the *LZ* sustained this provocative sense of humor while all the time forcing us to pay attention to the philosophical worldview sustaining the vision.

At some time in the future we may find a new treasure trove of ancient texts in a musty tomb that will reveal to us more about Liezi and his circle. But as noted above, for the moment this is not the case. The scholarly consensus is that the present text of the *LZ* is probably a compilation of the third or fourth centuries of the Common Era; again, generations of scholars have noted that the current text relies heavily on *Zhuangzi* for material. Nonetheless, the *LZ* does have a unique voice. Although not a literary masterpiece in the same class as the *Zhuangzi*, it is still a very stylish work. The *LZ* is as humorous and outrageous as its classical model—understandably because it borrows so much directly from the earlier text almost verbatim. But the humor is darker and the tone more ironic, sometimes almost sardonic. This style bespeaks of a world in decline, of the darkness of decay when Hegel's owl finally flies off into the dusk of history. Besides, it is a very good read; and this is not only the case in original classical Chinese[4] but also in the accurate and felicitous English translation of A. C. Graham (1960).

The preface of Zhang Zhan (fl. 370) to the received text tells us this about the history of the text. Even the text of the *Liezi* begins in the change and transformation of a complex and transforming period of Chinese history, the famous Wei-Jin transition from the classical epoch and Han dynasty to the long medieval age.

I have heard my late father say, "My late father (Zhang Zhan's grandfather), Liu Zhengyu, and Fu Yinggen were all maternal nephews of the Wang family. When they were young they played together in the maternal family's house. My father's maternal uncle was Wang Zizhou and his elder first paternal cousins Wang Zhengzong and Wang Fusu (Wang Bi), all liked to collect books. They had collectively secured Wang Chongxuan's library, which totaled almost ten thousand *juan* (NB: sections or chapters of texts). Mr. Fu's family has also been recognized scholars for generation. The three gentlemen had been friends from childhood and they competed in making copies of rare books. When they reached their maturity, having met the disorders of the Yongjia period (307–312 CE), my father, along with Fu Yinggen, escaped south in order to avoid the disaster. The carts were heavy and loaded to their capacity. Moreover, because the bandits were numerous and the road in front still long, my father said to Fu Yinggen: "Now it is unlikely that we will be able to preserve all that we are carrying, so let's merely select whatever items we estimate the world will want and each of us preserve and copy these works so that they will not be lost." Fu Yinggen therefore only saved his grandfather's Xuan's and his father Xian's collected works. Upon arriving south of the Yangze there was only a part of these works left. Of the *Liezi* there was only the "Yangzhu" and "Explaining Conjunctions" chapters and the report, in three *juan*. At the time of the disorder, Liu Zhengyu became the governor of Yangzhou and came across the river to our side. Afterwards my father obtained four *juan* from Liu's home, and subsequently also sought out six *juan* from Zhao Jizi, Wang Bi's son-in-law. By collating and comparing what was and was not in the various texts, only then was he able to compile the complete edition.

This book, in summary, attempts to show that total emptiness is the chief principle that governs all things, the evidence for which is that all things come to an end; divine wisdom is preserved constantly in the concentration of quietness, whereas the thoughts and reflections of desire come to grief in their own attachment to material things; but if one becomes enlightened that these thoughts and reflections of desire are like transformations and dreams, then one will not be limited, whether in matters large or small, to one realm; failure and success do not depend on mental power, and in self-governing it is best to let oneself go; if one follows his own

> nature then everything will be favorable wherever you go, and you will be able to tread on fire and water; and if one forgets oneself, there will be no mystery that is not illumined. This is the essence of the work. Thus what it makes manifest is often similar to the Buddhist scriptures, but its major conclusion accords with the *Laozi* and the *Zhuangzi*. Its choice of words and analogies particularly resemble the *Zhuangzi*. Zhuangzi, Shen Dao, Hanfei, Shizi, Huainanzi, the *Xuanshi*, and the *Zhigui* all quote its words, and therefore I have annotated it in this manner. (Yang 1965, 178–79)

This preface of the annotator of the received texts tells us a great deal about the nature and place of the text in the complicated world of Wei-Jin intellectual and social history. It situates the text for us in the difficult days at the beginning of the fourth century CE; and it does even more by telling us about the intellectual and social world of the text. Graham's best guess about the date and the composition of the text is that it was probably complied in the early fourth century and that there is one hand at work in the final redaction of the text (Graham 1986a). There is nothing in the preface that would contradict Graham's astute estimation of the received text. As he points out, much of the text is written in the form of "parables," a common genre for the third and fourth centuries.

The preface also paints a picture of the difficulties of life in the Wei-Jin period even for the rich elite. Civil wars abounded, and if the civil wars were not enough, bandits and foreign raiders compounded the difficulties. Many of the great Han clans did just what Zhang's family did: they moved south. The south at this time is not as we think of it today, or even in the Song period. It was a world of mystery, mists, and water; it was dramatically different from the dry north China plain that had been the cradle of Chinese culture and the seat of all the former Chinese states and imperial dynasties. As the elite families moved south, they tried to take as much of the treasured classical culture as possible with them. As Zhang tells the story, one of the things the family took was the text of the *LZ*.

Sadly from the perspective of the wandering elite, the *LZ* text suffered much from its move to the south. Most of the text was lost and had to be recreated from collections of books other exiled friends brought with them from north China. The preface makes it very clear that the present text is a reconstituted version of the original. The original text, however, was taken to be a genuine text from the heyday of the classical period. The proof for this was that other great classical Warring States texts quoted from the *LZ*. Even though critical scholars are dubious of the truth of these editorial assertions, the antiquity of the collected fragments was one of the reasons for preserving and publishing the new edition.

The other unmistakable note of change is the reference in Zhang's preface to the Buddha *dharma*. The Chinese recognition of the Buddha *dharma*, almost going with saying, marks a major transformation of the social, religious, and philosophic world of China. The Chinese had never before encountered, or even imagined, that there might be a civilized world beyond the boundaries of the Middle Kingdom that could produce something of cultural interest to them. Of course, as we now know, the Sinitic cultural world was never completely cut off from other parts of Asia, but compared to the contact between the European Greco-Roman world and India, the connections between China and the rest of Eurasia were scanty at best. What the Chinese did know, and which was crucial during the interregnum between the Han and the Sui-Tang restoration, was that the world beyond the traditional border of empire was filled stock full of warlike "barbarians." It would never have occurred to the Chinese that these barbarians had anything subtle to share with the educated elite. What had been shared, such as the introduction of the stirrup—which allowed for the creation of the much feared steppe heavy cavalry—did not count for much in the Sinitic inventory of civilized behavior or ritual.

Wei-Jin Philosophical Motifs

What then, can we identify as the governing motifs of the *LZ*? Arthur Wright, in his "A Historian's Reflections on the Taoist Tradition," outlined three defining traits for the entire spectrum of classical Daoist cultural forms. First, there is "an organic view of man and the universe, the notion that all phenomena (including man) are knit together in a seamless web of interacting forces, both visible and invisible. Interwoven with this is the idea of ceaseless flux: that the apogee of any of these forces engenders a reversion towards its opposite" (Wright 1970, 248). The second theme, also cataloged by A. C. Graham in his studies of the *Zhuangzi*, is the motif of primitivism (1986a). There is a longing on the part of Daoists for the freedom both for the individual and the society as a whole to return to a simple form of organization. Joseph Needham has also hypothesized that perhaps the Daoist hankering for the simplicities of rural blissful domesticity was the echo of a memory of life before the rise of urban strife.

The third trait defines the characteristic element of the Daoist religious quest. "A third element is the persisting belief that some men, by divers regimens—mystical, dietary, sexual, alchemical—can attain a kind of transcendence, which manifests itself in longevity, invulnerability, charisma, the ability to know and manipulate the forces around them" (Wright 1970, 248–49). Wright was not part of the group of scholars who divided Daoism neatly between the classical (Warring States texts) philosophical and (post-Han) religious visions and revelations. Wright, as a fine intellectual historian always does, had the knack of directing out attention to the obvious. Many scholars of Daoism had noticed that one of the persistent motifs of the tradition is a penchant for process—at least the kind of process made popular by Whitehead in the North Atlantic world. The question that needs to be asked is, what kind of "process" does Wright find in the ceaseless flux of the Daoist *imaginaire*? Wright certainly does not specify a robust Whiteheadian process but rather notes that we find a cosmology of ceaseless flux as one of the defining traits of philosophical Daoism.

Now, certainly a ceaseless flux and Whiteheadian process share movement, change, and transformation. However, in Whitehead there is a sense that the many become one in the process of self-generativity; there is an auto-telic feature to Whitehead's version of a creativity that generates actual entities without ceasing. Does a ceaseless flux define the same processive domain? Of course, Wright is trading on the ubiquitous pan-Sinitic world of yin-yang and the five forces. Given the late date of the received *LZ* text this is not a problem; the yin-yang/five *wuxing* 五行 phases cosmology had stabilized long before the *LZ* was given its final editing. In fact, it is such a commonplace feature of Chinese thought that most contemporary scholars assume that some form of the yin-yang/five phases format has been around ever since the beginning of Chinese second order self-reflection. However, it is well to remember that although prototypes of the mature yin-yang/five phases cosmology have informed the earliest records of Chinese culture, the maturation of the stable cosmology did not fall into place in its final form till the Han dynasty (Graham 1986b). Great Confucian scholars such as Dong Zongshu and Yang Xiong seem to have played an important role in fusing all of these cosmological traits into one attempt at systematic discourse, albeit with a Confucian cadence (Lloyd and Sivin 2002). But once in place it seemed so intuitive that it was assumed that this was about as cosmologically commonsensical as you could be.

For the sake of argument, let us ponder the ceaseless flux of all things and events a bit more. As Wright notes, this emphasis on flux is not entirely random. The flux is predicated on an organic viewpoint and is defined by a set of constant alternations. The alternations are aptly called yin and yang. The organic aspect is also linked to some of the central features of the yin-yang dyad. Yin and yang are organic in a deep sense because they are connected and constantly balanced. When the yang reaches its farthest point it reverts to a yin phase, and vice versa. The whole complicated technology of the *Yijing* lore is predicated on the alternation of the yin and yang in just this fashion.

It is the basis for what Graham, Geoffrey Lloyd, Nathan Sivin (Graham 1986b; Lloyd and Sivin 2002) and others have identified as the correlative structure of Chinese cosmology. It is not an agonistic battle between good or evil, light or heavy, male or female.[5] Rather, it is the oscillation between the two inseparable poles of reality in the making. Men and women, for instance, are an intricate balance of yin and yang, the five phases, and the social conditioning of the larger cultural world. In the 1950s Joseph Needham (Vol. II, 1956), so often a pioneer in Chinese intellectual history, followed Zhong Dongsun and named this typical Chinese cosmological approach correlative or dialectical thinking (see also Graham, 1986b). He argued that the classical Chinese intellectuals did not typically employ a subject-predicate proposition to frame their discourse and hence did not rely on the Aristotelian identity-difference logical framework. Rather, Needham said, "Relation (*lian* 連) was probably more fundamental in all Chinese thought than substance" (Needham 1956, 199). Needham elaborates the relational and organic sensibilities of the classical Chinese tradition in the following fashion: "Where Western minds ask '*What* essentially is it?', Chinese minds asked '*how* is it related in its beginnings, function, and endings with everything else, and *how* ought we to react to it?" (Needham 1956, 200).

Of course, the *LZ* does not adopt the philosophic motif of process as its main theme. Pride of place in this regard goes to *ziran* 自然 or spontaneity. However, the connection is very strong because without process as change and transformation, it is hard to see how the *LZ* could make *ziran* work at all, or vice versa. There is nothing surprising in this textual usage of *ziran* because the *LZ*, as we have already noted, is heavily derivative of the *Zhuangzi*, and *ziran* is a key in the *Zhuangzi* text. Along with *wuwei* 無為 or uncontrived action in the *Laozi*, *ziran* is probably as characteristic of classical Daoist thought as any term can be. Although spontaneity is not the same as process, such as the famous *shengsheng* 生生 or generativity [or creativity itself according to Mou Zongsan's reading the *Yijing* (1983, 1994)], it affords a processive sensibility to the *LZ*. These shared and even common set of motifs certainly move around in flux and refuse to stay the same whatever else we can say about them as thematic markers of process.

One important aspect of spontaneity is clearly presented when we think about the moral thinking of the *LZ*. Even as perceptive a scholar as H. G. Creel (1970) argued that there is nothing like ethical discourse in the Daoist tradition, at least when compared to the relentless focus on the ethical in the works of the Confucian masters. This is only true if we think of ethics as a deontological set of rules, and as we all know, the Daoists are congenitally allergic to rules of any kind, especially ethical rules so near and dear to the mind-hearts of Confucian worthies. In the "Explaining Conjunctions" chapter, it states that "[i]n any case, nowhere is there a principle which is right in all circumstances, or an action that is wrong in all circumstances" (Graham 1960, 163). The *LZ* goes on immediately to add a very pragmatic twist to its maxim about the nonefficacy of moral fixity. "The method we used yesterday we may discard today and use again in the future; there is no fixed right and wrong to decide whether we use it or not" (ibid.). At least one point to draw from the *LZ* narrative is that one does act in a moral fashion even if there is no fixed set of moral rules.

Daoist spontaneity is not a fixed moral norm. This is the point that Laozi, Zhuangzi, and Liezi constantly make to anyone bothering to listen to their stories of doing the right thing in the wrong way and vice versa. There is almost an endless list of such stories in the *LZ*. What is often amusing is that these stories are put in the mouth of Master Kong himself. Or there are times when a truly enlightened Daoist teacher confounds Master Kong as he blunders along in a typically constrained Confucian manner.

Transformations, Changes, and Generation

In the first place, the *LZ*'s cosmology is grounded firmly in the pan-Sinitic cosmology of *qi* 氣 vital force and the interaction of yin and yang and the five forces. According to the Liezi persona, the sages used the notion of yin and yang to order the cosmos. What is expansive and blowing out is yang and what is withdrawn and drawn within is yin. As Graham notes in his introduction to the opening chapter, "Heaven's Gifts," it is almost impossible to provide a univocal translation of *qi*. Almost four decades later, Hal Roth (1999) reconfirms Graham's estimation of the difficulty of translating *qi* consistently in English. Roth's informed surmise is that *qi* might originally have meant vapor, and then took on the connotation of breath, and moved on to even more cosmological glory as one of the key philosophical, spiritual, and medical concepts in the history of Chinese thought.

Along with the notion of polarity and reciprocity, mention of yin-yang in the *LZ* text also assumes various forms of change, transformation, birth, and flux. The *LZ* is not an organized metaphysical text by any stretch of the imagination. If challenged by such a notion, I can only imagine Liezi mocking the whole idea of metaphysics as a science. What physics? What science? And what things could we possibly be talking about would be the retort? Moreover, the aim of the work is not philosophical in a prepositional/assertive sense (Buchler 1974, 1990). Rather, the *LZ* text focuses its attention on questions of life and death and living in dangerous times in perilous situations. If it teaches anything, it is a perspective on the cosmos that allows us to be detached from the more common concerns generated by living toward death. It asks us to take the big picture and to take it with a pinch of salt and a willingness to laugh at our all too human pretensions of control and wisdom.

One of the most common themes found over and over again in the *LZ* is that things change. Nor is this an isolated insight in classical or post-Buddhist Chinese thought. The *Zhuangzi* proffered the same teaching. However, it is such a common theme in the *LZ* that some scholars have suggested a strong Buddhist influence on the text. The reasoning is that one of the central tenants of Mahayana Buddhism is the lack of any essential substance for any and all *dharmas* all the way down. There is no eternal entity and no subsisting essence to anything at all. All beings, even *dharmas*, arise and decline. Moreover, critics also note an inordinate interest in the question of dreaming or illusion in the *LZ* text. Dreaming, of course, was a famous part of the Butterfly-human dream recounted by Zhuangzi. Therefore, an accent on distinguishing, where possible, between the dream and waking state, was a perfectly presentable Daoist pastime. However, the linking of the dreaming world to the further speculation that all the cosmos may be an illusion based on dreaming suggested Buddhist influence. The counterclaim is that here again the internal logic of the Daoist discourse moves in a parallel fashion so it is impossible to say whether or not the *LZ* redactor was stimulated or influenced by Buddhist texts or ideas.

Whatever the outcome of such questions of intellectual influence are, this does not subtract from the point that in either scenario flux, birth, and transformation, in short, common metaphors for process, are very much in conceptual play throughout the text. In fact, anyone consulting either Graham's English translation (1960) or the critical Chinese edition of Yang Bojun (1965) will discover that themes of process and flux abound.

I will now track some of these processive themes. In order to delimit the search, I will focus on a set of important Chinese terms, for instance terms such as *sheng* 生, *hua* 化, *gai* 改, *shi* 勢, *bian* 變, *yi* 易, *ziran* 自然, and so forth.[6] These are most commonly translated verbally as to give birth, to transform, spontaneity, to change, to move, and so forth. For example, the graph *sheng*, according to the New Confucian Mou Zongsan (1983; 1990; 1994), is the prime candidate for the metaphysical notion of creative process in the Chinese philosophic tradition, broadly conceived. Mou cites as the *locus classicus* for the notion of creativity the famous passage in the Great Appendix of the *Yijing*, such that *shengsheng* [*buxi*] 生生不息 means creativity without ceasing in a strong metaphysical sense. By defining *shengsheng* as creativity itself, Mou means that the very nature of the cosmos is processive in nature, and that to have a cosmos means the generation of new and novel things and events. Some Chinese and Western critics argue that Mou has been reading too much process-oriented Western philosophy; while it is true that Mou was an amazingly learned scholar with a vast accumulation of knowledge of Western philosophy (he began his career as a logician who had an early interest in Whitehead and then an abiding passion for Kant), Chinese Buddhism, and every other form of Chinese thought, Mou would have demurred that his focus on *shengsheng buxi* was about as foundational and mainline to the development of all the various schools of Chinese thought as you could possibly find.[7] A literal translation of *shengsheng buxi* is generation (or birth) without ceasing. From this Mou makes the philosophic claim that this generation without ceasing is the pan-Sinitic metaphor for creativity itself as the cosmological signifier of universal process.

Before I review material from the opening sections of the *LZ*, I quote of my favorite lines about the ubiquity of change qua process from the chapter "Confucius." "Anything at all that we see, we always see changing. You are amused that other things never remain the same, but not know that you yourself never remain the same" (Graham 1960, 82). The dialogue in this parable is between Liezi and his teacher, Huzi. Liezi loves to travel. The tradition introduces Liezi as someone who wanders through the world by riding on the clouds. But of course, Huzi chides his student by missing the real point of the flux of the cosmos. True, Liezi observes the *bian* 變 or change of the cosmos, but fails to understand that his own personhood is as much in control of the *bian* of the cosmos as anything else whatsoever.

The opening chapter, "Heaven's Gifts," devotes a great deal of time to discerning various features about the ceaseless flux of the cosmos. The first section begins with Liezi living in the game preserve of Putian. Quoting the words of his own master Huzi, Liezi says, "There are the born and the Unborn, the changing and the Unchanging. The Unborn can give birth to the born, the Unchanging can change the changing" (Graham 1960, 17). The Chinese for birth is *sheng* 生and for change is *hua* 化. Therefore, two of the most important terms for a Daoist, or any Chinese philosophy for that matter, theory of process put in an appearance at the very beginning of the text. A moment later the text explains, "Things for which birth and change are the norm are at all times being born and changing. They simply follow the alternations of the Yin and Yang and the four seasons" (17–18).

One could hardly expect to find a more concise definition of the processive aspects of the mature classical pan-Sinitic cosmology than what is recorded in the opening section of "Heaven's Gifts." As we shall see, just after these opening sections, the next section then also gives us an example of a third linguistic marker for flux, change, and process, namely *bian*. But before we continue reading the *LZ*, I want to highlight one other aspect of the statement about the alternation of the yin and yang forces. The last phrase introduces the element of time. The four seasons are often invoked metaphorically as representing the temporal dimension of cosmic flux. For instance, the enigmatic first four graphs of the *Yijing* are exegeted as referring to the four seasons or even the four phases of the arising, success, favor, and faithfulness of anything whatsoever (Liu et al. 1995, 3–4). Whether or not this is an accurate rendition of what these opening phrases of the text meant to the original authors is almost impossible to say. What is important here is that this sense of temporal development from inception to mature faithfulness is what the classical self-reflective tradition believed was being said in this most universally respected of early texts.

There is another interesting turn of phrase in this early passage. This is the character Graham translates twice as "the norm." Actually the Chinese character *chang* occurs a number of times as the *chang* 常 of birth and the *chang* of change as it were. The semantic range of *chang* includes the notion of a norm, of a rule, of something constant. In modern Chinese it also means enduring, the general, certain, lawlike, etc. *Wuchang*, 五常 for instance, are the five cardinal Confucian virtues in the sense of being the five constants of moral lives. Birth and change are indeed the norm of anything that becomes and perishes.

The next cluster of passages in "Heaven's Gifts" continues this trend of thought. One of the commonplace statements I hear often about Chinese thought is that it lacks an interest in deductive explorations of topics such as the nature of being either in its ontological or cosmological form. There may be something of a statistical grain of truth in such assertions, but the following argument from the *LZ* should cause us to wonder if this lack of interest in the hot topics of Western metaphysics is really completely lacking from the Chinese scene. Of course, one of the difficulties in making my present claim is that the passage is ironic or perhaps even nonsensical in a humorous vein. It is not that the *LZ* text or its great model, the *Zhuangzi*, are uninterested in such questions, it is rather that they approach them with a characteristic sense of humor that masks the serious point they are making.

Liezi says at the beginning of the passage that "[f]ormerly the sages reduced heaven and earth to a system by means of the Yin and Yang" (Graham 1960, 18). The question then is posed, that "if all that has shape was born from the Shapeless, from what were heaven and earth born?" (ibid.). A sensible question indeed about how to determine what is the true nature of nature, and it is almost Socratic in method. If you merely provide me with examples of, let us say, virtuous action, I must still ask, what makes these virtuous actions and not just neutral behavior? It is the next set of statements that are very hard to interpret.

Liezi goes on to state that there were four "primal" traits: Primal Simplicity, Primal Commencement, Primal Beginnings, and Primal Material. I confess that I am never sure how seriously to take such lists in the *LZ*. Is the author just making fun of more serious cosmological thinking, half in jest, or is the author somewhat concerned to provide a vision, metaphor, or parable of how things work? I am not alone in enjoying such perplexing hermeneutical moments—East Asians have appreciated the ironic humor of this part of the Daoist world for more than two thousand years. But, if for a moment we take the underlying nomenclature of the list somewhat seriously, it is not without significance that the first segment of the list is the *taiyi* 太易. *Tai* is the term deployed in most Chinese thought when the author wants to indicate the highest, deepest, most profound manifestation of the topic at hand. For instance, within Song Confucian thought, following the *Yijing*, the ultimate is called the *taiji* 太極 or Supreme Polarity in Joseph Adler's felicitous and apt translation of the term (in de Bary 1999–2000). The old standard translation of *taiji* was Supreme Ultimate, but I hold Adler's new rendering to be more in line with the correlative dialectic of the Northern Song founders of a renewed Confucian philosophy such as Zhou Dunyi (de Bary 1999–2000, I: 669–78). The play, of course, is not on the first part of the binome, but on the second graph, *yi*. This graph, of course, is used as the name of the famous *Yijing* or the Classic of Changes as it is most often rendered in English. The range of meanings covers meanings such as easy, simple, gentle, change, exchange and so forth. For our point of view it would be wonderful to play on the notion that the simple or primal is actually change or the process of transformation. This is not far-fetched in terms of the history of the interpretation of the term in the history of Chinese thought. That is why the *Yijing* is translated as the *Classic of Changes* wherein change means transformation and process broadly conceived.

The passage in "Heaven's Gifts" goes on to state that "[t]he Primal Simplicity preceded the appearance of the breath" (Graham 1960, 19). Given the importance of breath or *qi* in all forms of Chinese self-reflexive thought, to be in some kind of state prior even to the perception of *qi* comes as a start. Among other citations, Yang's commentary notes that, of course, we immediately think of the Supreme Polarity of the *Yijing* when we try to interpret the cryptic remark about not even being able to sense the vital force, the breath, the vapor of the cosmos. In another passage in Yang's commentary, attention is directed to the *Zhuangzi*'s notion of *hundun* 混沌 or primeval chaos. This is the state of confusion wherein all black cows aren't even yet black, much less cows. In fact, as the *LZ* passage continues, it states that even after breath, shape, and substance are complete, there is still no distinction between things. This is the state that Graham translates as confusion, hence the repeated reference in the text and commentaries to the primal *hundun* or chaos.

The hermeneutical spirit that is always alive in reading classical Chinese texts tempts us to continue to limn out just what is going on in this passage. However, there is the suspicion, never far from the surface of the conscious mind-heart that the *LZ* text is toying with us. Of course, play is nothing to be neglected in the magic garden world of the *LZ*. Graham translates *hundun* as confusion. The *LZ* glosses the enigmatic terms as "that the myriad things are confounded and not yet separated from each other" (Graham 1960, 19).

The next section of this passage keeps probing the various twists and turns of a characteristic Wei-Jin cosmology. This state of confusion, we are told, can also be likened to the simple, and the simple has no bounds, no shape. However, the "simple" has a tendency to alter, to change—the Chinese term is another one of our glosses for process, *bian* or alter from shape to shape in this case. The "simple" becomes one, then becomes seven, then nine, and once ninefold, it reverts to unity. Graham translates it as "Then it (the final outcome of the nine fold alternation) reverted to unity" (19). Here again the sense of the phrase is one of motion, namely of the reversion of alternation that again become one—with the one standing for unity in Graham's reading. Yet the "one" is merely deemed a way of trying to designate the chaos of the confusion of the myriad things. The *LZ* then goes on to say that "unity is the beginning of the alternations of shape" (19). Even shapes, the forms of definiteness for the *LZ* text, are implicated in the dynamics of chaotic, creative generativity.

It is something hard to try to make the *LZ* fit the assertive (and mostly propositional) mode of exposition so popular in Western thought. As Justus Buchler taught however, not all love of wisdom need be expressed in assertive judgments. Along with the assertive mode of judgment are the active and the exhibitive. For instance, when we do something, when something changes or is transformed, attention, query, and judgment are directed such that 'bringing about' is the central trait attributable to our product, we produce in the mode of active judgment, we judge actively" (Buchler 1974, 97). Or when we focus our concern on the actual "process of shaping and the product as shaped is central, we produce in the mode of exhibitive judgment, we judge exhibitively" (ibid.). There is a suggestive parallel between Buchler's judgment of exhibition and some of the points in the last set of passages in the *LZ* text.

The exhibitive structure, of course, can take on different personas. The Daoist can be playful, amused, and even silly. The typical Confucian persona is serious. But both the playful and serious modes pile synchronic image upon synchronic image in order to exhibit a reality to which we are invited to pay attention. A. C. Graham has argued in a number of venues that Chinese philosophers often use the device of telling the student to pay attention to the world in order to discover all the facts relevant to the case at hand, and then choose the correct path of action (Graham 1989). The goal, certainly for Confucianism and even many Daoists, is to find a "way" to navigate through the dangers of a hostile environment. The diagnosis of the reasons for the danger differs from school to school and from philosopher to philosopher within a lineage. One need only remember the famous debate about whether or not human nature is good or debased, even odious, between Mencius and Xunzi. But it is not the point of the argument that is now of interest. Rather, it is what the philosophers share in common. It is the exhibitive style of exposition. It is the appeal to looking synchronically at a situation from as many viewpoints as possible in order to gather as many facts as are possible in order to find a way to act.

I will now turn to a montage of passages on process from other sites in the *LZ*, beginning with one more selection from "Heaven's

Gifts." The Chinese term in play in this selection is *sheng* or birth/generativity.

> Hence there are the begotten and the Begetter of the begotten, shapes and the Shaper of shapes, sounds and the Sounder of sounds, colours and the Colourer of colours, flavours and the Flavourer of flavours. What begetting begets dies, but the Begetter of the begotten never ends. . . . All are the Offices of That Which Does Nothing and. . . . It knows nothing is capable of nothing; yet there is nothing which it does not know, nothing of which it is incapable. (Graham 1960, 20)

This is another of those wonderfully challenging passages to translate from the Chinese into English. Reading Graham's rendition shows how choices must be made. For instance, Graham could have played on the lexicography of *sheng* to emphasize the notion of giving birth or arising. But if he had said something such as "the arising," the overtones of Buddhist *dharma* theory would have replaced the notion of being begotten. One can only wonder if Graham's early theological training, which he abandoned before ordination, and the cadences of the King James Bible with the poetry of the Gospel of John and the creative power of the logos influenced his translation. Could it have been otherwise? Beyond a wooden literalism, Graham made as good a choice as possible. There is no way to ever produce a one-to-one translation playing on the Chinese *sheng* within a sophisticated text such as the *LZ*.

I am inclined to take the whole passage as a perfect example of the *LZ* playing with *sheng* as yet another sedimented marker of process. The specific things that are begotten, made, become, definitely finally die. This is a motif that the *LZ* and classical Daoism share with Buddhism. As the Buddhists teach, it is the *dharma* of compound things to fall apart. Nothing every stays the same but all is subject to the cycle of birth and death. From the *LZ*'s perspective, this is the nature of That Which Does Nothing—it is the *wuwei* 無為 that engenders all, but is "what" per se in and of itself? Whereas if we could give an accurate definition of *wuwei* it would not be *wuwei*, it would not be true *wuwei* because it would simply then have become some one thing correlated to all the other myriad things. This is not the office, the *LZ* teaches, of That Which Does Nothing.

In the chapter titled "Confucius" the following Guanyin (a Daoist and not the Buddhist Guanyin) says:

> If nothing within you stays rigid,
> Outward things will disclose themselves,
> Move, be like water.
> Still, be like a mirror.
> Respond like an echo. (Graham 1960, 90)

The main protagonist of this chapter is Confucius. This may seem odd, but it really is not. Daoists generally deal with the First Sage in two different ways. The first is to make fun of Confucius or Confucians by showing, often through encounters with Daoist worthies, that they are not nearly as enlightened as they think they are. The second strategy is to make Confucius out to be a better Daoist than other sages; in short, to put Daoist teachings in the mouth of the greatest of the *ru* 儒 scholars.

What merits attention in this passage are the metaphors for the cultivated person. What Guanyin reveals is the typical Daoist teaching that if we are to live successfully in the world we must learn never to stay rigid in our mind-hearts, philosophic conceptualities, or bodies. As the *Laozi* taught, the mark of death is to become rigid and unable to respond to the world, whereas the mark of the living is to be supple. The *Laozi* went on to say that this is like becoming a baby, someone soft and without preconceived notions. Whether or not this is an accurate reading of the mind-heart of the infant according to second-generation cognitive science need not bother us at this point. The Daoist metaphors and images are priceless and one sure reason that the *Laozi* has enjoyed such cross-cultural attention wherever it has been translated from its original classical Chinese.

The last three metaphors in Guanyin's teachings are suggestive when viewed within the larger affirmation of process and flux posited by the *LZ* text. When we move, we must be like water. Of course, as Sarah Allan (1997) has shown, the motif or metaphor of water is one of the most powerful and pervasive traits of the pan-Chinese philosophic and literary world. Water is an important image for both Daoists and Confucians. Here we are told that we must be like water, and the characteristic of water we are asked to attend to is motion. The third metaphor, the response to an echo, trades upon the reciprocity of ear and sound. This is yet another metaphor that balances on the correlative polarity of so much classical Chinese thought.

The second metaphor of the mirror needs some more explanation in order to place it between the first and third line of the text. On the surface, itself often a metaphorical way of talking about a mirror, this seems to be much more static. A mirror, and the author here would have in mind the wonderful bronze mirrors of the Han dynasty, is most certainly a definite object. These mirrors were more than just objects on the nightstand of an aristocratic Han lady. They were often artistic representations of Han understandings of the cosmos. The still quality of the mirror was necessary for the person to be able to respond perfectly. We must remember that the semantics of images is linked to the correlative cosmology of the *Yijing*. Whereas a modern English reader might think of the fixed quality of an image as a literal representation of the object in question, the semantic undertones for the Wei-Jin intellectual could not help to be shaped by the teaching of the *Yijing* that the images point to the ceaseless creativity and motion of the yin-yang as emblematic of the Supreme Polarity, the *taiji*. The metaphor, inscribed as the middle of the three lines, is directed to the correlation of mirror and object more than to the idea of being still or placid. I take the *LZ* to be teaching that we must be perfectly receptive—the action is more important than the static nature of the mirror. The implications of a mirror qua bronze object depend on the rich interconnections of the culture itself and cannot always be emblematic of the static nature of reflection without appropriation.

The next passages come from "The Questions of T'ang" chapter. This is an intriguing text because it is an early analysis of infinity and its brush with a philosophy of relativity. Graham, in his introductory remarks to "The Questions of T'ang" argues that the discussion of infinity ought to be taken seriously as a philosophical meditation on the status and function of the infinite. The core of this question of the infinite begins this way:

> The ending and starting of things
> Have no limit from which they began.
> The start of one is the end of another,
> The end of one is the start of another.
> Who know which came first? (Graham 1960, 94)

This is a fascinating passage for a number of reasons. The topic of infinity, as we shall see, draws the author farther and farther into the murky depths of something and nothing. For our purposes, it is crucial to note that process is understood as endless. There is no fixed doctrine of substance to help things out in terms of ultimate beginnings or endings. It is just process all the way down.

The passage continues with one of the most convoluted answers in the whole of the *LZ* to the question of the infinite:

> It is nothing which is limitless, Something which is inexhaustible. How do I know this? [NB: Graham notes that there is a lacuna in the text here by noting that the Wei-Jin commentator Zhang writes "Since it is called Nothing, how can there be an outside? Since it is called Void, how can there be anything within it?" Graham then goes on to reconstruct what must have been the gist of the undamaged argument.] But also there is nothing limitless; there is no exhausting, but neither is there any inexhaustible. That is why I know that they are limitless and inexhaustible, yet I do not know whether they may be limited and exhaustible. (Graham 1960, 95)

This does make some sense when you place the passage in the context of classical Daoist thought that is loath of make something the origin of the process of the Dao. The limits, as Graham argues in the notes to this passage, are neither the something that is simply larger than anything else nor the smallest thing that is simply smaller than anything else. The problem with the above solution is that it is no solution at all because the infinite is without bounds of any kind. However, it is perhaps unwise to press the assertive point too far. As Graham states, "Chinese arguments of this kind present great difficulties of interpretation. In this section I have made a point of translating very literally, and confining my interpretation (which are disputable) as far as possible to the notes" (Graham 1960, 96).

The last passage of my montage of processive motifs in the *LZ* is found in the last chapter of the book, "Explaining Conjunctions." According to Graham, this is the most heterogeneous chapter in what is a very eclectic work. If there is an overall theme to the collected material, it is that we should be very skeptical about placing any trust in a fixed standard of judgment. The line in question here says, "Therefore the sage trusts the transforming process of the Way, and puts no trust in cunning or skill" (Graham 1960, 161). In all respects this is a typical Daoist admonition against using some kind of fixed convention, as would Confucians, to judge a situation. From the Daoist viewpoint of the *LZ* we know that there is neither any rule that is always right nor any action that is always wrong. This depends on their context for any interpretation tending toward action.

The passage also seems to cast a shadow of a doubt over the more commonly proffered Daoist take of "knowledge," namely, knack or spontaneous action without the willful, pernicious torque of self-interest to cause us to go astray. No, here even skill is rejected. But there is still an element of trust on the part of the sage in play. The Chinese term *xin* 信, which Graham translates as trust, has the connotation of relying on, depending on, to feeling secure with, and so forth. It is not the trust as one of the cardinal virtues of Confucianism, but certainly would be the state of someone with *xin* as trustworthiness. The image is apt. The sage relies or leans on the very process of the Dao 道 rather than any human cunning. In the end, it really is process all the way down or Dao if you like to pun.

Notes

1. This material for this study is drawn from a much longer chapter, which is in turn part of a study of the role of the trait or theme of process or transformation in work of certain Chinese philosophical texts and Western traditions. The Chinese material is taken from the work of Xunzi, the *Liezi* book, and the *daoxue* school of Zhu Xi and his students. Connections are then made to the closely allied modern North American schools of pragmatism, naturalism, and the process philosophical tradition that is traced to the work of A. N. Whitehead.
2. There are many fine studies of the thought of the period that can be pursued by anyone interested in the twists and turns of late Han and Wei-Jin intellectual life. For instance, see Berthrong 1998.
3. Even to speak of "philosophical Daoism" makes little sense to many of the best scholars in the field. Although it is hard to figure out what to call some of these early texts, most scholars of Daoism now resolutely reject as facile and completely misleading the dichotomy of "philosophical" and "religious" Daoism. Contemporary scholars simply like to call a text like the *LZ* a classical philosophical text; they would point out that such texts as the *Laozi*, *Zhuangzi*, and the *Liezi* are part of the ecumenical patrimony of all educated Chinese scholars regardless of their sectarian inclinations.
4. Along with A. C. Graham's fine English translation, we are lucky to have an excellent modern critical edition and commentary on the *LZ* by Yang Bojun published in Hong Kong in 1965.
5. Actually, according to Bret Hinsch (2002), Dong Zongshu defined yin-

yang as complementary but also added a highly stratified twist to the definitions. Without doubt yang was superior in position and authority to yin according to Dong. See pp. 143–57. According to Hinsch this marked a decline in the status of the feminine in Western Han thought, a tendency that sadly continued throughout much of Chinese social history.

6. Ames and Rosement (1998, 281) in their translation of the *Analects* have another list of key Chinese terms for change or process. They list five important terms: (1) *bian* or to gradually change over time; (2) *yi* as the change of one thing or pattern into another; (3) *hua* or the complete transformation one thing or event into another; (4) *qian* 遷 as the change from one place to another; and (5) *gai* or the correction or transformation of one thing or even based on some other principle or model. (6)Another important term, but not in the Hall and Rosemont list, is *sheng* or creative generativity. For someone like the redactor of the *Liezi*, (7) *ziran* qua spontaneity also should probably be added.
7. This is in fact just what Professor Mou told me in a personal interview in the early summer of 1974 in Hong Kong. Professor Mou graciously agreed to meet with me based on a letter of introduction provided by one of my professors. After about twenty minutes of drinking tea, Professor Mou walked me over to one of the small classrooms in New Asia College and asked me to explain to him my understanding of Zhu Xi. He knew from our short conversation and the letter of introduction that Zhu Xi was the focus of my dissertation. I threw caution to the winds and explained as much as I could about Zhu Xi, knowing all too well that this was probably the most important interpreter of Zhu Xi in the known universe. After I had talked about fifteen minutes, Professor Mou went on to discuss the issues at hand with me for about two hours. At one point he paused and asked me why I was using such a Whiteheadian reading of Zhu. I was beyond being amazed by his erudition at this point, but still went on to mutter that I thought that process philosophy was a good way to interpret Zhu's style of Song moral metaphysics in Western philosophic terms. Professor Mou agreed graciously, but then went on to say that while he has toyed with this idea for a while, he was presently more inclined to use Leibniz for this task. Mou's own favorite Western philosopher, of course, is Kant. I was properly impressed; awe would better describe my mental condition at that point.

References

Allan, Sarah. 1997. *The Way of Water and Sprouts of Virtue*. Albany: State University of New York Press.

Ames, Roger T., and Henry Rosemont Jr. 1998. *The Analects of Confucius: A Philosophic Translation*. New York: Ballantine Books.

Berthrong, John H. 1998. *Transformations of the Confucian Way*. Boulder: Westview Press.

Buchler, Justus. 1955. *Nature and Judgment*. New York: Columbia University Press.

———. 1961. *The Concept of Method*. New York: Columbia University Press.

———. 1974. *The Main of Light: On the Concept of Poetry*. New York: Oxford University Press.

———. 1979. *Toward a General Theory of Human Judgment*. 2nd ed. New York: Dover.

———. 1990. *Metaphysics of Natural Complexes*. 2nd, expanded ed. Albany: State University of New York Press.

A Concordance to the Liezi. 1996. Hong Kong: Commercial Press.

Creel, H. G. 1970. *What is Taoism and Other Studies in Chinese Cultural History*. Chicago: University of Chicago Press.

De Bary, Wm. Theodore, Irene Bloom, and Richard Lufrano, eds. 1999–2000. *Sources of Chinese Tradition*. 2 Vols. 2nd ed. New York: Columbia University Press.

Graham, A. C. 1960. *The Book of Lieh-tzu*. London: John Murray. Reprinted by Columbia University Press, 1990.

———, trans. 1981. *Chuang-tzu: The Seven Inner Chapters and other Writings from the Book Chuang-tzu*. London: George Allen and Unwin.

———. 1986a. *Studies in Chinese Philosophy and Philosophical Literature*. Singapore: The Institute for East Asian Philosophy.

———. 1986b. *Yin-yang and the Nature of Correlative Thinking*. Singapore: The Institute of East Asian Philosophy.

———. 1989. *Disputers of the Tao: Philosophical Argument in Ancient China*. La Salle, IL: Open Court.

Hinsch, Bret. 2002. *Women in Early Imperial China*. Blue Ridge Summit, PA: Rowan and Littlefield.

Liu Dajun et al., trans. 1995. *The I Ching: Text and Annotated Translation*. Jinan: Shandong Friendship Publishing House.

Lloyd, Geoffrey, and Nathan Sivin. 2002. *The Way and the Word: Science and Medicine in Early China and Greece*. New Haven and London: Yale University Press.

Needham, Joseph, et al. 1954–. *Science and Civilisation in China*. 8 Vols. Cambridge: Cambridge University Press.

Mou Zongsan. 1968–69. *Xindi yu Xingdi* [Mind and Nature]. 3 Vols. Taipei, Taiwan: Zhengjing Shuju.

———. 1983. *Zongguo Zhexue shijiu jiang* [*Nineteen Lectures on Chinese Philosophy*]. Taipei: Taiwan: The Student Book Company.

———. 1990. *Zhongxi zhexue zhi huitong shisi jiang* [Fourteen Lectures on Understanding Chinese and Western Philosophy]. Taipei, Taiwan: The Student Book Company.

———. 1994. *Zhongguo Zhexue de tezhi* [Special Traits/Features of Chinese Philosophy]. Taipei, Taiwan: The Student Book Company.

Roth, Harold D. 1999. *The Original Tao: Inward Training (Nei-yeh) and the Foundations of Taoist Mysticism*. New York: Columbia University Press.

Wagner, Rudolf G. 2000. *The Craft of a Chinese Commentator: Wang Bi on the Laozi*. Albany: State University of New York Press.

———. 2003. *Language, Ontology, and Political Philosophy in China: Wang Bi's Scholarly Explorations in the Dark (Xuanxue)*. Albany: State University of New York Press.

Watson, Burton, trans. 1968. *The Complete Works of Chuang Tzu*. New York: Columbia University Press.

Wong, Eva, trans. 1995. *Lieh-Tzu: A Taoist Guide to Practical Living*. Boston and London: Shambhala Publications.

Wright, Arthur F. 1970. "A Historian's Reflections on the Taoist Tradition." *History of Religions*. Vol 9, nos. 2 and 3 (Nov. 1969/Feb. 1970): 248–55.

Yang Bojun. 1965. *Liezi jishi* [Collected Commentaries on the *Liezi*]. Hong Kong: Taiping Book Company.

Ziporyn, Brook. 2000. *Evil and/or/as the Good: Omincentrism, Intersubjectivity, and Value Paradox in Tiantai Buddhist Thought*. Cambridge: Harvard University Press.

———. 2003. *The Penumbra Unbound: The Neo-Taoist Philosophy of Guo Xiang*. Albany: State University of New York Press.

Zürcher, Eric. 1959. The Buddhist Conquest of China: The Spread and Adaptation of Buddhism in Early Medieval China. 2 Vols. Leiden: E. J. Brill.

列子

The That-Beyond-Which of the Pristine Dao

Cosmogony in the Liezi

Thomas Michael

Culturally foundational notions mark the limits of what cultures are able to think, provide conceptual identity to its members, and clarify the mental categories that remain always outside of experience. When they are looked at and studied by outsiders, these notions typically fall into the category of religion or philosophy in the widest sense, because they appear first of all as disembodied entities existing in the conceptual space of culture. This first view is somewhat misleading because culturally foundational notions also play a major role in the material histories of different cultures.

Looking over the course of Western thought, in all probability the most dominant and influential culturally foundational notions are Truth with its source in Greek philosophy, and the monotheistic God with its source in Middle Eastern religion. Although the origins of these two notions can be traced back to very different realms of discourse and reference, one thing that the notions of Truth and God share in common is an ultimate open-endedness: neither will ever be completely grasped once and for all by the human mind. As well, Truth and God are ultimate notions, and represent, paraphrasing the famous words of Anselm, the that-beyond-which the human mind cannot go. In this sense, the notion of God possesses a certain priority over that of Truth, despite the fact that God is often identified with Truth. Truth describes a certain kind of metaphysical condition both eternal and unchanging, at least in the most philosophical portrayals of it, whereas the notion of God has an extra element of creativity not typically associated with the notion of Truth. Unlike Truth, God stands at the origins of the world and in some sense is implicate in its cosmogonic beginnings (and usually also implicate in its soteriological ending).

The implication of the notion of God with the beginning (and end) of the world is fairly standard in mainstream Western thought and belief, but various specific understandings place this notion somewhere along a continuum, one end of which is closure, and the other end of which is challenge. By "closure," I refer to the restrictive limits of various specifications applied to culturally foundational notions that delimit the general range of what can reasonably be thought of it; these specifications of detail can change but do so only with a tremendous amount of sustained cultural effort. By "challenge," I refer to the openness of various specifications applied to such notions; consciously or not, the relative underdetermination of these specifications challenges the mind to go beyond any of them, because, even in the case of negative theology, one must refer by designation to some target of discourses for there to be even a modicum of intelligibility. I will continue to use these two terms, *closure* and *challenge*, in these senses throughout this chapter.

As closure, the notion of God can be held to be more or less familiar, amenable to representation in terms of male, father, angry or compassionate, forgiving or judging, benevolent and patriotic or antagonistic toward nations and leaders. As closure, the notion of God can be almost fully known by human beings through revelation, imagination, or intuition. As challenge, the notion of God can be framed but never filled in; placed always beyond the farthest limits of human recognition, this form of the notion of God is beyond gender, beyond indeed any form of conditionality and determination. This stands as a challenge because it compels human beings always to sit on the edge of that existential angst so intimately experienced by the likes of Pascal and Kierkegaard and, one might add, Darwin and Einstein, that angst that is so conducive to contemplation when coupled with an absence of spiritual complacency commonly associated with the notion of God as closure. The challenge lies, first of all, in the compulsion to think the unthinkable, and also in the challenge to keep the notion open in the face of the constant tendency to give it closure through representation and familiarity.

Whether or not what is represented by the notion of God is a being, entity, or simply a place marker situated by human thought at the very origins, and whether or not what is presented by this notion can be fully known or never fathomed in terms of closure or challenge, this notion, like all notions, has a history. It is an extremely active notion, with what appears to be a life of its own; this can be seen, for example and most clearly, in the different formulations of the notion of God that we associate with the writings attributed to or associated with the likes of Abraham, Moses, Isaiah, Job, Jesus, Origen, Augustine, and Mohammad, to name only a few representative examples, each of whom had different things to say about it. Often these changes might be seen to follow the trends of changing historical circumstances, but at the same time there are certain other attributes that have constancy, including, most importantly, the placement of what is represented by the notion of God at the very beginnings. Typically, this placement is located at the beginning of this world and not earlier, although we do possess written records that describe the times before the world, for example the Canaanite *Enuma Elish* and the Greek *Theogony*, but then such works are far from representative of the monotheism at issue here. There are also traces or remnants of cosmogony in the opening lines of *Genesis*, and a lot of later Jewish theology does explore the times before the beginnings of this world. Probably no religion has taken the notion of God earlier than Buddhism; the *Lotus Sutra*, for example, provides a complete history of the adventures of Shakyamuni Buddha before he brought this world into existence.

These ruminations bring me to the traditions of East Asia, and China in particular. A. C. Graham once argued that the Chinese tradition has a particular affinity for the Dao, and that the notion of Truth did not hold a foundational position in Chinese thought and history.[1] The directions opened by his arguments have been explored to an even further degree by later scholars, maybe most notably David Hall and Roger Ames.[2] Their argument is that the Chinese tradition, and the Confucian tradition in particular, saw the world as an emerging aesthetic order without predetermination and lacking natural law. Ultimately, these sorts of arguments, if pursued far enough, can be taken as at least a partial explanation as to why the Chinese did not have a strong notion of God as the creator of the natural world. Some Chinese thinkers did have fairly general ideas about Tian (Heaven) as a transcendent deity overseeing human conduct, as evidenced by the writings associated with Mozi and even some sayings by Confucius, but the notion had no staying power. What did have staying power was a different notion, different from God and Truth in important ways: the notion of the Dao.

Early China, the so-called Golden Age of Chinese thought, represents one period in which there were many different and competing notions of the Dao, not unlike the period in early Greece when notions of Truth were debated and similar periods in the Western tradition when different notions of God also were debated: different people said different things about it, and what they said often built upon previous articulations.

Dao as a term has a long history stretching back to the oracle writings dating to the end of the Shang dynasty where it meant something like an intersection, but succeeding ages invested it with a tremendous amount of other meanings. Some of these later meanings include a path or to open a path, particularly a water channel; to guide, as a channel guides the flow of water through the fields; in an extended use of this meaning, it also means a path or way that guides one's actions, and thus to speak or say, but it also means speech that guides individual thought and action, for example the way of government or the way of seasonal progressions. Around the fifth century BC, two important and extended meanings of Dao coalesced around a more or less unified field of signification, the self and the world, as demonstrated by two separate writings that almost simultaneously began to be widely circulated in early China. These writings provided general ideas about the notion of the Dao and established its position as the most important culturally foundational notion of East Asia: the *Analects* attributed to Confucius and the *Daodejing* attributed to Laozi (hereafter called the *Laozi*). Although the two works appeared at virtually the same time, the notion of Dao opened up by each demonstrates some significant differences in its primary fields of reference creating a fault line that split the originally unified field of its ancient signification.[3] The *Analects* discusses the notion of the Dao as a predominately cultural phenomenon concerning the state and the family, and the *Laozi* discusses it as a predominately cosmic phenomenon that is simultaneously transcendent and immanent to human society and the natural world.

In the periods of the Warring States and Western Han, early Chinese writers examined, explored, and consciously negotiated the consequences of this original fault line in the notion of the Dao, and their textual records demonstrably show them tending to one of the two general regions originally pioneered by the *Analects* and the *Laozi*. Coming to terms with this original split appears to have been the driving force motivating the ideological developments and sociological formations of the several traditions of early China that were committed to establishing the priority of their own decisions to have the Dao signify one thing over another. Toward the end of the Warring States the two domains were brought together, as seen primarily in the *Xici Zhuan* and the *Zhuangzi*. In them, the Dao is something that exists on a continuum stretching from, on one side, the source from which all things come and to which all things return, to something that can be gained or lost by human culture or an individual person. But the two Daos are ultimately one and the same, because early China did not seem to possess a strong notion of transcendence; if they did have a notion of metaphysically distinct realms, then it too had no staying power. Thus, gods could ride their chariots to descend to where humans live, and humans, some of them anyway, could fly up the mountains to ascend to where gods live. There was no radical break with eternity on one side and temporality on the other. Yet the world still came from somewhere and, by relying on the cosmic field of the Dao discussed by the *Laozi* but not the social field discussed by the *Analects*, a satisfying answer was ready to hand.

For most of the period of the Warring States and early Han, thinkers showed the greatest interest in exploring the question about where the world came from, which was supplied by the writings of early Daoism, and it was *Laozi* 42 that provided what is quite probably the earliest solution: "Dao gave birth to One, One gave birth to Two, Two gave birth to Three, and Three gave birth to the ten thousand things" 道生一, 一生二, 二生三, 三生萬物.[4] This formulation presupposes the Dao as the original source from which all things first come into being and that preexists even Heaven and Earth. The notion of Dao in its signification as the original source of the world and beings holds an important place in early Daoist discourse, comparable at least in positional terms to the notion of God in mainstream Western writings about the origins of the world and beings. The positioning of these two culturally foundational notions in a cosmogonic period that preexisted the world, however, should not mask the many differences between them, one of which is that God is often seen as eternal and unchanging, whereas the Dao is seen as eternal but constantly changing. Another major difference in the two notions is that God is transcendent to the world and remains forever outside of it, although Christianity and some forms of Judaism try to bridge the chasm between transcendence and immanence by way of the notion of Sophia associated with the Wisdom tradition (but this seems to prove this rule), whereas the Dao is transcendent to the world but also immanent in it.

If we place this notion of the Dao on the spectrum previously applied to the notion of God, we can see that it also has two extremes, one standing as challenge and one as closure. As closure, we can witness the growing tendency among early Chinese writers to identify their notion of the Dao with a specific identity and characterization; this is already apparent in the *Laozi* 52 and quite possibly earlier, as for example in the *Taiyi Shengshui* writings, both of which identify it as a mother. *Laozi* 25 virtually identifies the Dao with another notion that had some currency in early China as the name of a powerful god, Taiyi; while other traditions held Taiyi to be a male god, as seen for example in the *Donghuang Taiyi* poem of the *Chuci*; the *Taiyi Shengshui* even identifies that god as a mother. In the Eastern Han, the notion of the Dao took on a thoroughly personified nature as the god Laojun, and even later the Dao was identified with a trinity of gods, one of whom was still Laojun. This is closure in the sense that the Dao was represented in ritual as one god among others, in art by statues and paintings, and maybe most pointedly in thought as a reified, more or less easily graspable notion.

On the other extreme, the notion of Dao stands as challenge. The major texts of the early Daoist tradition, the *Laozi*, *Zhuangzi*, and *Huainanzi*, directly discuss the notion as something uncontainable in language. In spite of this, they still continue to refer to the Dao in several ways, but doing so in the way that they did demonstrates that the writers were very conscious of the pitfall represented by closure. This is apparent both in the minimalist descriptions employed in talking about the cosmogonic past (compared to their relatively richer and fuller descriptions of the phenomenal present), and also in the language that they use. Maybe the clearest portrayal of this is seen in their use of a specialized vocabulary, one dominated by negative terms, a good example of which is provided by their discussions of the notion of Dao in its modalities as *wu* (variously translated as non-being, that-which-is-not, and nothing, but I also like to translate it at times as absence) and *you* (variously translated as being, that-which-is, and something, but I like to translate it at times as presence). This modality is taken up to describe the Dao's activity in both the phenomenal present and the cosmogonic past. In terms of the phenomenal present, *Laozi* 11 explicitly discusses *wu* and *you* in the context of immediate experience; for example, *wu* is the absence within that gives presence to a vase. *Laozi* 1 states: "*Wu* names the beginning of Heaven and Earth. *You* names the mother of the ten thousand things" 無名天地之始, 有名萬物之母.[5] *Zhuangzi* 2 expands on these ideas of *wu* and *you*.

> There is a state of *you*. There is a state of *wu*. There is a state in which "the state of *wu*" has not yet begun. There is a state in which "the state in which 'the state of *wu*' has not yet begun" itself has not yet begun. Suddenly there is *wu* and *you*.[6]
> 有有也者. 有無 也 者. 有 未 始 有 無 也者. 有未始 有夫未 始有 無 也者 .俄 而 有 無 矣 .

The opening lines of *Huainanzi* 2 provide a paraphrased quotation of the *Zhuangzi* passage, and its immediately following sections offer an interpretation that explicitly situates the ideas of *wu* and *you* in the time of the cosmogony.

What all of the discussions of the notion of the Dao in its cosmogonic modality of *wu* and *you* have in common is that they challenge the limits of human thought. They do this in several ways. First of all, the notion of the Dao is not given any closure or metaphorical representation and designation in terms of images, entities, or beings. Instead of saying something like, Dao is X, where X represents any kind of attribute or characteristic, these texts say only, Dao is (*you*)/is not (*wu*). We are not given any kind of mental content to grasp other than the very abstract qualities of is and is not. Second, the time and place to which this notion of Dao directs human thought is itself not amenable to any conceptual or linguistic designation in terms of human thought without in the process becoming subject to closure. It is not that that time and place do not exist in any sense of the word, nor that what human thought is being directed to is infinity in the abstract sense of the word, but rather that the time and place that is being discussed exists in a way that is simply beyond the limits of thought, both temporally because that time and place preexisted human beings and the world, and also conceptually because the notion of Dao is, as the texts commonly state, beyond language and surpasses the limits of what human thought can comprehend.

These two extremes, challenge and closure, are not exclusive and fundamentally separate ways of conceiving the very beginnings of the world and human existence, but represent "ideal types."[7] In practice, the two extremes can often be found within the same tradition, but they are nonetheless distinct at any moment of individual human thought, at least in theory. One cannot logically hold the idea that Dao, God, and Truth are essentially beyond predication and at the same time predicate them, but one can think any one of these three notions as beyond predication at one time but amenable to predication at another time. Humans are fickle.

This brings me to the *Liezi*. Although the *Liezi* was put together in what appears to be something very close to its final form sometime in the fourth century CE, some six hundred years after the appearance of the *Laozi* and *Zhuangzi*, and some four hundred years after the *Huainanzi*, many sections of it closely adhere to the spirit and conceptual content within them, so much so that the debate as to whether or not it was put together in the period of the Warring States has only recently achieved resolution (even if some sections can be considered earlier than others). The *Liezi* can be taken as a continuation of early Daoist discourse, in many ways a more authentic continuation than what is found in the commentaries of Wang Bi to the *Laozi* and Guo Xiang to the *Zhuangzi*. There is an active relation between many of the ideas found in the *Laozi* and the *Zhuangzi*'s extension and exploration of them, and the *Huainanzi*'s extension and exploration of the ideas of both the *Laozi* and the *Zhuangzi*. In a similar way, the *Liezi* demonstrates characteristics that allow us to see it as an extension and exploration of all three works, and this is particularly so in relation to the *Liezi*'s discussion of cosmogony.

Of the eight chapters of the *Liezi*, the text's discussion of cosmogony is given one fairly sophisticated presentation, which is found in the first chapter, *Tian Rui*. The chapter can be separated into two main parts, the first part consisting of five lectures given by Liezi, and the second part consisting of seven unrelated lectures and stories involving other people, of which Liezi gives one. The beginning and end of each of the five lectures given by Liezi in the first part of the chapter are fairly easy to recognize: the first lecture is prefaced by a question from a student, the second and third prefaced with the words, "Liezi said," the fourth by showing Liezi walking on the road, and the fifth by an initial quotation from the *Laozi*. The first and second lectures discuss the beginning of things before the existence of Heaven and Earth; the third lecture discusses the relation between Heaven and Earth, the Sage, and the ten thousand things; the fourth lecture presents Liezi's ideas about the evolution of creatures from germs to humans; and the fifth lecture discusses the life of an individual human from the time before birth to the time after death. Taken together, these five lectures provide a complete coverage of the progress of existence from the time before things to their present condition, so I think that these five lectures can be read as one more or less continuous lecture in five parts based on the progression of their themes. In the remainder of this chapter, I will primarily discuss the first two lectures, because they are the important sections in which we read about Liezi's ideas concerning cosmogony.

Maybe the most striking aspect of these first two lectures devoted to cosmogony is that Liezi hardly mentions the Dao directly; it is mentioned only once, where we read, "Its *dao* cannot be exhausted 其道不可窮," referring to the process of the unborn.[8] This usage of the term *dao* is very interesting, because it is in some ways just like a typical *dao* pertaining to some particular way or method, like the *dao* of the king or the *dao* of warfare. In other words, in the single instance in Liezi's cosmogony where he uses the term *dao*, there is nothing particularly cosmic about it in relation to the notion of the source from which all things come.

This is very interesting to notice because these two lectures are committed to an in-depth discussion of cosmogony that is anchored by and revolves around the notion of the pristine Dao, the original source of all things, and the *Laozi*, *Zhuangzi*, and *Huainanzi* exerted a lot of effort in establishing this usage of their notion of the Dao in relation to cosmogony, where they often directly name the Dao. It is an interesting question to ask, if the pristine Dao holds such an important position in Daoist cosmogony, why the *Liezi* hardly mentions it; I think the answer is fairly easily to guess because, so many centuries after the appearance of the *Laozi*, *Zhuangzi*, and *Huainanzi*, and considering also their popularity and currency in the literary, religious, and philosophical currents during that time, the pristine Dao had already come to be fully familiar and recognizable, whether or not one actually held those specific ideas, as the cosmogonic source from which time, space, the world, and all beings came.

But I think there is also another, internal reason why Liezi hardly mentions the Dao here. This has to do with what appears to be the text's recognition of the views of the *Laozi*, *Zhuangzi*, and *Huainanzi* concerning the idea that the Dao is beyond language and is something not accessible to human thought. This is demonstrated partly in the *Liezi*'s habit of using negative language to direct our thought to the what, how, and when of the cosmogony. The lectures, for example, give a central place to that which it calls the unborn 不生者 (*bushengzhe*), and the untransformed 不化者 (*buhuazhe*). Liezi discusses these two notions specifically in relation to the very beginnings of things and their continuation, both cosmically and cosmologically. As I will make clear, Liezi really is talking about the pristine Dao, but in a somewhat devious way because he does not use the term directly. Moreover, as I will discuss later, the *Liezi*'s assertions about "the unborn" and "the untransformed" can be construed as the text's peculiar gloss on the *Laozi*'s notions of absence and presence (*wu* and *you*), and the constant (*chang*) and the enduring (*jiu*). The conceptual difficulty of the two seemingly simple verbs of *sheng* and *hua*, like so many other ancient Chinese verbs, is complicated because they can be both transitive and intransitive, both active and passive in their nuanced meanings. Hence, the *busheng* does not merely mean that which has not gone through the birth process (for which the term *unborn* is already an inadequate translation) but also that which does not give birth to anything else. The same ambiguity is applicable to *hua* and *buhua*.

Liezi, however, does not maintain his characterization of this notion of the Dao as an absolute challenge, for example by saying that it is something beyond language or conceptualization. Instead of directly naming and discussing the Dao, he discusses it in terms of two of its modalities, the unborn and the untransformed, and then goes on to qualify and characterize those modalities. The complete portion of the section under discussion is given in the following. I provide this translation by relying on Rudolph Wagner's discovery of what he calls "interlocking parallel styles," for reasons that should be clear.[9]

有生不生,有化不化,不生者能生生,不化者能化化.生者不能不生,化者不能不化.故常生常化.常生(者)常化者無時不生,無時不化.陰陽爾,四時爾, 不生者疑獨,不化者往復.疑獨其道不可窮.往復,其際不可終.

There exists the born and the unborn,		the transforming and the untransformed.
The unborn gives birth to the born,		the untransformed transforms the transforming.
The born cannot not be born,		the transforming cannot not transform.
	Therefore,	
There is constant birth	and	there is constant transformation.
Things that are constantly born at no time stop being born,	and	things that constantly transform at no time stop transforming.
(Birth) follows from yin and yang,		(transformation) follows from the four seasons.
The unborn is indistinct and stands alone,		the untransformed comes and goes.
Indistinct and alone, its dao cannot be exhausted.		Departing and returning, its intervals cannot be arrested.[10]

In these lines, Liezi examines the unborn and the untransformed as the direct cause of existence and as the direct cause of change, respectively, for anything that exists. There is a certain priority involved with the birth of things, for without birth nothing would transform; however, there is also a certain sense in which the cause of birth and the cause of change both participate in or are separate parts of the same general category of thing, whatever that kind of thing might be. Liezi's inability to locate a term to name this general category of thing directly, or his unwillingness to invent one, is a function of the very high level of abstraction involved with the cosmogonic time and place of which he speaks. Clearly, Liezi is unwilling to use the term *Dao*, and he had plenty of opportunities to use it in any number of places in the passage. For him to name this category of thing by the term *Dao* would have the immediate effect of closing off the full scope of that to which he attempts to direct our thought. His conscious refraining from direct designation can be attributed, I believe, to his awareness of the limitations of this or any other selected word applied to the essence of the phenomenon of the cause of existence and change. In this way, Liezi's discussion of the Dao stands as challenge rather than closure, because he refuses to designate, and by designating thereby limit. In fact, the text is absolutely explicit on this point:

> It is wrong to call it the born, the transformed, the shaped, the formed, the informed, the empowered, the decreased, or the expanded.[11]
> 謂之生 化形 色 智 力 消息 者, 非 也.

In terms of cosmology in the period succeeding the existence of Heaven and Earth, the third lecture portrays either exactly the same mechanism, or a mechanism that is very similar, of the unborn and the untransformed in the present world of phenomenal experience. At this stage of the present world's existence, things and beings are born completely intact (meaning that their *de* 德 is at the height of perfection) but constantly undergo change and transformation. This dual reference of the location of the unborn and the untransformed in terms of cosmogonic time and the phenomenal world is fairly typical in Daoist writings, because both the origins and the present unfold according to more or less the same process that is identified with the activities of the pristine Dao. It is very interesting to note, however, that in the third lecture's discussion of the phenomenal world, we already find ourselves in an environment of seemingly vast multiplicity encompassing much more than the unborn and the untransformed.

> Therefore, there exists the born and also the birther of the born; there exists the shaped and also the shaper of the shaped; there exists sound and the sounder of sounds; there exists color and the colorer of colors; and there exists flavor and the flavorer of flavors.[12]
> 故有生者有生生者; 有形者有形形者; 有聲者有聲聲者; 有色者有色色者; 有味者有味味者.

These additional participants, the shaper, the sounder, the colorer, and the flavorer, were either not present in the cosmogonic period or existed only in potential form. I think it is most sensible to take them as further parts, semi-independent but not strictly separate from each other, of the total notion of the Dao that encompasses shape, sound, color, and flavor within the phenomenal world, in addition to birth and transformation. This is further borne out in the immediately following passage that demonstrates their association within the total field of the Dao, where we see their sum activity categorized under *wu-wei*, a common term in Daoist writings that describes the activity of the pristine Dao.

> What the birther gives birth to dies, but the birther of the born never ends; what the shaper shapes is real, but the shaper of shapes has never been; what the sounder sounds is heard but the sounder of sounds has never come forth; what the colorer colors is visible but the colorer of colors has never appeared; what the flavorer flavors is tasted but the flavorer of flavors has never manifested. These are all the functions of *wu-wei*.[13]
> 生之所生者死矣而生生者未嘗終；形之所形者實矣而形形者未嘗有；聲之所聲者聞矣而聲聲者未嘗發；色之所色者彰矣而色色者未嘗顯；味之所味者嘗矣而味味者未嘗呈：皆無為之職也.

Returning to the passages from the first lecture in which we are only dealing with the unborn and the untransformed, we can say that Liezi pushes the limits of what can be taken as challenge to human thought by directing our attention to the ultimate source of everything that exists without designating it directly. Nonetheless, its discussion of the unborn and the untransformed verges on becoming a closure through the application of certain attributes that limit their field. The lines "The unborn is indistinct and stands alone . . . its dao cannot be exhausted" 不生者疑獨…其道不可窮, and "The untransformed comes and goes . . . its intervals cannot be arrested" 不化者往復…其際不可終, already predicate with referential force: the unborn is separate from that which it gives birth to, and the untransformed is separate from that which it transforms.[14] In this way, Liezi guides our thought into thinking of the unborn and the untransformed as two separate things: they have different names and different fields, namely, the born and the transforming. On the other hand, we can easily imagine that what is born is also what transforms, but should that then lead us to think that the unborn and the untransformed are also to be thought as one and the same thing? Or are they, strictly speaking, two separate things? The unborn and the untransformed appear to me remarkably similar to the *wu* and the *you* discussed in *Laozi* 1, and a quick look at that passage will allow us to answer the question.

> *Wu* names the beginning of Heaven and Earth,
> *You* names the mother of the ten thousand things. . . .
> Hold to *wu* with the intent to witness its subtleties,
> Hold to *you* with the intent to witness its manifestations.
> These two emerge together but are called different names.
> Their sameness is the called the Mystery.
> Mystery upon Mystery: the Gateway of all mysteries.[15]
> 無，名天地之始；有，名萬物之母。故常無，欲以觀其秒；常有，欲以觀其徼。此兩者，同出而異名，同謂之玄。玄之又玄，眾秒之門.

Here the *Laozi* draws a separation between *wu* and *you*: *wu* is identified with the subtle beginnings of Heaven and Earth, while *you* is identified with the manifestations of the ten thousand things. Early Daoist discourse had two primary ways of analyzing the Dao, one in terms of *yin-yang*, and the other in terms of *wu* and *you*. Here, the *Laozi* is analyzing the Dao in terms of *wu* and *you*, terms that might be easily understood, as I mentioned earlier, as absence for *wu* and presence for *you*. The movement of the Dao, in this way of seeing it, is a constant movement of presence into absence. These ideas are given fuller expression in *Laozi* 11, with its images of the empty space in the middle of the hub, the empty space in the middle of a jug, and the empty spaces on walls making doorways and windows. But the question to ask is whether or not there is a sequential relation between *wu* and *you*. *Laozi* 40 answers: "The ten thousand things of the world are born from *you*, and *you* is born from *wu*" 天下萬物生於有，有生於無.[16] Here, *wu* as absence gives birth to *you* as presence, and *you* gives birth to the ten thousand things. What the language says is that both *wu* and *you* precede things, but I think this is a limitation imposed solely by the use of language, in that *Laozi* 1 appears to identify the birth of things with *wu* (subtleties), and the transformation of things with *you* (manifestations), in which subtleties refer to the invisible dynamics of things coming into presence from absence, and manifestations refers to what happens to those things after they have come into existence.

In this way, I think we can draw a direct relation between *Laozi* 1 and these passages from the *Liezi*: the unborn (giving birth to what is born) should be understood in terms of *wu*, and the untransformed (transforming what transforms) should be understood in terms of *you*. But the relation between *wu* and *you*, or the unborn and the untransformed, is not simply cosmogonically sequential, because although there does seem to be a sequence in the cosmogony, in relation to the present world *wu* and *you* and the unborn and the untransformed continually function, as seen for example in the image of the hub and the spokes.

Liezi makes this association between *wu* and *you* and the unborn and the untransformed explicit in the next passage, which is a direct quotation from the *Laozi* (which the *Liezi* cites as the *Book of the Yellow Emperor* 黃帝書):

> The Valley Spirit never dies,
> She is called the Mysterious Female.
> The Gate of the Mysterious Female
> Is called the root of Heaven and Earth.
> It goes on and on, something that almost exists,
> Use it and it never runs out.[17]
> 谷神不死，是謂玄牝。玄牝之門，是謂天地之根。綿綿若存，
> 用之不勤.

Here, the Gate of the Mysterious Female is not identical with the Gate of All Mysteries from *Laozi* 1.[18] The Gate of All Mysteries corresponds to an earlier stage of the cosmogony, from which *you* is born from *wu* at a time before the coming to be of Heaven and Earth, and the Gate of the Mysterious Female refers to a later stage, through which *wu* and *you* (but also *yin-yang*) together pass after the coming to be of Heaven and Earth, in which period, relying on the at least partial identification of *wu* and *you* with the unborn and the untransformed, things are born from the unborn and are transformed by the untransformed. Much later across the centuries to the late Ming, it is no surprise that sectarian Daoism invented an "Old Dame of No-Birth" 無生老母 (*Wusheng Laomu*) to personify part of this idea.[19] If this is not an improper line of reasoning, the *Liezi* can be understood yet again as another extension, significantly modified to be sure, of the ideas of the *Laozi*, *Zhuangzi*, and *Huainanzi*. For the *Zhuangzi* especially, birth and death and transformation are a perfectly "natural" and interminable continuum not to be tempered by humans. For the *Liezi*, not unlike the Augustine of *De civitae dei*, the truly permanent may be that which transcends the cycle of change. Without that shift, the obsessive quest for longevity in cultic Daoism is inexplicable and completely contradictory to these early Daoist ideas.

It is important to point out here that what Liezi has in mind are two and even three separate locations and times: the first is the absolute beginnings (but the absoluteness of those beginnings is relative to us from our standpoint based on the conceptual limitations of the human mind); the second is the formation and existence of Heaven and Earth, which preceded the existence of any of the ten thousand things; and third is the phenomenal world of the birth, transformations, and death of all things. These three locations unfold sequentially, as the following passage from the *Liezi* explicitly describes.

> But if all that has shape is born from the shapeless, then from what were Heaven and Earth born? I say: There is the Supreme Simplicity, the Supreme Origin, the Supreme Beginning, and the Supreme Elemental. In the Supreme Simplicity, *qi* had not yet begun to exist; the Supreme Original marked the first beginning of the existence of *qi*; the Supreme Beginning marked the first beginning of the existence of shapes; and the Supreme Elemental marked the first beginning of the existence of substance. *Qi*, shape, and substance were complete, but things were not yet separated from each other; this is Chaos. Chaos refers to when the ten thousand things were mutually intertwined and not yet separated from each other.[20]
> 有太易, 有太初, 有太始, 有太素。太易者, 未見氣也; 太初者, 氣之始也; 太始者, 形之始也; 太素者, 質之始也。氣形質具而未相離故曰渾淪。渾淪者, 言萬物相渾淪而未相離也.

There is a clear sequential progression through these four Supremes, culminating in the cosmogonic state called Chaos. Things can be said to exist at this stage, but not in the way we know things to exist phenomenally, namely as perduring objects and entities. In the state of Chaos, things exist in a state of pure potentiality, awaiting birth and transformation in the world, but the world itself has not yet come into existence. I should also point out that Chaos is, in the Daoist tradition, a very good thing, whereas in the Western tradition, Chaos is the epitome of horror.

How are we to understand the notion of "Supreme" 太 (*tai*) in these four cases? Do they refer to sites, periods, stages, or something else? The term *Supreme* is commonly seen as the first term in various names of different heavens, or different levels of the same all-encompassing heaven, in other Daoist writings, but maybe one of the first important uses of the term *Supreme* in early Daoist discourse did not refer to heaven at all but to a condition of this world in the phrase "Supreme Peace" 太平 (*taiping*). This phrase began to circulate around the end of the Warring States period to describe a utopian condition of deep harmony between the natural world and human society; it also provided the inspiration behind the many revolts from the Eastern Han onward.[21] Another related sense of Supreme is found in the compound *taishang*, the "supremely high" or "most high," and was used as a term of honor for exalted beings, particularly deities. The first use of this compound in Daoist writings is from *Laozi* 17: "The existence of the supremely high is not known."[22] In both of these compounds, *tai* carries a religiously charged meaning, referring to locations, conditions, or beings not readily accessible to human cognition.

There are two very interesting usages of the term *tai* in Eastern Han writings. The first comes from the *Baihutong*, and the second comes from the *Zhouyi Qian Zuodu*.

> At the beginning of Heaven, first there was the Supreme Origin, and then there was the Supreme Beginning. When the formative signs are completed, they name the Supreme Elemental.[23]
> 始起之天先有太初, 後有太始, 形兆既成名曰太素.

This passage from the *Tiandi* chapter of the *Baihutong* appears as a brief explanation of the origins of Heaven and Earth within its larger discussion of the superiority of Heaven over Earth, *yang* over *yin*, the ruler over the minister, and man over woman; this discussion is dominated by a thoroughly Confucian ideology. We might ask why this writing relies upon the cosmogonic terminology provided by the signification of the term *tai* in order to set forth its claims about superiority and inferiority? There is nothing specifically hierarchical about the *tai* cosmogony that would require any notion of superiority; on the contrary, the *tai* cosmogony tends to a vision of original unity not grounded in a foundational binary structure of superiority and inferiority. I imagine that this application of an originally Daoist-inspired cosmogony is an instance of the Confucian tradition's appropriation from this area of Daoist thought.[24] Cosmogony was not a strong point of the Confucian tradition until around the time of Song neo-Confucianism.

This is the passage from the *Zhouyi Qian Zuodu*:

> The Supreme Origin is the beginning of *qi*, the Supreme Beginning is the beginning of form, and the Supreme Elemental is the beginning of substance.[25]
> 太初者氣之始也, 太始者形之始也, 太素者質之始也.

This version of the *tai* cosmogony again relies upon the sequence from the Supreme Origin *taichu*, to the Supreme Beginning *taishi*, to the Supreme Elemental *taisu*. The *Zhouyi Qian Zuodu* is an Eastern Han "apocryphal text" (*weishu*). Many of these apocryphal texts explored correlative experiments in numerology, cosmography, and prognostication. Maybe the most dominant influence on their thought was provided by *Yijing* exegesis, which laid a general understanding of a formulaic and mathematical order of the cosmos. The content of the above quoted passage, however, seems to be not very apposite to the general thrust of *Yijing* exegesis; one can compare this *tai* cosmogony to the cosmogony found in the *Xici Zhuan*, in which the formation of the hard and soft lines immediately follows the transformations of *qi*.

I find it highly unlikely that the terms and general notions of the *tai* cosmogony originated with either the Confucian tradition or the *Yijing* tradition, although these two writings are the earliest surviving examples of it. I also think that one of the main reasons why these two traditions would appropriate it is because the *tai* cosmogony provides a set of categories or cosmogonic positions that could fill in a gap in the sequence leading from the absolute source of existence through cosmogony to cosmology that was not available in their own traditions. I would attribute the origins of the *tai* cosmogony to the Daoist tradition, because the earliest framework for it comes from the structures established by the *Laozi*, the *Zhuangzi*, and the *Huainanzi*. The *Liezi*, however, appears to take its notion of *taiyi* (Supreme Simplicity) as another term for the pristine Dao directly from the *weishu* writings, of which the *Zhouyi Qian Zuodu* is but one example.

The four *tai* named by Liezi clearly signify cosmogonic periods in sequential order, corresponding to the stages of the formation of *qi* born directly from the pristine Dao. *Qi* transforms into shapes, and shapes gather materiality through their transformation into substance. Liezi, like the *Baihutong* and the *Qian Kun Zuodu*, frames this cosmogonic movement in the general framework provided by *Laozi* 42: "Dao gave birth to One, One gave birth to Two, Two gave birth to Three." It is quite likely that the *Liezi* inherited the specific terms for the *tai* cosmogony from these and other Eastern Han texts, but the framework for the general sequence predates them all. One of the important consequences of the *Liezi*'s version of the *tai* cosmogony was to take back this cosmogony by grounding it within the parameters of a thoroughly Daoist discourse by eliminating all vestiges of both Confucian thought and *Yijing* exegesis (except for his retention of the term *taiyi* for the pristine Dao which, however, sounds a lot like *taiyi* 太一, another term in circulation that also referred sometimes to the pristine Dao).

I think it is important to keep in mind that the *Liezi* is playing a full language game here with these antecedent texts of the Chinese tradition by providing exegesis and commentary, much like Wang Bi, Heshanggong, and Guo Xiang. However, the important thing to notice here about both textual and publishing politics is that these three commentators never quite succeeded in publishing or transmitting their remarks as a work independent of the "host" texts, whereas the *Liezi* became an independent "classic."

Later appearances of the *tai* cosmogony are thoroughly imbued with a Daoist flavor, and I tend to attribute this to the influence exerted by the *Liezi* on institutionalized Daoism. A prime example of it is found in the *Taishang Laojun Kaitian Jing* (*The Scripture of the Most High Laojun Opening Heaven*). This piece begins with a series of claims about what there was not in the time of the very origins: "There was no Heaven no Earth, no *yin* no *yang*, no sun no moon. . ." 無天無地無陰無陽無日無月.[26] The text then lists some two dozen more instances of what there was not. Later, there were two kalpa 劫 (*jie*) periods of Chaos, called Hongyuan 洪元 and Hunyuan 混元.[27] Supreme Origin was formed from Hunyuan, which was followed by Supreme Beginning, which was followed by Supreme Elemental, and the sequence culminates in Chaos, Hundun 混沌. Although this text requires its own separate study, there are a few differences in this *tai* cosmogony compared to the *Liezi*. First, the formation of Heaven and Earth takes place in the time of the Supreme Origin: "During the Supreme Origin, Heaven and Earth began to be separated" 太初始分別天地.[28] Also during this time, the sun, moon, and even human beings first came to exist. In other words, the progress continues to use the terminology of the *tai* cosmogony, but the coming into existence of Heaven, Earth, and the ten thousand things is placed within that progress, not after. The second major difference is the presence of Laojun and his use of scriptures to actively form all things. In fact, the text explicitly identifies Laojun with the pristine Dao, and he appears with the dawn of each stage of the cosmogony. Most likely due to the lasting influence of the *Liezi*, the *tai* cosmogony was firmly established as one of the primary ways in which institutionalized Daoism explored the very beginnings of what exists, and provided a set of ideas enabling humans to imagine what could possibly have existed before the existence of Heaven and Earth, and before the existence of whatever it was that preceded the existence of Heaven and Earth. The cosmogony of the *Kaitian Jing*, however, has already fallen well into closure.

The living reality of the time and place that preceded whatever it was from which Heaven and Earth came into being is something entirely beyond the capacity of the human mind to realize; no humans were present, and the scope of what preceded Heaven and Earth is simply too big to be encompassed by thought. Even to raise the question of cosmogony as something to imagine means that we must necessarily do so by the extension of what it is we know, the categories, concepts, and experiences we have through our own embodiment, to what it is we do not know, in this case cosmogony. The *Liezi*, along with the many parts of the *Laozi*, *Zhuangzi*, and *Huainanzi*, appear perfectly aware of these limits on the human mind to realize the very beginnings directly. We can compare this with ideas pertaining to mainstream Western access to the cosmogony. In this tradition, the human mind is also taken to be incapable of realizing the very beginnings directly but nonetheless has indirect knowledge of it primarily through the revelations of God, particularly in the biblical writings in the opening pages of Genesis.

In the Western case, first there is a state of chaos that is not usually described or represented in the writings, from which God creates heaven and earth, and then there is the creation of cosmos, followed by the creation of all things. The later Christian tradition would attempt to ignore chaos altogether in the theory of creation ex nihilo. In the Daoist case, first there is a state of chaos represented in terms of only absence and presence, and then there is the formation of cosmos followed by the formation of all things. The later Daoist tradition would insert the formation of several heavens populated with various gods chronologically before the formation of earth, and this is, indeed, an almost predictable development following from the insertion of the several heavens as seen for example in these writings of the *Liezi*. In the Western example, there is no discussion of what preceded God, or what God was doing in some other place before the creation of this world. In the case of Mahayana Buddhism, we do have the history of Shakyamuni Buddha, who is said to have achieved enlightenment under a previous Buddha in another world system before he formed this world system, but that only pushes back the issue: What about the time before that previous Buddha in that other world system?

This brings me back to one of the central issues of this chapter, the relation between challenge and closure in relation to the culturally foundational notions pertaining to the very beginning of all that exists. The early Daoist notion of the Dao is in some ways more amenable to challenge than to closure, because the notion already seems to come ready-built with a referential field preceding the existence of that from which Heaven and Earth came into formation. In the Western case there is a tendency to closure already given with the Genesis account of God that begins with that being's existence in the midst of chaos, followed by the separation of heaven and earth on the third day of creation, according to Genesis. I do not mean to say that the Daoist cosmogony reflects a more archaic view of the cosmogony, because the first textual appearances of the early Daoist cosmogony were consciously placed on top of an earlier body of Chinese myths that explored the beginnings of the world, but those myths, which seem to appear historically earlier than the early Daoist writings, only go back to the beginnings of the world and not all the way back to the periods that preceded its formation. Further, the Daoist cosmogony quickly fell into the tendency to closure long before the appearance of the *Liezi*, with the deification of the god Laojun as the personification of the pristine Dao in the Eastern Han.[29] The *Liezi* in this way can be seen as a kind of reform work, and it nowhere discusses the Dao in anthropomorphic terms or images, notions that surely would have been known by the author or authors of the text.

The concluding sections of the second lecture rapidly recapitulate the process of the entire cosmogony, and end with an explicit statement of the formation of the world leading directly into the cosmology of the third, fourth, and fifth lectures. This concluding section begins by referring to a short passage from *Laozi* 14 that describes some aspects of the Dao and, at the end of the chapter, also directly names the Dao. The reference in the *Liezi* truncates the passage, and it identifies what the *Laozi* calls the Dao with the term *yi*. In the following, I put the words from the *Laozi* changed by or omitted from the *Liezi* in brackets.

> Looked for but not seen [it is called minute], listened to but not heard [it is called rarefied], and reached for [felt for] but not touched [it is called smooth]: this refers to Simplicity *yi*.[30]
> 視之不見，聽之不聞，循(搏)之不得，故曰易也.

We have already seen Liezi use the term *Supreme Simplicity* in the passage quoted above to represent the notion of the pristine Dao. In this passage, Liezi fills out his ideas about Supreme Simplicity (and thus the pristine Dao) by applying to it the characteristics of invisibility, inaudibility, and untouchability from the *Laozi*. As mentioned above, Liezi apparently gets the term *Supreme Simplicity* from Eastern Han period *weishu*, where it refers to both the *yi* of the *Yijing* and the source from which all things come. Still, we need to ask why Liezi chooses this term instead of some other term, especially Dao, in his discussion of the ultimate source. *Yi* has several meanings, the most important of which include simplicity, change, and the name of the divinatory text the *Yijing*. As simplicity, this refers to the ease of the movements of the Dao; as change, this refers to the nature of the Dao; and as the title of the *Yijing*, it supports an identification of the Dao with the source of creativity guiding the world and analyzable in terms of *yin-yang* that was first made in the *Xici Zhuan*, a text appended to the *Yijing* at the end of the Warring States. The term *yi*, however, is much more vague than the term *Dao*, which had by this time become thoroughly identified with cosmogony and in a sense had become too overdetermined, judging from the texts of popular religion in which the Dao was already identified with Laojun. The referential field of *yi* was much larger than that of Dao, and Liezi clearly wants to avoid simple designation and the threat of closure in this instance. The passage from the *Liezi* continues by, again, rewriting another passage from the *Laozi*, *Laozi* 42, which reads: "Dao gave birth to One, One gave birth to Two, Two gave birth to Three, and Three gave birth to the ten thousand things."

> Simplicity is without shape and boundary. Simplicity changed and became One; One changed and became Seven; Seven changed and became Nine; the change of Nine is the limit, and thereupon returned to change back into One.[31]
> 易無形埒，易變而為一，一變而為七, 七變而為九, 九變者, 究也; 乃復變而為一.

Traditional Chinese commentators have seen in this passage a clear reference to *Laozi* 42, but the *Liezi*'s changes are interesting.[32] The passage begins by naming that ultimate source by a negative characterization, saying in essence that there is nothing we can say or know about it other than that it simply was something. Simplicity became One, a common Daoist technical designation for *qi*. The progression is from *qi* to Seven and Nine; Seven and Nine are *yang* numbers that share in the creative and expanding qualities of *yang*. The progress then completes by reverting back to *qi*. In this, we seem to have a closed system forever folding back in on itself, but Liezi does not stop there; he moves the process out of its internal cycles to say something about the first formation of the world. These numbers, in part because of their *yang* associations, also commonly refer to the cycles of returning demanded by the many alchemical stages in the production of various elixirs so dear to institutional Daoism, so I think we might also understand the numbers Seven and Nine, as referring to the number of cycles necessary in order to complete the progress from one stage to the next. The section concludes in the following.

> One is the beginning of the changes of shape. The pure and light ascended to become Heaven, the turbid and heavy descended to become Earth, and the harmoniously balanced *qi* became the Human. Thus, Heaven and Earth encompass *jing*, and the ten thousand things transform and are born.[33]
> 一者, 形變之始也。清輕者上為天, 濁重者下為地, 沖和氣者為人。故天地含精, 萬物化生.

In these final lines of the second lecture, *Liezi* again relies upon the cosmogonic structure of the *Laozi* 42, specifically at the stage of Two (*yin-yang*) forming Three (the realms of Heaven, Earth, and the Human), finally resulting in the birth and transformation of the ten thousand things. At this point, the activities of the unborn and the untransformed reactivate, in a manner of speaking, such that what is born and transforms now not only includes *qi* and *yin-yang*, but also all things. With this, the *Liezi*'s cosmogony draws to a close.

These first two lectures of the *Tian Rui* chapter of the *Liezi* focus on the cosmogonic aspect of the culturally foundational notion of Dao. These lectures, surprisingly, only mention the term *dao* one time, in an instance that has nothing particularly cosmogonic about it. Certainly the author of these lectures was not unaware that he was talking about the pristine Dao, but he refrains, consciously I claim, from naming it directly and thereby leaves the notion to stand as a challenge to the limits of human thought. The fact that the *Liezi* attempts, as far as possible, not to designate and thereby give this notion closure, is not a weakness specific to its vocabulary or to the Chinese language; there is no notion in English to use to directly name it either, and I can't imagine a different human language that would make such a notion available, although some cultural and religious traditions maintain that they do have the words for exactly this purpose.[34] By this I mean a word that could somehow cut through time to designate directly the reality of the time before the origins, a word that could process the absolute inaccessibility of the time before the origins to provide knowledge of that environment for the human mind. But in the end, the words we have are never able to transcend the categories of human thought. The best that can be attempted is to rely upon the categories of our own experience and through some combination of projection and imagination to sound out the that-beyond-which of signification, if for no other reason than simply to challenge the mind to confront the limits of human possibility.

Notes

1. See A. C. Graham, *Disputers of the Tao* (LaSalle, IL: Open Court Press, 1989).
2. See David Hall and Roger Ames, *Thinking Through Confucius* (Albany: State University of New York Press, 1987).
3. See Thomas Michael, "Confucius and Laozi: Two Visions of the Dao

of Antiquity," in *Metaphilosophy and Chinese Thought: Interpreting David Hall*, ed. Ewing Chinn and Henry Rosemont, 169–77. (New York: Global Scholarly Publications, 2005).

4. *Laozi Zhushi ji Pingjie* (Chen Guying: Zhonghua Shuju, 1984), 232.
5. Ibid., 53.
6. *Zhuangzi Jishi* (Guo Qingfan: Zhonghua Shuju, 2004), 79.
7. I use this notion in Weber's sense, where it refers to a logical ideal, not a moral ideal. Weber, however, typically applied this idea to social action with the intent to reveal the analytical consistency of the general features of concrete social institutions; I use this idea to reveal the analytic consistency of culturally foundational notions.
8. *Liezi Jishi*, Yang Bojun (Beijing: Zhonghua Shuju, 1979), 3.
9. See Rudolf Wagner, *The Craft of A Chinese Commentator: Wang Bi on the Laozi* (Albany: State University of New York Press, 2000), 53–114.
10. *Liezi*, 1979, 2–3. Another feature in this passage, characteristic of a great deal of the *Liezi*, is the use of end rhymes: the repetitions of *sheng* (birth) and *hua* (transform) obviously, as well as *er* ("follows"), but also *du* ("alone") and *fu* ("come"), and *qiong* ("exhausted") and *zhong* ("arrested"). These patterns rhymes and repetitions alone direct the dating almost definitively to the late fourth century and beyond.
11. *Liezi*, 1979, 5.
12. Ibid., 9–10.
13. Ibid., 10.
14. Ibid., 3.
15. *Laozi Zhushi ji Pingjie*, 1984, 53.
16. Ibid., 223.
17. *Liezi*, 1979, 3–4.
18. Thomas Michael, *The Pristine Dao: Metaphysics in Early Daoist Discourse* (Albany: State University of New York Press, 2005), 61–68.
19. See, for example, David Jordan and Daniel Overmyer, *The Flying Phoenix: Aspects of Sectarianism in Taiwan* (Princeton: Princeton University Press, 1986).
20. *Liezi*, 1979, 6.
21. Max Kaltenmark, "The Ideology of the T'ai-p'ing ching," in *Facets of Taoism: Essays in Chinese Religion*, ed. Holmes Welch and Anna Seidel, 21–24. (New Haven: Yale University Press, 1979).
22. *Laozi Zhushi ji Pingjie*, 1984, 130.
23. *Baihutong Shuzheng* (Chen Lizhuan, Zhonghua Shuju, 1994),v. 1, 421.
24. See Michael, 2005, 13–15.
25. *Zhouyi Qian Zuodu*, in *Weishu Jicheng* (Shanghai Guji Chubanshe, 1994), 46.
26. *Taishang Laojun Kaitian Jing*. In *Yunji qiqian* (Taibei: Ziyou Chubanshe, 1992), 18.
27. The term *kalpa* clearly indicates a Buddhist influence in view of this text's date, whereas the term *hun* is imbued with a heavy Daoist flavor. This whole notion finds fictional textualization in the opening chapter of the *Shuihu zhuan* (*Outlaws of the Marsh*) from the Ming Dynasty.

28. *Kaitian Jing*, 1992, 18.
29. See Anna Seidel, *La divinisation de Lao tseu dans le Taoisme des Han* (Paris: École Française d'Extrême-Orient, 1992).
30. *Liezi*, 1979, 6–7.
31. Ibid., 7.
32. The passage here is also directly echoed and paraphrased in the opening of *Xiyou ji* (*Journey to the West*).
33. *Liezi*, 1979, 8.
34. See Barbara Holdrege, *Veda and Torah: Transcending the Textuality of Scripture* (Albany: State University of New York Press, 1996).

列子

The Theme of Unselfconsciousness in the *Liezi*

Philip J. Ivanhoe

> It is ironic that the one thing that all religions recognize as separating us from our creator—our very self-consciousness—is also the one thing that divides us from our fellow creatures.
>
> —Annie Dillard[1]

> It is especially dangerous to be conscious of oneself.
>
> —A. C. Graham[2]

Introduction

An important theme in the *Liezi* and in early Daoist texts in general is that those who have mastered the Way are in some important sense unselfconscious about their actions and themselves. This elusive state of mind is a distinctive feature of several of the most memorable characters and events described in early Daoism. Similar ideas can be found in the writings of the Confucian school as well, and in this case it is clear that what is most valued is a certain lack of self-consciousness about one's ethical achievements and moral worth. For many traditional Chinese thinkers, a particular type of unselfconsciousness is a critical feature of proper human action and a constitutive characteristic of those acts that express the spiritual ideal known as *wuwei* "non-action" or "effortless action."

Such ideas strike many Western readers as particularly strange and exotic, and at least some philosophers will regard such teachings as odd and perhaps muddled. After all, how could it be a good thing to be *less* aware of what you are doing? Most scholars of Chinese thought would agree that what I will call the *theme of unselfconsciousness* is important for a wide range of Chinese thinkers, but there is as yet no careful and systematic philosophical analysis of what this kind of claim entails. In particular, earlier studies of topics such as *wuwei* have not endeavored to describe the nature of the kind of unselfconsciousness that one must cultivate in order to reach the ideal state of action or being.[3] I will argue that this is the key to appreciating the particular *value* of this ideal.

In this chapter, I offer a sketch of the theme of unselfconsciousness, exploring several distinct but related senses of it, describing the nature of the desired form of unselfconsciousness, and offering an explanation for *why* many traditional Chinese thinkers have tended to value this state. I will argue that there are two distinct, though related, senses of unselfconsciousness in the *Liezi* and other early texts. In contrast to most studies of this general theme, I will argue that the intuitions motivating the first sense, what I will call the *everyday sense*, entail nothing particularly mysterious or exotic. Rather, this sense of unselfconsciousness describes important though often misunderstood aspects of human life. I will go on to argue that the second, *religious sense* of unselfconsciousness involves much more subtle and less self-evident claims. As one approaches this latter ideal, the precise nature of the desired state and the value it purportedly has become increasingly elusive and inaccessible to the uninitiated. I will show that the author of the *Liezi*, like other traditional Chinese thinkers, presents this more dramatic sense of the theme of unselfconsciousness as a natural extension of the more prosaic *everyday sense* but that this move is not justified in any clear way. I will defend the view that while we have good reasons to endorse the everyday sense, we need something like faith to embrace the more dramatic religious claims about the value of unselfconsciousness. Nevertheless, understanding the former will help us appreciate the nature of the life described by the latter.

Three Expressions of the Theme of Unselfconsciousness

A certain kind of excessive self-consciousness can corrupt and undermine the quality of a wide range of human activities. We see such intuitions expressed in our own culture in a variety of ways. Most of us accept the idea that sometimes we only succeed in understanding some problem or in finding something we are seeking when we *stop looking*. One may become so obsessed with *solving* a problem or so worried about past or potential failure, that one's attention and energies are drawn away from the problem itself and are dissipated in a dysfunctional preoccupation with being the person who solves it. When we finally find what we are looking for, we often admit that "it was right there in front of me all along." In such cases, excessive self-consciousness plays a role in preventing us from *seeing* well, in the sense of making full use of our faculty of perception or understanding.[4]

Most of us would also agree that being overly concerned with *how one is doing* or *how one's action or behavior is being perceived* by others often can corrupt and undermine one's performance. If we are engaged in a competition but are focused on the agony of possible failure or the enjoyment of potential rewards, our attention and energies are misdirected. They are being siphoned away from the important thing—the task at hand—and directed toward aims that do not in any direct way help us perform better and that may in fact interfere with our success. If we are singing a song, dancing a dance, or making love with someone we cherish, we can be inhibited and made clumsy by thoughts of how others—even those we love—might be thinking of us. In such cases, too much attention to our selves stymies our attempts to *do* well.[5]

Finally, most of us would agree that a certain kind of excessive self-consciousness often corrupts and undermines our attempts to realize certain emotional states or traits of character. If, for example I want to be more "laid-back" and carefree, this very thought can lead to an obsessive desire that only exacerbates my present uptight and harried existence. My desire to *make myself* feel a certain way can prevent that very feeling from coming into being. I might aspire to cultivate a certain virtue such as compassion. But my very desire to be a more caring person may fatally hamstring my efforts to realize this laudable ideal. In extreme cases, it can lead me to squander my attention and energy in devising self-aggrandizing fantasies about how sweet and caring I already am or to deploy my time, energy, and skill at devising complex explanations of how my apparently selfish actions really are expressions of care. In any event, excessive concern with *my self* and *what I want* misdirects my attention and energy. If I want to be more sensitive and caring, I should be thinking more about those in need and less about myself.

In such cases, too much concern with my self undermines my ability to *be* a certain way.

In each of the three types described above, our *seeing*, *doing*, or *being* is corrupted and diminished by excessive consciousness of one's self. Such misguided attention to the self can be expressed as a form of "self-fulfilling prophesy"—a dysfunctional preoccupation with the possibility of failure that serves as the source of one's lack of success.[6] In such cases, as Graham put it in the line that serves as one of the epigraphs to this essay, "It is especially dangerous to be conscious of oneself." As seen in these examples, and as I will explain in greater detail below, the *theme of unselfconsciousness* concerns where one's attention lies and where one's energies are directed. It insists that at least under some conditions and in certain situations an excessive attention to one's own success, well-being, or psychological state undermines one's efforts to see, do, or be well. Notice, though, that this does not in any way imply that one must be inattentive, much less *oblivious*, to the goals of seeing, doing, or being. Those seeking to *see* well must focus their faculties on the problem before them. Those seeking to *do* well must apply themselves to the best of their abilities. Those seeking to *be* a certain way must take steps and strive to realize the state to which they aspire. But they must make these efforts in ways that avoid allowing the focus of their attention and energy to drift back and remained fixed upon themselves.[7]

In order to facilitate my analysis, I want to develop and deploy the distinction, mentioned above, between *everyday* and *religious* expressions of the theme of unselfconsciousness.[8] By the former, I mean a set of related claims about the value of unselfconsciousness that are more limited in scope and modest in force. The *everyday* sense does not entail that unselfconsciousness should characterize every moment of one's life, that it will protect one from every threat or danger, or that it has value beyond specific conditions and circumstances. In contrast, discussions of the *religious* sense of unselfconsciousness describe the proper way to live not just under certain conditions or circumstances but always. It describes a way of life that purportedly protects one from all physical and psychological harm. Moreover, the religious sense not only requires a lack of excessive self-consciousness but a more radical and thoroughgoing loss of self. In order to achieve the everyday ideal of unselfconsciousness, one must train oneself to be significantly less concerned with one's own desires and well-being and learn to focus one's attention and energies on other people, activities, or goals. In order to achieve the religious ideal, one must dramatically expand one's sense of self. One must come to see oneself as but a part of the greater patterns and processes that constitute the *dao* and one's actions as flowing out of and contributing to the harmonious operation of this grand scheme. The everyday sense appeals to events, states, and activities that most of us have experienced or seen in the course of our daily lives. The religious sense holds forth an ideal that only the most advanced spiritual virtuosi have experienced and that purportedly even they cannot adequately describe.

One can find examples in the *Liezi* and the other early classics of Daoism of each of the three types or expressions of the theme of unselfconsciousness that I earlier endeavored to describe. Let us look at some of these passages and see how they relate to the everyday or religious senses that I have sketched immediately above.[9]

Examples from the *Liezi*

In the second chapter of the *Liezi* we find the story of the mythical Yellow Emperor, who avidly was searching for the ideal way to lead his life (Graham, 33–35). For fifteen years, he served himself, enjoying his power, position, and privilege. He discovered, though, that this only led to the dissolution of his spirit, and so he changed his ways and for the next fifteen years dedicated himself to serving his people and the welfare of his kingdom. Unfortunately, this course yielded a similar result, which led him to exclaim, "Deep is my error! It is an affliction to care for oneself alone, and as great an affliction to govern the myriad things!" (Graham, 33). Having exhausted the paths of hedonistic egoism and altruism, he turned to spiritual cultivation: "He retired to live undisturbed in a hut in his main courtyard, where he fasted to discipline mind and body, and for three months had nothing to do with the affairs of state" (Graham, 34). This course too proved unproductive and brought only exhaustion. At that point, worn out by his efforts to find the perfect form of life, the Yellow Emperor fell asleep and dreamed of the ideal state of Huaxu, where the people "do not know how to prefer themselves to others, and so they neither love nor hate. They do not know how to turn their faces to things or turn their backs, go with the stream or push against it, so nothing benefits or harms them" (Graham, 34). For the first time, he saw clearly what was before him all along: the Way.

Understanding—in the form of a vision—comes to the Yellow Emperor when, like the people of Huaxu, he stops thinking about *himself*.[10] His earlier attempts proved futile because of his excessive self-concern. His quest was foiled not simply by striving but by striving *in a particular way*. He was self-consciously trying to improve *himself*—hedonistically, ethically, and spiritually—but this concern with his own well-being, success, and psychological state prevented him from finding the answer he sought. For the answer is the Way and the Way is not *for* him; it is not for anyone or anything in the sense of having a special concern or utility for a given individual or class of things. If one follows the Way, one does not do so in order to get something but as an expression of what one by nature is. One can only realize and enjoy the carefree and contented life it offers when one abandons oneself to it.[11]

This passage clearly concerns the religious sense of unselfconsciousness. It describes the proper way to live not just under some conditions or certain circumstances but always, a way that purportedly protects one from all physical as well as psychological harm. It requires not only a lack of excessive self-consciousness but also a more radical and thoroughgoing loss of self. The passage concludes with the emperor bringing peace and prosperity to his entire state—through the power of his virtue—at which point he then "rose into the sky"—that is, became an immortal. What is more, the people of his state "did not stop wailing for him for more than two hundred years" (Graham, 35).

And yet, what lends these more radical religious claims some air of plausibility is an earlier, less prominent expression of the everyday sense of unselfconsciousness. The passage begins with a ruler who confronts not a religious quest but the paradox of hedonism. Self-consciously seeking directly for his own happiness was leading him to ruin. Not only was he not happy, he was damaging his health and making himself miserable. This is not an arcane spiritual matter but a common and well-known human predicament. One cannot even please oneself *if one has excessive concern with one's self*. The story takes an interesting turn when it insists that the same unhappy result occurred when the emperor pursued the paths of strict altruism and spiritual cultivation. It seems that one cannot live a satisfying life in service to others or some higher religious cause if one has excessive concern with one's self.[12] All three of these paths led to unhappiness and a loss of vitality—sure signs that he was working against the Way.

There is nothing particularly mysterious about the claims advanced on behalf of the everyday sense of unselfconsciousness. Many people would and all should accept the idea that an excessive concern with one's own pleasure, goodness, or spiritual well-being is not the way to the best life and can lead one to failure and harm. While not all of us practice it, most of us tend to endorse the ideal of a middle or moderate path in life and believe that the best life is found by sincerely serving the interests of other people and ideals as well as oneself. The Yellow Emperor is not unlike those who run from one self-help fad to another looking for a "meaningful life," while their friends wonder why they don't just "get over" themselves and enjoy the good life they have. This more prosaic, though by no means unimportant, perspective on the value of unselfconsciousness does not entail that one practice it in *every* situation and circumstance. It does not promise to protect one from *every* threat nor provide one with complete contentment, much less immortality. It does not require the more radical loss of self that is characteristic of the religious sense; in fact it requires one to show a balanced concern for oneself as well as other people and principles. It does, though, promise to help one see more clearly and understand more deeply important truths about what makes a human life good, and it at least opens the door to the possibility that a life organized around a more radical loss of self might hold considerable promise.

In the *Zhuangzi* we find several passages concerning the character Liezi.[13] In the longest and most detailed of these, Liezi appears as the apprentice or disciple of a man named Huzi. I take it to be important that in this story, Liezi is presented as someone who, like the Yellow Emperor in the story above, is seeking wisdom and actively engaged in spiritual study. The *Zhuangzi* passage opens with Liezi becoming infatuated with a shaman named Ji Xian, "[w]ho could tell whether men would live or die, survive or perish, be fortunate or unfortunate, live a long time or die young, and he would predict the year, month, week, and day as though he were a god himself" (Watson, 94–95).

Such skill would indeed be highly valued and Liezi deems it as superior even to the knowledge his teacher possesses: "I used to think, Master, that your Way was perfect. But now I see there is something even higher!" (Watson, 95). Huzi responds by chastising his disciple for ignorance and, of particular note for the theme we are exploring, for excessive pride and boastfulness: "You take what you know of the Way and wave it in the face of the world, expecting to be believed! This is the reason men can see right through you" (Watson, 95). He invites Liezi to bring Ji Xian around to take a look at him. Ji Xian attempts to physiognomize Huzi on several different occasions, but each time he comes up with a different assessment and prediction. This lack of consistent diagnosis is the result of Huzi's ability to present different aspects of himself to the shaman trying to "see through him." In their last meeting, Huzi presents himself as "Not Yet Emerged from My Source. I came to him empty, wriggling and turning, not knowing anything about 'who' or 'what,' now dipping and bending, now flowing in waves . . ." (Watson, 96–97). Ji Xian is so overwhelmed by what he sees that "his wits left him and he fled" (Watson, 96). Liezi was dispatched to bring him back but could not catch up with the fleeing shaman. As a result, Liezi

> concluded that he had never really begun to learn anything. He went home and for three years did not go out. He replaced his wife at the stove, fed the pigs as though he were feeding people, and showed no preferences in the things he did. He got rid of the carving and polishing and returned to plainness, letting his body stand alone like a clod . . . (Watson, 97)

This story offers a clear example of the religious sense of the value of unselfconsciousness. As in the earlier passage about the Yellow Emperor, the protagonist begins by trying to understand or see some higher truth and ends by turning away from any self-conscious attempt to improve himself. Liezi's Master chides him for his early fascination with Huzi, attributing it to Liezi's overriding desire to present *himself* as someone with great knowledge and power. It should not go without notice that Ji Xian's power is concerned exclusively with various aspects of personal well-being and success. As in our earlier story, Liezi's excessive concern with the self impedes his understanding. Huzi quite literally illustrates this when he undoes the slick shaman by presenting him with a vision of chaos and unending change. While this story lacks any overt transition from the everyday to religious sense of unselfconsciousness, it clearly presents the latter as superior to *any* mundane knowledge or ability. By overwhelming the shaman, Huzi implies the superiority of knowledge of the Way. This is a theme we will see repeated in several of the other stories we shall explore below.

In early Daoist texts, there are more examples of unselfconsciousness in regard to *doing* than to any other kind of project, state, or activity. Perhaps this is because "doing" in general is the most common opportunity we have for experiencing the general phenomenon we are seeking to understand; perhaps it is because of the competitive advantage that one obtains by demonstrating the practical superiority of one's way; or perhaps it reflects the fact that Daoists sought to describe a *way of life* not just a theory about how to live. In any event, the idea that excessive concern with *how one is doing* or *how one's actions might look* to others can interfere with or even fatally undermine our ability to succeed at what we are doing is a widespread theme. The ideal mode of action is simply to lose oneself in the flow of one's activity.[14]

The idea that someone who is less or even not at all conscious of himself can in fact be better off is brought out in the anecdote about a drunken man who is thrown from a cart.

> When a drunken man is thrown from a cart, swiftly though he falls it does not kill him. His bones and joints are the same as another mans yet he is not harmed as another man would be, because of the integrity of his spirit. He rides without knowing it, falls without knowing it; life and death, astonishment and fear, find no entry into his breast, and so he does not shrink from hitting things. If this is true even of a man who gets his integrity from wine, how much more is it true of those who get it from Heaven! The sage hides himself in Heaven, therefore no thing can harm him. (Graham, 38)

This passage offers an excellent example of the *value* of the everyday sense of unselfconsciousness. The general idea is that in certain situations or circumstances, thinking about oneself makes one less likely to succeed or fare well. The story relies upon the common impression that drunkenness can make one more supple, flexible, and fearless, thus enabling one to survive a fall that would likely kill those in full possession of their senses. While most of us think that a sense of self-preservation is critically important to us, this passage suggests that our dearest interest—our very survival—is at least in some cases best served by *not* thinking about ourselves. Here we have a commonsense experience that at least makes problematic the idea that it is always best to have a clear and distinct sense and be fully in control of oneself. The passage further implies that there is much greater preservative power to be found in an integrity that comes from Heaven—rather than mere wine. This of course points toward the more religious sense of unselfconsciousness.

A similar idea is expressed in a different way in the following story about an archery contest between Bohun Wuren and Liezi.[15] This anecdote begins with Liezi showing off his skill to Bohun Wuren. The latter, though, remained unimpressed and asked Liezi if he could shoot as well "overlooking an abyss a thousand feet deep" (Graham, 38). Bohun Wuren then proceeded to climb a high mountain and walk backward out onto a perilous cliff overlooking an immense abyss until his feet hung halfway over the edge. He then bowed to Liezi inviting him to follow suit. But Liezi was paralyzed with fear and "lay on his face with the sweat streaming down to his heels" (Graham, 38–39).

This story offers a dramatic example of the value of unselfconsciousness. It remains on the plane of the everyday but conveys a hint of the more sublime religious realm through its complete conquest of the fear of death. The underlying point, seen in several stories throughout the early Daoist corpus, is that common skill can become clumsy if not rooted in an understanding of the Way.[16] For the Way enables one to shed the excessive concern with one's self that can cause the less enlightened to become unglued. What remains is a heightened ability to focus on the task at hand that enables such skillful exemplars to achieve a preternatural level of success.

A similar point is made in the story of the Ferryman who is so at home on the water and so absorbed in his work that he wastes no attention or energy worrying about potential danger: "Though ten thousand ways of slipping and overturning spread out before him, they cannot enter the doors of his mind; he is relaxed wherever he goes" (Graham, 43). Not paying attention to potential danger to one's self is a paradigm for the more general idea of not letting "outside things"—that is, things outside of the task at hand—interfere with one's performance. As the Ferryman explains, "Gamble for tiles and you play skillfully; for the clasp of your belt, and you have lost confidence; for gold, and you get flustered. You have not lost your skill; but you hold yourself back, you give weight to something outside you; and whoever does that is inwardly clumsy" (Graham, 43–44). Worrying about whether one will succeed or fail or how others will judge one are additional expressions of excessive self-concern. They draw one's attention and energies away from what is most important and interfere with one's performance. The stories that follow, about the man who swims at ease in the treacherous waters below Luliang Falls and the Old Cicada Catcher who catches his prey "as though he were picking them up off the ground" make a similar point (Graham, 44–45). These passages offer examples of the everyday sense of the value of unselfconsciousness. While these exemplars of the Way are remarkable, there is nothing mysterious or supernatural about them or their abilities. Nevertheless, all of these stories point toward the more dramatic claims of the religious sense. To varying degrees, these different masters of the Way distance themselves from our normal concern for the self. In so doing, they are traveling on a trajectory that leads to the more radical loss of self that is characteristic of the religious sense. This is particularly clear in the last story, where the cicada catcher describes his attitude toward his own body and its effect on his art: "I hold my body like a wood-chopper hacking at a root, I hold my arm as steady as a branch on a withered tree; out of all the myriad things in the vastness of heaven and earth, I am conscious only of the wings of a cicada" (Graham, 45). The cicada catcher's disregard for himself leads him naturally to liken his torso and limbs to mere things. In so doing he expresses the Daoist ideal of the equality of things.

Our final expression of the theme of unselfconsciousness concerns its value for attaining certain desirable states of being. By a "state of being" I mean a fairly specific state of character, emotion, or attitude. For the religious sense of unselfconsciousness, the goal will be to attain a state of being in which one is in harmony with the *dao*. Such a state purportedly enables one to act in an effortless and frictionless manner and achieve remarkable results. It guarantees that one will not be harmed, for one will avoid any conflict with the other creatures and things of the world.[17] A sure sign that one has attained this desired state of being is a wholly harmonious relationship with other creatures, as shown in the following passage from the *Liezi*.[18]

> There was a man living by the seashore who loved seagulls. Every morning he went down to the sea to roam with the seagulls, and more birds came to him than you could count in hundreds. His father said to him: "I hear the seagulls all come roaming with you. Bring me some to play with." Next day, when he went down to the sea, the seagulls danced above him and would not come down . . . (Graham, 45)

At the start of the story, the man lived in harmony with the Way and thus had a special and harmonious relationship with the seagulls. The birds could sense that he was not a threat and therefore frolicked freely with him by the side of the sea. He did not *self-consciously* strive to be friends with the seagulls; their relationship was simply a result of being in harmony with the Way. However, when his father asked the man to bring him some of the birds, all of this changed. Now, he was *trying* to befriend the seagulls in order to capture them. The point is similar to what we have seen earlier. Being a friend is not something one can aim at directly. I can *act like* your friend, but that is not being your friend. Nevertheless, being a friend, to another person or to the birds, is something one can self-consciously cultivate. If one focuses one's attention and energy *on the birds* and accepts and loves them for what they are, one will exude the desired quality. If one tries to cultivate such love *in order to catch them*, then one's attention and energy are not focused on loving the birds; one is focused on catching them, and they will fail to come to you.

A short passage about two concubines offers another example of the value of unselfconsciousness in regard to *being*.

> When Yang Zhu was passing through Song, he spent the night at an inn. The innkeeper had two concubines, one beautiful and the other ugly. The ugly one he valued, the beautiful one he neglected. When Yang Zhu asked the reason, the fellow answered: "The beautiful one thinks herself beautiful, and I do not notice her beauty. The ugly one thinks herself ugly, and I do not notice her ugliness."
>
> "Remember this, my disciples!" said Yang Zhu. "If you act nobly and banish from your mind the thought that you are noble, where can you go and not be loved?" (Graham, 52)

This passage offers direct testimony both to the right way to be—unselfconscious of one's virtues—and the right way to cultivate oneself—by working to focus one's attention on the proper action and not on one's self. The beautiful concubine was too aware of her beauty, and this made her less lovable.[19] The ugly concubine had no thoughts of being beautiful, and this made her more appealing. Yang Zhu counsels his disciples to emulate the ugly concubine, in the sense that they should do what is noble but not with the thought of how noble they are or may become. They should do what is noble because that is what one who follows the Way does—as a matter of course.[20]

Both these examples of the value of unselfconscious in regard to being concern the everyday sense; neither of these passages describes people or events that are beyond ordinary experience. And yet both point toward the more elusive religious sense of unselfconsciousness, a state where the self is lost in the activity of following the Way. The religious goal is to act without any sense of oneself as distinct from the greater patterns and processes of the *dao*. One is still the "site" of action, but the source of action lies in the Way. This is difficult for most of us to understand, but I do not think it is beyond the reach of our imagination or that we completely lack an ability to appreciate what is valuable about this quality. We have some sense of it from our experiences of the more everyday form of unselfconsciousness, for example, we all have felt the distinctive joy of letting ourselves go in the course of some activity such as dancing or playing some sport. To be absorbed in an activity in this way not only tends to make our performance *better,* it gives us a special expanded sense of ourselves. We don't shrink into nothing but rather expand to fill up the entire activity. In such moments, we feel connected to and part of something much more grand, powerful, and important than our everyday self. We also feel a poignant sense of security, peace, and ease. If one can extrapolate from such everyday experiences along a trajectory that transcends any particular activity, one approaches the sense of oneness with the *dao* that is the goal of the religious sense of unselfconsciousness.[21]

Those who attain the religious ideal combine all three of the expressions of unselfconsciousness that we have been exploring. Such people are able to see, do, and be in the proper way. The Yellow Emperor *after* his attainment of the Way offers a good example of this type of achievement. Such spiritual paragons exhibit the more radical loss of self that is the distinctive mark of the religious sense. Their activity appears purposeless in the sense of lacking any individual desires or designs that could be construed as unnatural or contrary to the Way.

One of the most interesting and distinctive aspects of early Daoism is its rejection of the value of direct, magical control over Nature. We saw this in the earlier passage about the shaman Ji Xian and his "defeat" by Liezi's master Huzi. In that story, Liezi is presented as someone who is naively enthralled with the more practical or *purposive* abilities that accrue to one who has attained some type of control over Nature.[22] This is not the only story in which Liezi is portrayed as lacking in true vision—an interesting and distinctive theme within the early Daoism corpus.[23] For example, in the *Zhuangzi*, we find the following story about Liezi riding the wind.

> Liezi could ride the wind and go soaring around with cool and breezy skill, but after fifteen days he came back to earth. As far as the searching for good fortune went, he didn't fret and worry. He escaped the trouble of walking, but he still had to depend on something to get around. If he had only mounted on the truth of Heaven and Earth, ridden the changes of the six breaths, and thus wandered through the boundless, then what would he have had to depend on? Therefore I say, the Perfect Man has no self; the Holy Man has no merit; the Sage has no fame. (Watson, 32)[24]

Like the earlier story about Ji Xian's shamanistic powers, this passage describes but dismisses Liezi's remarkable ability to ride upon the wind. What, though, is the basis of such criticism? Perhaps it is that concern with such abilities reveals an excessive concern with one's self and specifically with one's power and superiority.[25] Rather than harnessing the wind for *himself*, the passage tells us that Liezi should simply have surrendered to the Dao and ridden upon the transformations of Heaven and Earth. In harnessing the wind, Liezi is imposing his own desires and will upon the world, and this shows that he falls short of the religious ideal of unselfconsciousness that we have been exploring. We can see this ideal writ large as the distinctively Daoist view that imposing a general human perspective upon the world will disrupt and interfere with the Way. We need to be receptive and attentive to the world. We are to respond "like a mirror" to what comes before us, and we are to avoid imposing our expectations and values upon the natural world.[26]

Conclusion

I have argued that the value of unselfconsciousness is an important theme in the *Liezi* and suggested that this claim can be extended to a large range of traditional Chinese thinkers. It would take much more time to defend the broader claim, and it would take us away from the *Liezi*, which is the focus of the present volume. Let me, though, offer two examples from the Confucian tradition as evidence that such a case could be made. The first comes from the *Analects*.

> The Master said, "Do not be concerned that you do not have an [eminent] position; be concerned about having what it takes to fulfill such a position. Do not be concerned that no one knows you; be concerned about being worthy of being known." (*Analects* 4.14)

In this short but powerful passage, Kongzi advises us to cultivate a particular kind of unselfconsciousness. I am not to think about my self in terms of my station or renown; rather, I am advised to be concerned about ensuring that I am qualified to gain and fulfill an important position and that I am worthy of being well known. His point is that we must be mindful of ourselves but not in a self-centered way. We are to strive to be worthy and to develop ourselves as best we can, but we are to do so in service to the greater cause of the *dao*. In other words, we are to work at becoming better because this is the right way to be. We are not to look to the fruits that such efforts often bear, for the fruits are not the proper object of concern and focusing upon them will draw attention and energy away from our true task.

My second example is a commentary on the figure of Kongzi as described in a famous passage from the *Analects*. In his *Collected Commentaries on the Analects*, Zhu Xi (1130–1200) offers the following explanation and analysis of *Analects* 7.1, in which Kongzi describes himself as one who *transmits but does not create*:

> To transmit is to do no more than pass down the old, while to create is to invent something new. Only a sage is capable of creating, while transmitting is something a worthy can achieve. . . . Kongzi edited the *Book of Poetry* and produced the definitive editions of the *Book of Rites* and the *Book of Music*. He elucidated the *Book of Changes* and enhanced the *Spring and Autumn Annals*. In every one of these cases, he passed on the old [teachings] of the former kings; in no case did he create anything [new] of his own. And so, he described himself in this way. Not only did he not dare to compare himself to the creating sages, he did not dare to directly rank himself among the ancient worthies. The greater his virtue grew, the less conscious he was of it; he was not even aware of how humble his own words were . . .

Taken on its own, the idea expressed in the last line of Zhu Xi's commentary is subtle but not in any way mysterious or paradoxical. It is wholly consistent with our own intuitions about moral worth. For most of us would agree that a genuinely good person does not spend a great deal of time thinking about her own goodness. Part of what *makes* one good is the disposition to think more about the needs and desires of *other people* and less about one's own good. This is very clear in the case of virtues such as compassion. In order to show compassion, to perform a genuinely compassionate act that expresses the virtue, I need to be focused on *helping the needy*—not on the goodness of my action or character.

I have also argued that in the *Liezi* and other early Chinese texts there is a latent and largely unnoticed distinction between everyday and religious senses of the value of unselfconsciousness. By the former, I mean a set of related claims about the value of unselfconsciousness that does not entail that unselfconsciousness should characterize every aspect of one's life, that it will protect one from every threat or danger, or that it has value beyond specific conditions and circumstances. In contrast, discussions of the religious sense describe the proper way to live not just under certain conditions or circumstances but always. It describes a way of life that purportedly protects one from all physical as well as psychological harm, and it requires a more radical and thoroughgoing loss of self. The everyday sense appeals to events, states, and activities that most of us have experienced or seen in the course of our daily lives. The religious sense holds out an ideal that only the most advanced spiritual virtuosi have experienced and that purportedly even they cannot adequately describe or convey.

Distinguishing between an everyday and religious sense of the value of unselfconsciousness helps us to appreciate how the former is used to make the latter more accessible and perhaps more plausible. Traditional Chinese advocates of the religious sense of unselfconsciousness deploy descriptions of the more prosaic everyday sense both to argue for the value of unselfconsciousness and to give readers a sense of what the more arcane religious ideal might be like. Nevertheless, one can accept the former without believing in the latter and recognizing the value of the former is not alone sufficient for establishing the value of the latter. Failing to see and appreciate the difference between the everyday and religious senses of unselfconsciousness will tend to lead one to overlook important aspects of the shared ideal. It is easy for the value of the everyday sense of unselfconsciousness to be lost in a gathering sense of mystery.

Another distinction that helps to dispel at least some of the mystery that tends to obscure an understanding of the value of unselfconsciousness concerns the difference between the process of developing unselfconsciousness and unselfconsciousness as the end goal or ultimate aim of self-cultivation. Failing to distinguish between the *course of development* and the *ultimate end state* can multiply the aura of mystery around the value of unselfconsciousness, even in the case of the everyday sense. For example, one might accept that in particular situations and under certain circumstances, unselfconsciousness is a valuable and desirable trait. It does not seem unreasonable to believe that unselfconscious play with one's child is better—both for one's child and for oneself—than play that results from the reluctant obedience to a sense of parental duty. Those who endorse such a claim though might bemoan the fact that they just can't *will* themselves into the state that is their ultimate goal; they can't immediately and directly become the kind of people who engage in unselfconscious play. This makes perfect sense; to develop a disposition takes time. One can no more immediately and directly will oneself to be more playful than one can immediately and directly will oneself to be physically fit. In another respect, though, the challenge before such a person might seem to present a paradox.[27] For the *mere thought* that it would be better if I were simply to give myself over to the to-and-fro of play may impede my ability to engage in such activity. Our earlier analysis of the value of unselfconsciousness provides us with a clearer understanding of how this can happen. When I think about how badly *I* need to be less self-conscious or how much *I* wish I could let myself go, the focus of my attention and the flow of my energy tends to shift from playing with my children to working on myself. If I allow this to happen and become obsessed with my self or anxious and self-conscious about my performance or my progress, then I can indeed undo my attempts to improve myself. What I need to do instead is to shift the focus of my attention and devote my energies to playing and specifically to playing with my children. If I can do this it will lead me, at least to some extent, to *forget about myself*.[28]

Some may think that the process described above just moves the problem up one level. I am undone because I am left worrying about how badly *I* need to focus less on me, and this leaves me still absorbed with myself. But one need not fall into such a dysfunctional trap—and if one can avoid tight linkage here, one avoids the strong sense of intractable paradox that distorts the nature of such cases. Understood in the right light, the desire to become more playful or the desire to play with my children are enough to move me toward the kind of change to which I aspire without involving an obsessive concern with myself. Such desires are not about me; they are about the value of carefree play and the right way to spend time with my children.

If I am *trying* to develop a certain ability or disposition, there is no gainsaying that I still have work to do. But trying is not necessarily an impediment to progress; it is simply a sign that I have not yet attained the desired aim or end state. In such cases, what I must do is to engage in practices and follow policies that tend to generate the desired ability or disposition. If I want to develop a greater ability to engage in unselfconscious play, I must remind myself of the virtues of play and be on the lookout for good opportunities for play. I must work to be attentive to types of behavior or thoughts that prevent me from engaging in play. In other words, I need to develop and maintain standing dispositions that will guide me and help me to achieve my goal.[29] But these dispositions need not be constant, obsessive thoughts about the need to *make myself* more playful—that indeed would undo my efforts. Rather, they can remain in the background of my thoughts and concerns until an appropriate circumstance brings them and me into play. Indeed, this is how they *must* function if they are to serve as effective means to my desired end. The point is that I have many more resources at my disposal than an inner voice commanding me constantly to "engage in unselfconscious play!"

It makes perfect sense to say that those of us who still have to remind ourselves to be attentive to opportunities, the needs and desires of others, and errant tendencies etc. still have not fully attained a particular desired end state. As noted above, our need to make a self-conscious effort is a sign that we still have work to do. But that does not show that there is any intractable paradox involved in making the right kind of effort. It does, though, show the importance of distinguishing between the process of development and the end state.[30] For there is no effective way to attain the latter in a sudden burst of will and attempting to do so will tend to lead one into the kinds of self-defeating tensions that we have discussed.[31] Nevertheless, as shown above, the same tension does not haunt the process of development. Striving to enjoy the value of unselfconsciousness remains a riddle, but the riddle has a solution.

Notes

Thanks to Erin M. Cline, Eric L. Hutton, Paul Kjellbeg, and T. C. Kline for comments and suggestions on earlier drafts of this chapter.

1. From chapter 6, "The Present" (Dillard, 79).
2. From the introduction to chapter 2 of the *Liezi*, "The Yellow Emperor" (Graham, 32).
3. Roger Ames (1994) has produced a valuable study of *wuwei* as an ideal form of government in the early Confucian tradition. Edward Slingerland (2003) has written a comprehensive analysis of *wuwei* as a "spiritual ideal" among early Chinese thinkers. Neither of these authors has offered an analysis of the kind that I propose in this chapter.
4. Sometimes what prevents us from finding what we are looking for is a stubborn adherence to some preconceived idea of *what* we need or *how* to find it. Daoists discuss this type of case as well. For example, consider the story of Huizi and the huge gourds in chapter 1 of the *Zhuangzi*. What I have in mind though are cases in which an excessive concern with *one's own success* serves as the primary impediment to one seeing or understanding.
5. While we often imagine such concerns in terms of being seen by others, this is not a necessary feature of the phenomenon in question. While self-consciousness often occurs in a real or imagined social setting, it can exist apart from such contexts. We can be self-conscious of ourselves in regard to a personal ideal or standard that does not involve being seen or evaluated by others. In this respect, self-consciousness is similar to shame.
6. I owe this point to Erin M. Cline.
7. As I will argue below, failing to pay attention to this aspect of the theme of unselfconsciousness easily leads to an excessive mystification of topics such as *wuwei*.
8. This distinction is an ideal type that is useful for analysis. I do not intend to posit some hard and fast distinction between "religious" and "philosophical" Daoism or anything like that. My point will be that these two types represent a continuum, and that the former is invoked to make the latter more plausible and accessible.
9. I will illustrate each of the three types with examples from the *Liezi* but will augment these examples with additional passages concerning the figure Liezi taken from the *Zhuangzi*.
10. This revelation occurs when he falls asleep and moves to a state in which at least a certain form of self-consciousness is no longer in play. This may explain an important feature of at least some of the passages about dreaming that one finds in early Daoist texts.

11. One is free of anxiety by virtue of not having to choose, one is content because one follows one's natural inclinations and tendencies within a larger harmonious order, and one enjoys a sense of being part of something much more grand and meaningful than one's individual self. I have described these and other goods related to following the Way in regard to Zhuangzi's philosophy (Carr and Ivanhoe, 53-55).
12. Susan Wolf (Wolf 1982, 419–39) argues that moral saints end up living deeply unappealing lives because they make every effort to be perfectly good. One could argue that such people are in the grip of a moral ideal or that they are excessively concerned with their own moral worth. Robert Adams (Adams 1984, 392–401) offers a sensitive and revealing response.
13. There are six such passages in the complete *Zhuangzi*. I will refer to one of them below in my discussion of the value of unselfconsciousness and *doing* and two others in my later discussion of *being*. Of the six, only two present Liezi as someone with true spiritual understanding (Watson 195, 313–14).
14. For a contemporary defense of the value of unselfconscious action, see Csikszentmihalyi (Csikszentmihalyi 1990).
15. (Graham, 38–39). The same story appears in chapter 21 of the *Zhuangzi* (Watson, 230–31).
16. Like the last story, versions of the following three also are found in the *Zhuangzi* (Watson, 200–201, 204–205, and 199–200).
17. In the *Liezi* we are told, "The highest man walks under-water and does not suffocate, Treads fire and does not burn, Walks above the myriad things and does not tremble" (Graham, 37). See also chapter 55 of the *Daodejing*, etc.
18. In this passage, the natural harmony between humans and other animals is manifested as mutual trust and a kind of friendship. In other passages, however, such as the one concerning the fisherman Zhan He, natural harmony does not preclude humans preying upon other creatures. Perhaps the difference is that fish were seen as a natural source of food for humans whereas capturing the seagulls was regarded as a fundamentally unnatural action and aim. In the latter case, the very idea of capturing the birds is something the man's father—not the man himself—desires. See the essay by Erin M. Cline in this volume for a study of the Zhan He passage.
19. Compare the opening lines of the second chapter of the *Daodejing*: "Everyone in the world knows that when the beautiful strives to be (or regards itself as) beautiful, it is repulsive. Everyone in the world knows that when the good strives to be (or regards itself as) good, it is no good."
20. Here and in several other passages that I will examine below, from both the Daoist and Confucian tradition, those who attain an advanced degree of unselfconsciousness gain the distinctive qualities of one with *de* "virtue" or "power." Among these qualities is a natural attractiveness or moral charisma. This idea is also evident in the story of the Yellow Emperor, discussed above. I explore early Confucian and Daoist concep-

tions of virtue in "The Concept of *De* ('Virtue') in the *Laozi*" (Ivanhoe 1998a).

21. I have described this as a sense of "metaphysical comfort" both in relation to Zhuangzi's ideal state (Carr and Ivanhoe, 87) and as a general psychological good (Ivanhoe 1998b).
22. I have in mind the sense of "purposive" described by Herrlee G. Creel when he suggested that there are "purposive" and "contemplative" aspects to early Daoism (Creel, 37–47).
23. There is a story about Zhuangzi lacking true understanding, which may portray his "conversion" or "enlightenment" to the Daoist Way. For a study of this passage and its reception among Western scholars, see Ivanhoe (Ivanhoe, 13–25). Nevertheless, Liezi is unique as a character within the early Daoist sagely pantheon for having a number of stories about him lacking true discernment. This seems to distinguish him as serving a distinctive literary and philosophical role that is not fully appreciated by contemporary scholars.
24. As reflected in the title of this volume, Liezi is renowned for his ability to ride the wind (Graham, 35–36).
25. I take this to be the main point of the final story about Liezi in the *Zhuangzi* (Watson, 353–54) in which Liezi is critized by Bohun Wuren for his inability to hide his virtue. In this passage, Liezi shows both that he understands what he should do and that he still is unable to achieve the desired state of being.
26. We see a similar idea in the writings of Annie Dillard (Dillard, 32–33) who singles out the ability to "see truly" as "the pearl of great price." Like early Daoists, she thinks that this involves, "a discipline requiring a lifetime of dedicated struggle....But although the pearl may be found, it may not be sought . . . the secret of seeing is to sail on solar wind." While there are important similarities between these views, there are also significant differences. Dillard writes within a theistic tradition in which a true vision of Nature leads one to an appreciation of God. Nevertheless, like the early Daoists, she insists on the need for a distinctive kind of humility in order to see and orient oneself properly within the world.
27. In several essays, David S. Nivison describes what he calls "the paradox of virtue," (Nivison 1996) and in his book, *Effortless Action*, (Slingerland 2003) Ted Slingerland develops a parallel argument for what he calls "the paradox of *wuwei*." My analysis differs from both of these in significant ways. Most important, I focus on the character of the kind of self-consciousness that is to be avoided and seek to explain why it is problematic for the achievement of certain goals, and I distinguish between everyday and religious expressions of this ideal. I believe that the cultivation of at least the everyday sense of unselfconsciousness, in either the case of virtue or *wuwei*, is a paradox but one that can be solved. The solution is subtle but in no way mysterious. As I have implied above, a revealing analysis of these phenomena can be developed by drawing an analogy with the paradox of hedonism, but pursuing this point would take me too far from the more limited concerns of this chapter. For a discussion of Nivison's and Slingerland's views, see my

"The Paradox of *Wuwei?*" *The Journal of Chinese Philosophy* 34, no. 2 (June 2007): 277–87.

28. "Forgetting the self" is an important spiritual goal in a number of early Daoist texts and is clearly related to the theme of unselfconsciousness. The goal of forgetting the self may at first seem to represent another example of the "paradox" that some scholars see at the heart of this cluster of issues. For how can *I* make an effort to forget about *myself*? I am always there putting forth any such effort. But the work of forgetting the self need not be so direct. I can forget about my self by thinking more about others, by becoming absorbed in reading a book, watching a play, listening to music, practicing a rite, or, as the author of the *Zhuangzi* would have me do, by losing myself in the cadence and rhythm of the *dao*.
29. In the case of Daoism and to some extent the Mengzian strain of early Confucianism as well, the task of self-cultivation is aided by natural and spontaneous impulses. The challenge is more to *stop* doing what interferes with these tendencies and ensure that they guide and inform our actions.
30. Certain thinkers espouse a more radical "discovery" model of self-cultivation, in contrast to the kind of "development" model that I have been describing. On such a model, one must suddenly wake up to or realize the ideal spiritual state. Nevertheless, even such thinkers recognize that certain techniques and regimens facilitate the attainment of their ideal and that certain behavior and ways of thinking inhibit or work against spiritual progress. The discovery model was first described by A. C. Graham (Graham 1992). I have developed this distinction at much greater length in Ivanhoe 2002 and extended the range of self-cultivation models in Ivanhoe 2000. Thanks to T. C. Kline for pointing out the importance of this distinction for the set of issues I am concerned with here.
31. One might on a given occasion get close to behaving in the way that one desires through an act of will, however, this does not constitute the stable disposition that is one's true aim. The disposition is needed in order to reliably guide one to and enable one to enjoy the desired end state.

References

Adams, Robert. 1984 "Saints." *The Journal of Philosophy* 81, no. 7.

Ames, Roger T. 1994. *The Art of Rulership: A Study of Ancient Chinese Political Thought*. Albany: State University of New York Press.

Carr, Karen L., and Philip J. Ivanhoe. 2010. Revised Second Edition. *The Sense of Anti-rationalism: Zhuangzi and Kierkegaard's Religious Thought*. Createspace.com.

Creel, Herrlee G. 1970. *What is Taoism? And Other Studies in Chinese Cultural History*. Chicago: University of Chicago Press.

Csikszentmihalyi, Mihaly. 1990. *Flow: The Psychology of Optimal Experience*. New York: Harper and Row.

Dillard, Annie. 1974. *Pilgrim at Tinker Creek*. New York: Harper and Row.

Graham, A. C., trans. 1973. *The Book of Liezi*. Reprint. London: John Murray.

———. 1992. *Two Chinese Philosophers*. Reprint. LaSalle, IL: Open Court Press.

Ivanhoe, Philip J. 1991. "Zhuangzi's Conversion Experience." *The Journal of Chinese Religions* 19.

———. 1998a. "The Concept of *De* ('Virtue') in the *Laozi*," in *Religious and Philosophical Aspects of the Laozi*, 239–57. Albany: State University of New York Press.

———. 1998b. "Nature, Awe, and the Sublime." *Midwest Studies in Philosophy, Volume 21: The Philosophy of Religion*. Notre Dame: University of Notre Dame Press: 98–117.

———. 2000. *Confucian Moral Self Cultivation*. Revised second edition. Indianapolis: Hackett.

———. 2002. *Ethics in the Confucian Tradition: The Thought of Mengzi and Wang Yangming*. Revised second edition. Indianapolis: Hackett.

———. 2007. "The Paradox of *Wuwei*?" *The Journal of Chinese Philosophy* 34, no. 2: 277–87.

Nivison, David S. 1996. *The Ways of Confucianism*, ed. Bryan W. Van Norden. La Salle, IL: Open Court Press.

Slingerland, Edward. 2003. *Effortless Action: Wu-wei as Conceptual Metaphor and Spiritual Ideal in Early China*. New York: Oxford University Press.

Watson, Burton. 1968. *The Complete Works of Chuang Tzu*. New York: Columbia University Press.

Wolf, Susan. 1982. "Moral Saints." *The Journal of Philosophy* 79, no. 8: 416–39.

列子

Reading the *Zhuangzi* in *Liezi*

Redefining Xian*ship*

Jeffrey Dippmann

The research for, and subsequent content of, this chapter has undergone an almost complete about-face since its inception. What initially began as an attempt to demonstrate that the Daoist classic, the *Liezi*, represents an aristocratic reaction to the emergence of sectarian Daoism and a rejection of its magico-religious practices, has slowly evolved into the conviction that the text subtly accepts and implicitly endorses the basic tenets of sectarian Daoism. Whereas previous scholarship in the West has seen the *Liezi* as openly hostile to the so-called cult of immortality and the attendant practices of "religious Daoism," I am increasingly convinced that the pursuit of becoming a *xian* 仙, or immortal, was part and parcel of the *Liezi*'s principal message. Far from excoriating those who sought to lengthen their lives and attain a state of untrammeled freedom and miraculous powers, the author highlighted their achievements and accepted the path to immortality as one viable option for Daoist practitioners. Along with presenting positive imagery of immortals such as the Yellow Emperor, the *Liezi*'s author also creatively manipulates and edits the Daoist classic, the *Zhuangzi*, in such a way that the magical propensities of the latter's Perfected become further embellished.

As the readers of this volume are well aware, the *Liezi* is a work of eight chapters, traditionally attributed to the hand of an ancient Daoist sage who, according to some accounts, was a contemporary of Guan Yin, or gatekeeper Yin, involved in the legendary encounter with Laozi as the latter rode off to the west. As A. C. Graham demonstrated in his landmark essay on "The Date and Compliation of the Liehtzyy," the earliest known version of the *Liezi* is clearly a composite work, with much of it borrowed directly from other well-known texts such as the *Xunzi*, *Daodejing*, *Mozi*, and most commonly the *Zhuangzi*. In fact, twenty-five stories or fragments can be clearly identified as derivative of the *Zhuangzi*, by far the largest such borrowing within the text.

Due to fragmentary and wholly unverifiable biographical details, the life of Liezi, if he ever existed, is shrouded in uncertainty. If we use the *Liezi*'s own evidence, he would be placed somewhere in the fifth century BCE. In addition to the supposed relationship with Guan Yin, the text makes it clear that Liezi knew of the works of Mozi (479–381 BCE). While the *Mozi* never mentions *Liezi*, and while the *Zhuangzi* has numerous tales concerning *Liezi*, the latter never mentions Zhuang Zhou (369–286). The earliest mention of such a text comes in the work of Liu Xiang who in 14 BCE describes an eight-chapter work seemingly corresponding to the present text. Thus, tradition holds that the present text is the work of the late fifth or early fourth century BCE. By contrast, current Western scholarship, beginning with the groundbreaking work of Graham in the early 1960s, places the text nearly six hundred years later, with most evidence pointing to a final redaction appearing for the first time with a commentary authored by Zhang Zhan in the late fourth century CE.

In his commentary, Zhang claims that the text is part of a rare collection belonging to his family, one that his grandfather Zhang Yi carried with him across the Yangtze River as he fled south during the chaos of the Western Jin dynasty's collapse in the early fourth century. Zhang hints that this particular text was little known outside his family circle, perhaps to those in Southern China in particular, and goes to great lengths to demonstrate a chain of possession. As Graham points out, however, this chain does not extend beyond his grandfather's contemporaries, and leads us to conclude that, in its present state, the *Liezi*'s provenance could be neither proved nor disproved by Zhang's own contemporaries.

Based on this evidence, many scholars such as Graham and T. H. Barrett have suggested that the *Liezi*'s mixture of fantastical stories and sometimes hard-line realism, especially in the face of death, reflect a distinctively fourth-century Chinese worldview prevalent among the educated elite. Arguing that the shock of the Han dynasty's demise at the hands of religiously inspired rebellions led the elite to interpret the primary Daoist texts (such as *Daodejing*, *Zhuangzi*, *Yijing*) in a decidedly nonreligious manner, they have made the case that the *Liezi*, as a product of this period, both presented its "original" material and read (and interpreted) its earlier predecessors in like manner. Fearing that the "religious" elements of Daoism encouraged a "dangerous fanaticism" based on the certitude of immortality, the educated milieu of which Zhang was part supposedly eradicated and discouraged anything that "might promote religious enthusiasm" (Barrett, 399). If such is the case, in some small way perhaps, this attitude may be seen as the germination point for the long-standing perception that there are two Daoisms, *daojia* and *daojiao*, philosophy and religion. Indeed, Graham asserts in his seminal translation of the *Liezi* that the 3rd and 4th century "philosophers still kept aloof from the alchemists who had usurped the name of Taoist. With one dubious exception, references in the *Liezi* to the cult of immortality are hostile" (Graham 1960, 16).

A closer look, however, one untainted by the supposition of two distinct Daoisms, challenges this conventional wisdom. My reading of the *Liezi*, both in its "original" portions and its reliance on prior material such as the *Zhuangzi*, suggests that the *Liezi* did not necessarily disparage the pursuit of *xian*-ship, or immortality, but rather may have actually advocated its pursuit à la so-called religious Daoism. Amidst its unbridled skepticism and whimsical tales of monsters, far-off lands, and bizarre customs I find a spirit of endorsement, albeit one tempered by the customary Daoist caution that achieving immortality is not an ordinary feat. We may "know" the relevant arts, but their successful application is reserved for the skilled practitioner.

Part of my argument, admittedly speculative in nature, relies on another element of China's religious history. While true that the aftermath of the fall of the Han's reign led to a retrenchment of the ruling elite's attitude toward "religious fanaticism," it is also the case that Zhang worked within the religious milieu of southern China. Here, the attitudes toward the religio-magical efficacy of Daoism remained, and remains to the present, very positive and accommodating. Indeed, the remnants of the early *Tianshi* (Heavenly Masters) sect found a home in southern China during the late third and early fourth centuries, eventually reformulating themselves into the *Zhengyi* (Orthodox Unity) sect, the dominant school of Daoism in southern China up to the present day. In addition, the region served as one of the principal homes for the rise and ongoing presence of *fangshi* 方士 (prescription masters). One of the hallmarks of both the earlier *Tianshi* and later *Zhengyi* schools is the reliance on *daoshi* (Daoist priests) to perform efficacious works of religious magic, through prescribed rituals and access to the spiritual world, for the benefit of the larger community. And recent scholarship has shown clear links between the practices of *fangshi* and the rise and dissemination of the so-called cult of immortality.

The south was also the provenance of Ge Hong's *Baopuzi* (*Master Who Embraces Simplicity*) one of the earliest Chinese texts detailing the work and activities of the alchemical tradition. Written in the early fourth century, the *Baopuzi* is a veritable compendium of alchemical tales, recipes, and preparatory prescriptions for the practice of *weidan*, or external alchemy. Ge Hong also compiled an exhaustive body of hagiographical materials on ancient and contemporary *xian* (immortals), replete with tales of the miraculous powers and eccentric behaviors associated with the three standard types of *xian*: earthbound (some living to five thousand years of age), those "delivered from the corpse" (presumably dying but then ascending to heaven from the coffin, leaving tokens of clothing or other accoutrements), and the celestial *xian* who are taken up in the clouds during broad daylight by a train of immortals or dragons. Taken together, these works represent both the ongoing tradition of *xian*-ship and the foundations for later practice within Daoism. Therefore, alongside the hostility of the educated elite (among whom Ge Hong can be counted) existed a rich and vital acknowledgment of and encouragement to emulate the pursuit of *xian*-ship. One piece of Graham's argument for the late compilation of the *Liezi* is that Ge Hong bemoans the lack of relevant material in the standard Daoist works, citing the *Daodejing*, *Zhuangzi* and *Yijing*, but never mentioning the *Liezi*, despite its later elevation to the status of Daoist classic.

And so, while there are indeed signs within the *Liezi* that its "editor," whether Zhang Zhan or his grandfather, was skeptical about the claims put forth by Daoist practitioners (as it is, by the way, about almost every other phenomenon in the world), it nevertheless also conveys a sense of wonderment and implicit acceptance of the possibilities associated with the pursuit of longevity and immortality. Indeed, not only does the *Liezi* provide positive portraits of immortals such as the Yellow Emperor, it also adds episodic elements to the sections derived from the *Zhuangzi*.

The genesis of the *xian* has been effectively linked to the presence of *wu*/shamans (such as the legendary Yu) and *fangshi* (prescription masters) in Chinese society. As Mircea Eliade has demonstrated, the cross-cultural shamanic tradition has several unifying themes or characteristics: among the most important are the ability to communicate with or shape shift into animals (Yu's transformation into a bear to relieve China's flooding most readily comes to mind); ecstatic journeys into the underworld and heavens (again, Yu's limping gait as a model for Daoist excursions to the nine stars of the Great Dipper serves as an example); the ability to control the five elements/phases; a reliance on and ability to interpret dreams; and being adept at healing (Eliade, 3–7). In addition, the *fangshi* tradition added the use of talismans as curative agents and the claim of expanded power over the five phases to the point of being able to fashion elixirs of immortality out of base materials such as cinnabar, lead, mercury, and pine nuts. *Fangshi* appear to have been commissioned by several emperors for the sole purpose of concocting recipes designed to immortalize their patrons, while at the same time serving their local communities in the realms of demon expulsion, rites of cosmic and familial renewal, and of course healing.[1]

When we examine the *Liezi* closely, we find many of these basic elements represented and placed into an almost celebratory context of fabulous tales and miraculous occurrences associated with *xian*-like individuals. I want to simply highlight what I see as several of the more interesting examples of how the *Liezi*'s author reread or edited his main source of redaction, the *Zhuangzi*. One of the most prominent is the legendary Yellow Emperor (*Huangdi* 黃帝), an early model for and exemplar of the Daoist *xian*. Long revered by the tradition for his embodiment of Daoist ideals and supposed authorship of China's first medical treatise (*Yellow Emperor's Classic of Medicine*), the teachings attributed to the Yellow Emperor are thought by many to be one half of the earliest form of incipient Daoism, so-called Huang-Lao thought.

Both texts contain an extended narrative relating the story of Huangdi's inquiry into the proper way of ruling and attunement with the Dao. This episode occurs in the eleventh chapter of the *Zhuangzi* and chapter 2 of the *Liezi*. In both cases, the Emperor has ruled for several decades (nineteen years in *Zhuangzi*, fifteen and then an additional fifteen in the *Liezi*). Concerned about learning how to govern more efficiently, the Yellow Emperor sets out to discover what the *Zhuangzi* calls "the Perfect Way." At this juncture, the story takes different turns. The *Zhuangzi* records that he seeks the sagely advice of a Master residing in the Mountain of Emptiness and Oneness. Upon inquiry, he is reviled by the Master, who refuses to counsel him as an unworthy disciple. Under his rule the entire world has declined, and the unfortunate Emperor is dismissed with the words: "shallow and vapid, with the mind of a prattling knave—what good would it do to tell YOU about the perfect way?" At this juncture, the Yellow Emperor "withdrew, gave up his throne, built a solitary hut, spread a mat of white rushes and lived for three months in retirement" (Watson, 118–20). He subsequently returns to the Master and inquires about instruction in the method for attaining long life, which he finally receives in a kind of philosophical litany and presumably (though not explicitly stated in this episode) successfully implements (*Zhuangzi* 6 records that he "got the Way and ascended into Heaven").

In the *Liezi*, Huangdi has led a life of successive hedonism and worry over the rule of his empire, until he finally reaches his pivotal existential moment, decrying his previous errors and seeking release from the burden of caring for himself and others. Rather than going to a sage, however, he immediately "refused to concern himself with decisions of policy, left the Imperial chambers, dismissed his attendants, discarded his orchestra of bells and drums, reduced the delicacies of his kitchen. He retired to live undisturbed in a hut in his main courtyard, where he fasted to discipline mind and body, and for three months had nothing to do with the affairs of the state. Falling asleep in the daytime, he dreamed that he was wandering in a far off country." There he encounters a world of beings living out the natural course of all things, following their true natures, and exhibiting many of the characteristics of immortals: "[T]hey go into water without drowning, into fire without burning; hack them, flog them, there is no wound nor pain; they ride space as though walking the solid earth, sleep on the void as though in their beds . . . they only undertake journeys of the spirit." After declaring that he has finally found himself, the Yellow Emperor returns to rule for another twenty-eight years, after which he "rose into the sky," a standard metaphor for ascension as an immortal.

I find several intriguing elements to the revisions in *Liezi*'s account, the most interesting being the method by which the Yellow Emperor found the true way. The presumably earlier account, which scholars presuppose sanctions the pursuit of immortality, contains a fairly standard encounter between a seeker and master. Seemingly humiliated, or at least chastised, the Yellow Emperor departs and goes into seclusion for reflection. Upon his second audience, he is schooled in the philosophical reality of the Way/Dao and is now prepared to "get it." In the *Liezi* on the other hand, that realization comes not through the intervention of a wise sage, but through an ecstatic journey of the mind during a dream. While preparing himself through fasting and discipline, he acknowledges that he could not find the proper method; it is only through the dream world that he finally is able to acknowledge, "I know it, I have found it, but I cannot convey it to you."

In addition to the potential allusions to the dream excursions of the early shamanic tradition, it must also be noted that the dream traditionally plays a critical role in the attainment of immortality. Hagiographic tales of a multitude of immortals, including those portrayed in Ge Hong's work, focus on the centrality of dreams and their critical role in breaking through the fixation on the conventional world of phenomena and entry into realms of the immortals.[2] Perhaps the most famous instance involves Lu Dongbin, one of the Eight Immortals of traditional Chinese lore. In an episode known as the Yellow Millet Dream, Lu Dongbin's transformative moment follows hard upon the heels of a dream, during which he lived an entire life span and through which he awakens to the futility and worthlessness of conventionality. Much like Huang-di, Lu Dongbin then abandons his pursuit of earthly success and devotes himself to becoming a *xian*.

One other interesting rereading of the *Zhuangzi* also occurs in the second (*Yellow Emperor*) chapter of the *Liezi*. Here the text essentially recreates the story known as "Three in the Morning." One of the most familiar stories in the text, this episode is also found in the *Zhuangzi's* second chapter, and reads in part: "When the monkey trainer was handing out acorns, he said, 'You get three in the morning and four at night.' This made all the monkeys furious. 'Well, then,' he said, 'you get four in the morning and three at night.' The monkeys were all delighted. There was no change in the reality behind the words, and yet the monkeys responded with joy and anger. Let them, if they want to." The reality of the situation never changed, but perception did; in this way the wise sage harmonizes and equalizes all things (again, a more "philosophical" agenda, if you will).

In the *Liezi*, the episode is preceded by an account of the sages of old, and their ability to communicate with the beasts and birds of the world. In a very straightforward manner, the author reports that even today, in the East, there are many "who understand the speech of domestic animals; this is a discovery possible even to our own limited knowledge." With this preface, the *Liezi* then introduces the story of three in the morning, but with a very interesting emendation. This keeper of monkeys "could interpret the thoughts of the monkeys and they too caught what was in his mind." Because he gave too much to the monkeys, his family suffered and he steadily became impoverished, finally resorting to the tactic of reducing the monkeys' daily allotment. The standard story is then repeated. Once again, I find this rather small emendation intriguing. Whereas the *Zhuangzi* uses it as a lesson for philosophical reflection, the *Liezi* incorporates an element, namely, mind-to-mind communication with different species, which again parallels many standard accounts of the abilities of *fangshi* and *xian* adepts. And it is all done with complete aplomb and apparent seriousness. If the author were seeking to purge the *Zhuangzi* of "religious elements" as suggested by Barrett and Graham, one would not expect to see such additions to the older story, nor placed into a context of extolling the practices of the ancient sages, many of whom were again exemplars of immortals.

This episode raises two questions that remain unresolved in my own mind. First, it is possible that Zhang Zhan had at his disposal a full copy of the *Zhuangzi* (edited by Guo Xiang into its present form), for which we have some evidence elsewhere, and that this version contained the fuller account just surveyed.[3] Until we discover the original *Zhuangzi*, that question will be left unresolved. The second question over which I am still puzzling is: Why is it that the keeper was able to trick the monkeys if they also understood the trainer's thoughts? One would presume that they would see through the trick and remain angry. The *Liezi* may be trying to emphasize the superiority of the human mind over that of beasts, as it concludes "it is always the same when the cleverer of two things traps the sillier," but questions still remain in my own mind.

The above are just two intriguing examples of how "religio-magical" elements appear to have crept into the *Liezi*'s reading of the *Zhuangzi*. Outside of these borrowings, the *Liezi* also offers us another seeming anomaly to the supposed rejection of Daoist practices. Chapter 5 presents us with the *Questions of T'ang*, an extended soliloquy on the wondrous cosmos and the futility of human reason to grasp its true nature through discursive, discriminative thought. Indeed, while virtually devoid of any direct quotations from the *Zhuangzi*, the chapter emulates and extends one of its predecessor's main themes: the relativity of all knowledge and the dangers of our unfortunate reliance on such an unreliable faculty. Two of this volume's contributions also address episodes from the chapter (Cline and Richey), which includes some of the most fantastic and seemingly fanciful tales in the entire work. In addition to the introductory and concluding episodes, the *Questions* presents seventeen distinctive tales and narrative-driven lessons drawn from the vast riches of Chinese folklore and mythology. Included in this collection is the tale of the five mountains of the *xian*, to which we will turn shortly.

Thematically, and earnestly, bracketing the seemingly whimsical fables are two straightforward, rationalistic accounts presented with neither the *Liezi's* usual skepticism nor its tongue in cheek approach. As Graham notes in his translation, the chapter opens with the text's only significant extended foray into analytical reasoning, "which, against all the author's principles, is intended seriously" (Graham 1960, 92). Strikingly reminiscent of similar arguments in the *Zhuangzi*,[4] this relatively short introduction establishes a tone of intellectual inquiry and reasoned analysis into the nature of the cosmos and all that is contained within its bounds. While possibly fragmentary in its present state,[5] the text nevertheless systematically walks us through the Emperor Tang's questions regarding space and time, and their relation to the world of forms, as posed to the philosopher-sage Ji of Xia. As the argument demonstrates, and clearly seeks to establish in the mind of the reader, our ordinary point of view, freighted as it is by presuppositions and discriminatory thinking, limits us to a surprisingly narrow vision of the world. Analogous to the side blinders attached to stereoscope viewers, our everyday sight narrowly circumscribes our world, establishing un-Dao-like limitations on space, time, and the ten thousand things. And in true Daoist fashion, even positing the limitless limits our worldview: "'There is no limit, but neither is there anything limitless; there is no exhausting, but neither is there anything inexhaustible.'" Even rational argumentation, Ji seems to say, forces us to acknowledge the paucity of our supposedly reasoned outlook on the world.

As noted above, what follows next is a series of seventeen narrative tales of bizarre events, beings and places, including an extended mythology concerning the world outside of the four seas. In an attempt to answer Emperor Tang's query concerning the relativity of things, Ji relates a series of tales describing the various lands outside the pale of ordinary apprehension. Among these lands, lying to the east of Zhili, is found a bottomless ravine containing five mountains (including the legendary peaks of Penglai and Yingzhou). Vast and immeasurable, the valley and its sacred peaks, continuously fed by the Milky Way, serve as the abode of an immortal race, nourished by pure fruits and living the free and untrammeled life universally celebrated as the ultimate goal of "religious" Daoism: "Amidst verandas and towers of gold and jade, beasts of unblemished white, and forests of pearl and garnet . . . . Its inhabitants are all immortal sages, flying from mountain to mountain throughout day and night in numbers too vast to count." The unfortunate actions of an unruly giant in the far recesses of time disrupted the harmony of the five sacred mountains, but all indications are that the immortals continue to reside and frolic within the "Entry to the Void."

Bookending Ji's analytical cautionary to our reliance on commonsensical views of the world, and closing out the chapter's lineup of awe-inspiring, head-scratching tales of robots, bizarre customs, Daoist anglers, and masterful musicians, is a final tale designed to completely overturn the staid, conservatively oriented Confucian worldview. Instead of offering one more, rationalistically improbable myth, however, the *Liezi* pulls a literary sleight of hand on its reader. The episode is worth recounting in full:

> When King Mu of Chou made his great expedition against the Jung tribes of the West, they presented him with a knife from K'un-wu and a fire-proof cloth. The knife was one foot eight inches long with a red blade of tempered steel; cutting jade with it was as easy as

> cutting mud. The fire-proof cloth could be washed only by throwing it into fire; the cloth turned the colour of the fire, the dirt the colour of ash; take it from the fire and shake it, and it glistened like snow. A Prince thought there were no such things, that the tradition was mistaken. Hsiao Shu said: "How obstinate the Prince is in trusting his own judgement, how obstinate in his false reasoning!" (Graham 1960, 117)

As Graham rightly notes, the elements within the story remind the reader of Emperor Wen's (220–226) skepticism concerning such implements, only to later find that they did in truth exist. In addition, as Graham also points out, Zhang Zhan's commentary draws out the fact that by "concluding the chapter with this section . . . is to show that, since there is nothing fabulous about these two things, everything recounted earlier is fact also" (Graham 1960, 117). I would further suggest that the true import of the chapter lies in its overall structure. As with any good argument, the chapter begins with an introductory claim: common sense does not always provide us with an accurate picture of our surroundings. Readers are thus set up in the first section with an analytical appraisal of the cosmos, and walked step by step through a demonstration on how our presuppositions do not stand up under critical review. This is followed by evidentiary material designed to bolster that claim, including the tale of flying immortals. By way of conclusion, we have a final, indisputable case of the limits of common sense (the Prince's skepticism), which both seals the deal and provides the *Liezi* with its fundamental premise: if you recognize this example of credulity gone wrong, then you ought to recognize the fact that all of the other preceding tales are within the realm of possibility as well, including the art of immortality.

I would offer one final example of how the *Liezi* presents an affirmative image of the immortal arts, one that Graham inexplicably refers to as "dubious" (Graham 1960, 16). In its closing chapter, the *Liezi* presents a series of episodes and anecdotes ostensibly revolving around the idea of chance, coincidence, and happenstance. Essentially arguing that we must abandon our reliance on preestablished norms and moral/social guidelines in favor of situational responses to the natural flow of events, the chapter includes a final discussion of those who pursue immortality. Acting upon rumors that a certain man knew the Dao of immortality, the Lord of Yen sent an emissary to retrieve the secret. Before he could reveal his secret, however, the man died, prompting a series of exchanges over whether the man truly did know the secret to longevity or not. After the standard, commonsensical reactions are voiced (basically that he died, so obviously he knew nothing), the section concludes with the words of Huzi:[6]

> There are always men who possess a theory they cannot act on, or who can act without possessing the theory. There was a man of Wei who was good at mathematics. When he was near death he disclosed his secrets to his son, who remembered the words but could not apply them. Another man questioned the son, who told him what his father had said. The other man went by what he said and applied the theory as successfully as his father had done. Why then should not a mortal be able to talk about the theory of living for ever? (Graham 1960, 177–78)

Once again, there is no sense that the *Liezi's* author rejects the art of immortality, or is seeking to convince the reader that its pursuit is disreputable or unseemly. Rather, the moral seems to be that the pursuit of immortality, like any other endeavor requiring skill and/or knowledge, is dependent on the successful application of the art. Knowledge is insufficient, and in fact may be dangerous. This theme reverberates throughout the literature on immortality, with would-be *xian* encouraged to exercise extreme caution, lest they achieve the opposite results with their experimentation. Daoist practice does not simply involve knowing the right Way/Dao. Particularly in the case of immortality, there are often "preconditions" necessary for its achievement. Such prerequisites include the proper physiognomy, astrological confluences, morality, and so on.[7] Now, I am not claiming that the *Liezi* necessarily has these standards in mind when relating the tale above. However, at the same time, the text does not repudiate the pursuit of *xian*-ship nor does it argue that adherents are fanatical radicals misappropriating or misapplying the teachings of "philosophical" Daoism. Just as a mathematical formula can work in the proper, skillful hands, and be completely ineffectual when employed by the naïve, so too does the art of immortality and its secrets for life without death require care and skill. Why does this seem so far-fetched?

Indeed, for many, myself included, and perhaps the text's intended audience as well, the application of a mathematical formula is far more abstract, mysterious, and incomprehensible than many of the tales embedded in the *Liezi*. In fact, numerous stories of the immortals reveal a similar type of certainty, again leading me to believe that the *Liezi*, far from ridiculing the practices of *xian*-ship, may have instead accepted and ultimately endorsed them.

Notes

1. The best summary of the history and function of *fangshi* is found in DeWoskin 1983. The entries by Penny and Pregadio in the *Daoism Handbook* are also valuable synopses.
2. For further reading, see the translations of Ge Hong's *Traditions of Divine Transcendents* by Robert F. Campany, and Chen Shiyuan's *Encyclopedia of Dreams* by Richard E. Strassberg.
3. For more information, see Ronnie Littlejohn's contribution to this volume.
4. For example, those contained in chapters 2 and 17.
5. In his original translation, Graham posited a missing segment within the argument, but resolved the apparent lacuna in the presentation of the same argument in his 1989 *Disputers of the Tao* (79–80).
6. The Huzi 胡子 quoted here is apparently not the Huzi 壺子 associated with Liezi as his teacher and master; see *Liezi* chapter 1 and passim for references to their relationship.
7. Again, for a brief summary, see Penny's entry in the *Daoism Handbook*.

References

Barrett, T. H. 2003. *Liezi (Lieh Tzu)*. In *Encyclopedia of Chinese Philosophy*, ed. Cua, 397–400.

Campany, Robert Ford. 2002. *To Live as Long as Heaven and Earth: Ge Hong's* Traditions of Divine Transcendents. Berkeley: University of California Press.

Cua, Antonio S., ed. 2003. *Encyclopedia of Chinese Philosophy*. New York, London: Routledge.

DeWoskin, Kenneth J. 1983. *Doctors, Diviners, and Magicians of Ancient China: Biographies of Fang-shih*. New York: Columbia University Press.

Eliade, Mircea. 1964. *Shamanism*. Princeton: Princeton University Press.

Graham, A. C. 1960. *The Book of Lieh-tzu*. London: A. Murray.

———. 1961. "The Date and Compilation of the Liehtzyy." *Asia Major* 2, ser. 8: 139–98.

———. 1989. *Disputers of the Tao*. Chicago: Open Court.

Kohn, Livia, ed. 2000. *Daoism Handbook*. Leiden; Brill.

Penny, Benjamin. 2000. "Immortality and Transcendence." In *Daoism Handbook*, ed. Kohn, 109–133.

Pregadio, Fabrizio. 2000. "Elixirs and Alchemy." In *Daoism Handbook*, ed. Kohn, 165–95.

Strassberg, Richard E. 2008. *Wandering Spirits: Chen Shiyuan's* Encyclopedia of Dreams. Berkeley: University of California Press.

Watson, Burton. 1968. *The Complete Works of Chuang Tzu*. New York: Columbia University Press.

Applying the Teachings of the Liezi

列子

Body and Identity

Livia Kohn

It is a truism by now that Daoism, in comparison to other religions, has a rather positive view of the body and places great emphasis on physical cultivation. The body in Daoism is the key to understanding and transforming the self, through basic healing, the attainment of long life, and the eventual transformation of the person into a spirit entity or immortal. Daoists do not view the body as a mechanical entity governed by base instincts but follow the Chinese medical understanding that it consists of various aspects of *qi* and the phase-energetics of the inner organs and meridians. The healing practices of Chinese medicine are accordingly at the root of various Daoist practices, and many acupuncture points have Daoist connotations. Based on this dynamic medical conception of the body yet going beyond it, Daoists, moreover, view the body as a network of celestial passageways and starry palaces, allowing adepts to move beyond the physicality of their existence toward a greater, more spiritual realm, reaching out for the gods in the stars and the Dao at the center of creation (see Kohn 1991).[1]

Physical practices, therefore, not only form an essential part of the religion but also serve to transform the mind and spirit, which form an integral part of the person and are not fundamentally separate from the body. Physical energies, forms of mentation, psychological activities, and spiritual states are not opposing forces but form different aspects of the vital energy of *qi* that vibrate at different speeds and manifest at somewhat subtler or grosser levels.

Neither medical nor religious texts, therefore, separate mental from bodily phenomena but take both as indications of the person's overall state. "Mind" (*xin*) in this context can generally indicate the various aspects of consciousness and mental activity, seen as subtler manifestations of *qi*. It can also, more specifically, refer to people's evaluation of the world in terms of good and bad, likes and dislikes, the way we relate to ourselves and others, based on sensory stimuli, emotions, and classificatory schemes.

In this second sense, "mind" is often contrasted with "spirit" (*shen*). Spirit is a yet subtler form of *qi*, understood as the primordial, formless, and ever-changing force of life, which in connection with the physical body causes human beings to be alive. It occurs in its most concentrated form in the heart and ideally works through the mind in its more general sense to govern life perfectly. However, people get sidetracked through their involvement with sensory attractions and the pure spirit is transformed into an opinionated and limited mind through the senses and emotions. Confused and defiled, human beings need to be taught how to recover the primordial state—a work that begins and ends again with the body, similarly seen in twofold division, as an original, cosmic entity known as the "physical body" (*xing*), on the one hand, and a more evaluative, sense-determined aspect described as the "personal body" (*shen*), on the other (see Kohn 1989). Much of Daoist physical cultivation aims to reclaim the sense of cosmic physicality, thereby allowing the transformation of grosser into subtler forms of *qi* and the eventual attainment of a state of pure spirit and everlasting life.

The *Liezi* is in many respects a Daoist text, shown not only in its contents but also in the fact that its author was formally deified along with Laozi and Zhuangzi by Emperor Xuanzong in 742 and that it is contained variously in the Ming dynasty Daoist canon (DZ 729–733)[2] and other later collections. Given this fact, it should contain some reflection of the overall general Daoist understanding of the body and spiritual transformation. What, then, is the view of the body in the text? Or does it contain different views of the body? How does the text relate to the overall Daoist understanding of body-mind unity and the ultimate goal of self-transformation? What kind of an identity, ordinary, spiritual, and otherwise, does the *Liezi* propose? More than that, given the fact that its first commentator Zhang Zhan of the fourth century is also known as the author of the *Yangsheng yaoji* (Long Life Compendium) in ten sections, how does it relate to physical cultivation practices? Where can we place the *Liezi* in the overall context of Daoist schools and lineages, world visions and cultivation practices?

To answer these questions, the following contribution will first outline the various visions of the body found in the *Liezi* as we have it today. It will then examine the biography of Zhang Zhan and his authorship of both the *Liezi* commentary and the *Yangsheng yaoji*. Looking third at the practices and body visions expressed in the cultivation text, it will reach some conclusion about the position of the *Liezi* in the larger context of Daoist body visions and physical practices.

Liezi on the Body

There are two fundamental positions on the body in the *Liezi*. The first could be called the adaptive attitude. It states that the body is not a personal possession but forms part of the energetic system of heaven and earth, that it changes and develops according to laws greater than itself over which the individual has no control, and that one needs to adapt to the body's processes, either by resigning oneself to fate or by enjoying any given state as much as possible. The other we might call the transformative position. According to this, the body is made of *qi* and as such participates in the changes of heaven and earth, but is not entirely beyond control; rather, through various methods of self-cultivation and meditation the body's *qi* can be controlled, ordered, and transformed to subtler levels, so that the attainment of higher states is possible. In both cases, personal identity is closely linked to the cosmos, but one is more passive and resigned to universal patterns that occur without the individual's input while the other is more active and engages in a productive interchange with the cosmic forces. Both are, moreover, part of Daoism, although they come from a different background and appear in different community contexts.

The Adaptive Position

The adaptive position is present mainly in chapters 1 ("Heaven's Gifts"), 6 ("Endeavor and Destiny"), and 7 ("Yang Zhu"), the former two emphasizing the need to resign oneself to the vagaries of fate while the latter focuses on the joy one can receive from being embodied. In chapter 1, for example, we have:

> [The body] is the shape lent to you by heaven and earth. Your life is not your possession; it is harmony between your forces, granted for a time by heaven and earth. Your inner nature and destiny are not your possessions; they are the course laid down for you by heaven and earth. Your children and grandchildren are not your possessions; they are lent to you by heaven and earth to cast off from your body like an insect casts its skin. Therefore you travel without knowing where you go, stay without knowing what you cling to, are fed without knowing how. You are the *qi* of heaven and earth which goes to and fro. How can you ever possess it? (Graham 1960, 29)

Here it is made very clear that the body is part of a larger entity that we have no possession or control over—not only the body, moreover, but all life, destiny, and offspring. The ideal is to move through life with an attitude of acceptance, in a mental state of unknown and no-mind, part of the *qi* of heaven and earth as it moves along following its own paths. All active involvement with the body will ultimately be futile. As chapter 6 notes:

> Valuing life cannot preserve it; taking care of the body cannot do it good. Similarly, scorning life cannot shorten it; neglecting the body cannot do it harm. Hence some who value life do not live, some who scorn it do not die, some who take care of the body do it no good, and some who neglect it do it no harm. This seems unreasonable, but it is not. In all these cases, life and death, good and harm, just come of themselves. (Graham 1960, 129)

Here any kind of self-cultivation and active effort at transforming or developing the self through physical practices is completely rejected, the various ways in which people deal with the body being seen as ultimately without consequence or effect. There is no way in which one can predict what the body is going to do and any way of helping or obstructing it will not result in any serious, personally determined change.

This understanding of the body and life is very similar to the thought of the *Zhuangzi* commentator Guo Xiang (d. 312), who is well known for his deterministic attitude to life as part of an encompassing mystical Daoist vision of human beings and the world achieving perfection in the Dao or, as Isabelle Robinet put it, "le monde comme absolu" (1983).[3] Quite consonant with the *Liezi*, he emphasizes in his commentary (DZ 745) that people ultimately are the Dao in a microcosmic form. More specifically, he outlines a theory that human beings share in the Dao through allotment (*fen*) and are structured by its cosmic principle (*li*). The share that everyone has in the Dao, moreover, determines the individual's "inner nature" (*xing*); everybody's principle is found in his or her "fate" (*ming*).

Inner nature, says Guo Xiang, "is what people rely on spontaneously without ever being conscious of it" (2.35b). Given to them as their share in the Dao, it is the way people are naturally, their inherent psychological makeup, which is entirely independent of knowledge or consciousness. It has nothing to do with people's subjective wishes or concrete hopes, but is there and cannot be changed. Obtained at birth, any enforced change of inner nature must result in suffering, as much as any development along its lines will be to the good. Inner nature restricts and limits the person, but in a positive way, since everyone subconsciously knows what is good for him or her and can thus live life to perfection. However, people tend to distort their inner natures, gaining an erroneous sense of identity and striving for things that are not appropriate for them, thus creating difficulties, havoc, and misfortune.

Fate modifies inner nature; it is the life that one is ordered (*ming*) to have by heaven (Kaltenmark 1965, 657). "That which one is given is one's fate" (4.11a), Guo Xiang says. Fate is there to be accepted, not to be changed. It orders human existence in exactly the same way that principle structures the universe. It determines every individual's birth, age, opportunities, chances—all the outer circumstances of life. While fate shapes the concrete (outer) conditions of life, inner nature determines the psychological (inner) pattern of the individual. Representing nurture and nature, fate and inner nature are responsible for the development of the individual—body, mind, and fortune. They both need to be accepted and fulfilled, not counteracted. The more one works along with one's destiny, the better one realizes oneself, and the more contentment, happiness, and perfection one experiences. The more one tries to avoid it, the harsher the realities of life appear.

The proper attitude toward inner nature and fate is accordance, harmony, adaptation, and even resignation to the given realities. The more spontaneously such accordance is achieved, the better.

Conscious knowledge and active decision making have no part in this, since they cause a rift between subject and object and make spontaneity impossible. To overcome conscious knowledge, Guo Xiang advocates increasing forgetfulness to the point where opposites are no longer perceived. Instead of knowledge, there is "unknowing"; instead of conscious mental activity and feeling, there is "no-mind." Once all things are forgotten, one proceeds to forget the forgetting. One "forgets and again forgets" or "decreases and again decreases," as the *Daode jing* has it (ch. 48). All beings are then the same in one's perception; there is no more good and evil, no more right and wrong. One has attained the state at which all beings are made equal. Then, whatever "I" may develop, whatever state the "I" may find itself in, forgetfulness pervades all, all is one. Guo Xiang says,

> Taking shape is "I" arising,
> Being alive is "I" at work;
> Growing old is "I" decaying,
> Being dead is "I" at rest.
> All these states are different,
> and yet they are the same,
> because they are all "I."
> Though all four are changes,
> They never are not "I."
> How could this "I" be cherished? (7.23b)

Here he documents how he sees the ultimate oneness of the Dao at work within and through body, mind, and person. By becoming fully one with all, the individual dissolves in the flow of life. He or she attains perfect oneness and harmony with the Dao. At this stage, a new sense of self emerges, a self no longer limited to the ego or defined by the body, but identical with universal principle. As Guo Xiang describes it,

> This life of mine, I did not bring it forth. Thus all that occurs throughout my life of perhaps a hundred years, all my sitting, getting up, walking, and staying, all my movements, all my quiet, all hurrying and resting of mine—even all the feelings, characteristics, knowledge, and abilities I have—all that I have, all that I do not have, all that I do, all that I encounter: it is never me, but principle only. (6.16a)

Once having reached this ideal state, the person at one with the Dao no longer acts according to individual feelings, wishes, and intentions. Rather, the pure creative force of the universe, the radiant spirit of the Dao, acts through him or her. The Dao takes care that the person fulfills his or her inner nature and fate to perfection. Everyone has such access to the Dao in the realized mind within. This mind is pure spirit, the individual's inborn virtue of the Dao. It guides people perfectly and ensures their happiness. Guo Xiang says,

> The ways of the human mind are such that naturally there is nothing that is not done. Going along with them and just following and complying with them, people will naturally be tranquil and fulfill their duties spontaneously. (13.10b)

Forgetfulness thus leads to a new life in harmony with the perfect rhythm of the universe. The sage, the fully realized human being, emerges—on the inside filled with a mind of tranquil freedom and unified perception, on the outside acting in alignment with the flow of life. His movements are like natural processes; his actions appear spontaneous, yet are in fact inevitable. Free from self, free from merit, free from fame (*Zhuangzi* 2/1/22), the sage leaves no traces. He does not change anything in the world, nor does he become an example for others. "A good traveler leaves no track or trace," as the *Daode jing* has it (ch. 27). He has certainly no attachment to the body or desires to change and modify it in any way.

A similar attitude is also present in chapter 7 of the *Liezi*, but with a slightly different twist and a more hedonistic perspective. Agreeing fundamentally that the body is "not my possession" and that "it is impossible to prolong life, valuing life cannot preserve it and taking care of the body can do it no good" (Graham 1960, 153, 147), the text in this chapter yet sees it as a potential source of great discomfort that is by no means the idyllic harmony of Guo Xiang. It says:

> Even if one should live out one's destined span, infancy and senility take nearly half of it. The nights lost in sleep, the days wasted even when we are awake, take nearly half the rest. Pain and sickness, sorrow and toil, ruin and loss, anxiety and fear, take nearly half the rest of this. Of the dozen or so years that remain, if we reckon how

long we are at ease and content, without the least care, it does not even amount to the space of an hour. (Graham 1960, 139)

The conclusion reached from this rather dismal evaluation of the human condition is that one should enjoy the body and its pleasures as much as possible while one has them. "Only in fine clothes and good food, music and beautiful women" will you find happiness, the text says. Act upon the whims of your heart and give in to all spontaneous desires—you may never get another chance. Do not refuse the pleasures of life while it lasts and follow the whims of inner nature freely, while disentangling from care and remaining untouched by considerations of reward and punishment, praise and scorn (Graham 1960, 140–41).

The position expressed here is not completely alien to that of Guo Xiang and the attitude to the body dominant in chapters 1 and 6 of the *Liezi*. It rests on the same foundation—that the body is part of heaven and earth and cannot be controlled—but puts a different slant on how we know what inner nature requires for personal fulfillment. Where Guo Xiang demands a withdrawal of the senses in favor of a state of intuitive insight or unknowing for the realization of inner nature, Yang Zhu according to chapter 7 sees the senses as the immediate messengers of the Dao. As the text says:

> Give yourself up to whatever your ears wish to listen to, your eyes to look on, your nostrils to turn to, your mouth to say, your body to find ease it, and your will to achieve. . . . Restricting any of these you serve oppressive masters. If you can rid yourself of all oppressive masters and wait serenely for death, whether you last a day, a month, a year, ten years, you will succeed at "nourishing your life." . . .
>
> Enjoy this life to the fullest and drain the utmost pleasure from its best years. The greatest misfortune then is a belly too weak to drink without restraint or potency which fails before lust is satisfied. (Graham 1960, 142, 145)

Again, the body has to be accepted for what it is and cannot be changed, and all that human beings can do is to adapt to its changing states and different abilities with as easy a mind as possible. This position—whether meekly accepting bodily patterns or maximizing physical enjoyment—is ultimately a passive approach to being embodied. It sees identity as fluid and intangible, the person a mere flicker in the ongoing processes of heaven and earth, a transient, ephemeral splash in the ocean of cosmic eternity. There is nothing to hold on to, nothing to strive for, nothing that can ever be a definitive self or "I." Human beings in this adaptive view have to come to terms with their ultimate nothingness as individuals, their complete dependence on and participation in the flow of the Dao.

The Transformative Position

The adaptive view contrasts significantly with the transformative position, according to which human beings, graced by individual consciousness, can mentally separate themselves from the constant process of change, learn to understand its underlying dynamics, and set out to use it to their advantage. Especially in chapter 2 ("The Yellow Emperor"), the *Liezi* notes a distinction between body and heart, virtue, or spirit. It stresses that the physical form alone does not make a human being, but that there is a higher level of energy that creates life and proper humanity. The text says:

> Anything with a skeleton six feet high, hands different from its feet, hair on its head and front teeth hidden inside its mouth, which leans forward as it runs, is called "human." Yet a human being may well have the heart of a beast. (ch. 2; Graham 1960, 53)

Vice versa, anything that looks like a beast "with wings at its sides and horns on its head, with teeth and nails wide apart, which flies into the air or walks on all fours" is considered an animal notwithstanding the mind within, and yet there may in some cases be no great difference in mind and intelligence between living species. To be human, one has to have an inner power, called "virtue" (*de*) or "spirit" (*shen*) in the *Zhuangzi* and commonly associated with *qi* in Chinese medicine and Daoism.

In addition to these terms which it also applies, the *Liezi* sees the inner human power as "integrity" or "sincerity" (*cheng*) and notes that it emits a vibration or light (*guang*) from the body. It says,

> When a person's inner integrity is not firm, something oozes from his body and becomes a radiance which outside him presses on the

> hearts of others. It makes others honor him more than their elders and betters and eventually gets him into trouble. (ch. 2; Graham 1960, 49)

Here the inner power allows energy to "ooze" out and determine the person's relation to the world. If the integrity is stable, the person's "radiance" will be harmonious and unthreatening and people will largely ignore him. But if it is not firm, people will pay more attention to him than is appropriate, leading to all sorts of potential trouble.

To stabilize integrity or virtue, people need to practice meditative and physical methods of self-transformation, thereby learning to see things differently and reorganize their body toward more subtle energetic patterns. For this, they have to "unify inner nature, tend the *qi*, maintain virtue on the inside, and penetrate to the place where beings are created" (Graham 1960, 38). This, as outlined in both chapters 2 and 4 ("Confucius"), can occur in a nine-year process. After three years of practice, the mind no longer dares to think of right and wrong and the mouth no longer dares to speak of benefit and harm; after five years, the mind is again thinking of right and wrong, while the mouth again speaks of benefit and harm; after seven years, the person thinks whatever comes into the mind and speaks whatever comes into the mouth without distinguishing between right and wrong, benefit and harm; and after nine years, he thinks and speaks without restraint whatever enters his sphere and without knowing whether the right and wrong, benefit and harm are his or another's (Graham 1960, 36, 81).

It can also be part of the advanced training in technical skills, as for example in chapter 5 ("The Questions of Tang") where the charioteer Taidou instructs his disciple Zaofu. He says:

> If you respond with the bridle to what you feel in the bit, with the hand to what you feel in the bridle, with the mind to what you feel in the hand, then you will see without eyes and urge without a goad. Relaxed in mind and straight in posture, you will place the twenty-four hooves exactly where you want them, and swing around, advance, and withdraw with perfect precision. (Graham 1960, 113–14)

The idea is that by systematically training the mind away from relying on the senses and toward using subtler, more immediate perception and by reorganizing the body toward finer attunement with the energies and actions of the outside world, a deep mental calm and inner stability is reached. As in the adaptive position described earlier, this is described as a state of relaxation and unknowing. However, it is not mindless, inevitable, and resigned. On the contrary, it leads to an in-depth control over the body which becomes invulnerable and immune to sensory impulses, able to go beyond the solidity of earthbound existence and to tune into the cosmic vibrations of all.

An example in the text is the ancient sage Gengsangzi who has transcended the senses and is able to look and listen without using eyes and ears. He says:

> My body is in accord with my mind, my mind with my *qi*, my *qi* with my spirit, and my spirit with great nonbeing. Whenever the minutest existing thing or the faintest sound affects me . . . I am bound to know it. However, I do not know whether I perceived it with the seven holes in my head and my four limbs, or knew it through my heart and inner organs. It is simply spontaneous knowledge. (ch. 4; Graham 1960, 77)

This passage describes the perception and mental state the practitioner strives for. In perfect alignment, the person's body, mind, *qi*, and spirit are matched harmoniously with the Dao, so finely attuned to everything that perception is absolute and does not come through one or the other sense organ but through the very fabric of the person's being, a being that is in complete attunement with the vibrations of the greater universe. Again the key motif is one of unknowing, but it does not lead to a passive, receptive, resigned acceptance.

Instead, practitioners learn to control their own minds and bodies to the point of being able to show different patterns at will. The classic story about this is when Liezi urges the Daoist master Huzi to let himself be analyzed by a physiognomist shaman. At each visit of the shaman, Huzi consciously presents him with a different mind which leads to varying diagnoses from imminent death through looming misfortunes to highest sageliness. Eventually the shaman is so confused that he is completely demoralized, "his wits left him and he fled" (ch. 2; Graham 1960, 47–49). Another classic is the description of powers over the body that allow the adept "to enter fire and water, pierce metal and stone, overturn mountains, turn back rivers, shift walled cities, rise the empty air without falling, and pass unhindered through solid objects; there is no end to the thousands and myriads of ways in which one can alter things and transform them" (Graham 1960, 61). Similarly, the denizens of the wondrous western country of Huaxu

> go into water without drowning, into fire without burning. Hack them, flog them, there is no wound nor pain; poke them, scratch them, there is no ache nor itch. They ride space as though walking the solid earth, sleep in mid-air as though on their beds. Clouds and mist do not hinder their sight, thunder does not confuse their hearing, beauty and ugliness do not disturb their hearts, mountains and valleys do not trip their feet. (ch. 2; Graham 1960, 34)

Having undergone the transformation of *qi* into pure spirit, people such as these have overcome all limitations of their physical existence. Although still embodied, they are predominantly spirit beings; although part of the Dao, they are neither unconscious nor passive in their actions. No longer earthbound, they can converse with the denizens of the otherworld and, as described in chapter 3 ("King Mu of Zhou"), undertake spirit travels into the celestial realms.

When they turn their attention to earth, moreover, they actively control nature. Thus, the ancient sage Laochengzi was not only able to appear and disappear at will but he also could "exchange the four seasons, call up thunder in winter, create ice in summer, make flying things run and running creatures fly" (ch. 3; Graham 1960, 65). The craftsman Yanshi even went so far as to construct a homunculus, a semi-animated creature that looked like a person and moved about when pushed in the right spots. King Mu of Zhou marveled at it and experimented with it. After inspecting its insides and finding all organs present and accounted for, "he tried taking out its heart, and the mouth could not speak; tried taking out its liver, and the eyes could not see; tried taking out its kidneys, and the feet could not walk." Satisfied, he sighed, "Is it then possible for human skill to achieve as much as the creator?" (ch. 5; Graham 1960, 110–11).

This is the nub of the transformative position on the human body: practitioners become one with the Dao as do their adaptive counterparts, but instead of only joining the Dao in its ongoing changes they become one with its creative core and begin to control not only their bodies but the natural environment around them, mastering the changes and taking charge of the processes of creation.

In Daoist history, this position—together with many of the stories and metaphors used in the *Liezi*—is formulated dominantly in the *Zhuangzi*. Here, too, we find an emphasis on an inner power that animates beings, as for example in the story of the piglets running away from their mother's corpse because "they loved not her body but the thing that moved her body" (ch. 5; Watson 1968, 73). We find stages of attainment that reach from the forgetting of "benevolence and righteousness" through that of "rites and music" to the complete oblivion of everything (ch. 6; 1968, 90) or from placing the world, things, and life outside oneself to reaching the "brightness of dawn" and "seeing one's own aloneness" (ch. 6; 1968, 83). We have tales of superb and enlightened craftsmen such as Cook Ding who cuts up oxen using only pure spirit and not looking with the eyes (ch. 3; 1968, 50–51) and Woodworker Qing who seeks the raw materials for his bell stands after a seven-day fast in a state of mind "so still that I forget I have four limbs and a form and body," (ch. 19; 1968, 205–206). And we find the transition from sensory to *qi* and spirit perception when Confucius admonishes Yan Hui: "Make your will one. Don't listen with your ears, listen with your mind. No, don't listen with your mind, but listen with your spirit. Listening stops with the ears, the mind stops with recognition, but spirit is empty and waits on all things" (ch. 3; 1968, 57). Many of the ideas and images of the *Zhuangzi*, as well as its transformative position on the human body, later made their way into Highest Clarity Daoism (see Robinet 1983b). Founded in the mid-fourth century on the basis of a series of revelations granted to Yang Xi, a medium residing among local southern aristocrats near Nanjing, the new capital of the Eastern Jin, it emphasized direct communication with the otherworld through visualizations and ecstatic meditations. Practitioners strove to transform into cosmic beings and attain high ranks in the otherwordly hierarchy. No longer limited by their earthly environment, they increasingly made the heavens their true home, wandering freely throughout the far ends of the world and soaring up into the stars. They hoped to develop "a new personality of cosmic dimensions, where the physical and the imaginary body, the individual and the cosmos, are intimately merged, where the ordinary human being has become a true Daoist saint, such as described by Zhuangzi" (Robinet 1989, 160).

The *Yangsheng Yaoji*

How, then, do physical practices come into this? How is the body treated by the different kinds of practitioners? What kind of practices were undertaken in the early middle ages? And where do the *Liezi*'s views of the body fit in with the larger context of Chinese physical practices? To answer these questions, I propose to look at the *Yangsheng yaoji* (Long Life Compendium), a manual of physical longevity techniques dated to the fourth century and connected to the *Liezi* through its author Zhang Zhan, who is also the *Liezi's* main commentator.

The *Yangsheng yaoji* does not survive as an integrated text. Lost after the rebellion of An Lushan in 755 (Barrett 1980, 172), it is extant in fragments and citations (collected in Stein 1999), found mainly in three sources:

the *Zhubing yuanhou lun* (Origins and Symptoms of Medical Disorders), a medical compendium in 50 *juan* put together by a committee headed by the court physician Chao Yuanfang and presented to Emperor Yang of the Sui in 610 (see Despeux and Obringer 1997);

the *Yangxing yanming lu* (Record on Nourishing Inner Nature and Extending Life, DZ 838), a Daoist collection of meditative, breathing, and physical practices in two *juan*, ascribed to Sun Simiao and probably of the mid-seventh century (see Switkin 1987);

and the *Ishinpō* (Essential Medical Methods), an extensive Japanese medical collection by the court physician Tamba no Yasuyori (912–995), which was presented to the emperor in 984 (see Sakade 1989).

Its ten sections are listed in the *Yangxing yanming lu* (1.9b-10a) and mentioned in Sun Simiao's *Qianjin yaofang* (Essential Prescriptions Worth a Thousand Gold [Pieces], DZ 1163), which dates from 652 (Stein 1999, 103). They are

1. Harboring Spirit
2. Loving *Qi*
3. Maintaining the Body
4. Practicing Gymnastics

5. Proper Language
6. Food and Drink
7. Bedchamber Arts
8. Rejecting Common Habits
9. Herbal Medicines
10. Taboos and Prohibitions

In many ways this list of practices continues information on how to conserve the body and ease the mind found in the early medical manuscripts, unearthed in Zhangjiashan and Mawangdui and dated to 186 and 168 BCE respectively (see Harper 1998). The manuscripts include texts on ways to harmonize yin and yang, find alignment with the Dao, nourish life through herbs, breathing exercises, sexual techniques, as well as methods of absorbing *qi*, abstaining from grains, and undertaking therapeutic gymnastics. Predominantly medical and often geared toward the alleviation of symptoms, they also describe practices for enhanced longevity and a more harmonious life.

The *Yangsheng yaoji* as extant today contains citations and summaries of more than thirty earlier works, some of which are otherwise unknown while others are Daoist immortality texts also cited in Ge Hong's (283–343) *Baopuzi* (Book of the Master Who Embraces Simplicity, DZ 1185; trans. Ware 1966), thus allowing a fourth-century dating of the text (Stein 1999, 110–13). This is also borne out by the authors and masters mentioned, which include many second- and third-century figures, among them well-known authors of medical works such as Zhang Zhongqing (142–200), the author of the *Shanghan lun* (On Cold-Induced Disorders; trans. Mitchell and Wiseman 1999), together with various alchemists and immortality seekers described by Ge Hong in his *Shenxian zhuan* (Biographies of Spirit Immortals; trans. Campany 2002).

The ascription of the *Yangsheng yaoji* to Zhang Zhan is based on the bibliography of the *Suishu* (History of the Sui Dynasty). Zhang Zhan, unfortunately, is not an unusual appellation, and there are three known persons by this name in medieval China. A first Zhang Zhan lived in the Eastern Han but cannot be our author, because of the fourth-century dating of the text. A second Zhang Zhan, alias Ziran, has a biography in the *Weishu* (History of the Wei Dynasty) and could well be the author, except that he has no known relation to either Daoist thought or medical practice. Despite this, he is the favorite candidate of Zhu Yueli on the grounds that philosophically minded aristocrats of the Dark Learning (Xuanxue) tradition would not be involved in Daoist immortality practices (Zhu 1986, 102). This, as Sakade point out, is not necessarily the case, arguing for the authorship of the third Zhang Zhan, better known for his commentary on the *Liezi* (1986, 5).

Zhang Zhan, alias Chudu, does not have an official biography despite the fact that he apparently wrote several philosophical commentaries and two compendia on longevity practice (listed in the *Suishu*), that he served as imperial secretary under the Eastern Jin in their newly established capital at Nanjing, and that both his father and grandfather were senior officials in the Western Jin (Despeux 1989, 228). Rather, information about him is anecdotal, partly contained in the *Shishuo xinyu* (A New Account of Tales of the World; trans. Mather 1976), and partly in the biographies of contemporary officials and later descendants.

From these sources, it appears that Zhang Zhan was philosophically minded and a follower of Dark Learning thinkers such as Guo Xiang, whom he frequently cites in his *Liezi* commentary. He also had medical knowledge and was eager to improve the *qi* in his residence by planting various kinds of pine trees. The *Jinshu* (History of the Jin Dynasty) biography of Fan Ning further mentions that he was susceptible to a longevity recipe.for eyestrain consisting of six ingredients: read less, think less, focus inward, scan outward, sleep late, and go to bed early. He was to mix these ingredients with his *qi* and take them into the heart for seven days. This would enhance his vision and extend his life (Stein 1999, 101).

It is thus more than likely that the commentator of the *Liezi* and Dark Learning thinker Zhang Zhan was also the compiler of a work on longevity practices, emphasizing the active treatment of the body in pursuit of harmony with the Dao.

Working with the Body

The ten sections of the *Yangsheng yaoji* cover the major topics of traditional longevity practice and for the most part provide remedies to improve bodily functioning. The text, as collected and arranged by Stephan Stein (1999), gives numerous instructions regarding food and herbal remedies together with prescriptions for proper sleep, hygiene, sexual activity, and exercises. It places a strong emphasis on seasonal taboos and doing things on the right days and at the right times. For example, one had best take a bath and wash one's hair when the moon is in the constellation *dongjing* (Stein 1999, 180); one should avoid eating raw onions in the first month because they can cause diseases and not take any intestines on days with the cyclical signs *ren* and *zi* (1999, 189). Also, specific combinations of food should be avoided, such as anything hot and cold, sweet and raw, as well as wheat and oats, onions and honey, celery and pig's liver, dried ginger and rabbit, and so on (1999, 200–204). Alcohol should be used only in moderation, water should be boiled before drinking, and great care should be taken not to get cold when sweaty. The text also has specific recipes for beneficial food combinations, descriptions of the qualities and healing properties of herbs and foodstuffs, as well as a series of instructions for pregnancy (1999, 208–10). In many cases, it provides specific remedies for certain conditions, notably stomach and digestive problems, including cramps, flatulence, constipation, and diarrhea (1999, 226–28).

The overall goal of the presentation is to encourage people to live as healthily as possible, working closely in harmony with nature and the four seasons. Citing the ancient immortal Pengzu, the text says:

> The method of nourishing longevity consists mainly in not doing harm to oneself. Keep warm in winter and cool in summer, and never lose your harmony with the four seasons—that is how you can align yourself with the body. Do not allow sensuous beauty, provocative postures, easy leisure, and enticing entertainments to incite yearnings and desires—that is how you come to pervade the spirit. (*Ishinpō* 23.3a; Stein 1999, 169)

The most important advice is to remain moderate in everything: to eat and drink with control, to stay away from various luxuries that lead to a weakness of *qi*, and to keep speech and laughter within limits—since any excess will harm the lungs and kidneys (1999, 179, 186). Citing Pengzu once more, the text points out especially that heavy clothing and thick comforters, spicy foods and heavy meats, sexual attraction and beautiful women, melodious voices and enticing sounds, wild hunting and exciting outings, as well as all strivings for success and ambition, will inevitably lead to a weakening of the body and thus a reduction in life expectancy

(1999,178). In the same vein, the more mental activities of thinking and reflection, desires and engagements, speech and laughter, yearning and relishing, joy and anger, likes and dislikes will harm various psychological forces, such as the spirit, will, intention, heart, and spirit and material souls (1999, 170–71). This, in turn, leads to an overall diminishing of *qi*, which brings one farther away from the Dao and reduces long life.

The conception here is that harmony with the Dao is expressed in mental stability and physical wellness and that any form of agitation or sickness indicates a decline in alignment with the forces of nature. Thus, the text advises that "going along with heaven and earth brings good fortune; going against heaven and earth brings misfortune" (*Ishinpō* 23.29b; Stein 1999, 182), and notes: "The Dao is *qi*. Preserving *qi* you can attain the Dao, and through attaining the Dao you can live long. Spirit is essence. Preserving essence you can reach spirit brightness, and once you have spirit brightness, you can live long" (23.17ab; Stein 1999, 172). This thought essentially reverses the thinking of Daoist immortality practice, where you preserve the *qi* to reach long life, and once you live long can reach out farther into transcendence and attain the Dao, reaching the spirit brightness of the celestials above.

Very much functioning in the adaptive mode of relating to the body, the text closely echoes Guo Xiang's thinking. It states:

> Being equipped with the five constants [phases], everyone has an inner nature that is dominantly calm or reckless, strong or weak. Those inherently calm cannot be made reckless; those inherently reckless cannot be made calm: they each have their inner natures. Going against inner nature means losing one's allotment [*fen*], desiring more than appropriate means harming one's life [*sheng*]. . . .
>
> The way of ordering life, therefore, is to follow along with inner nature and give and take in accordance with what is appropriate, let loss and gain unfold in gradual flow. This way each person can fully attain his or her perfect alignment [*shi*]. (*Ishinpō* 23.2a; Stein 1999, 170)

Referring clearly to Guo Xiang's key concepts and using his terms, such as allotment and alignment, this passage states the fundamental outlook of the *Yangsheng yaoji*. It does not claim to bring people to higher states or help them reach perfection in the creative center of the Dao, but serves to prevent them from losing their steady course and provides remedies for ailments and disharmonies that may already have manifested. Nor is it addressed to religious seekers, such as the followers of Highest Clarity whose main activity was meditation and the search for ecstatic visions. Rather, it focuses on literati—thinkers, writers, and officials who wish to live securely and peacefully. The readership is made clear when the text comments on the potential harm of too much thinking and reflection. It says that "reading books leads to reflection, and that can diminish inner nature," but of course, since "it is impossible not to read books," it is best to stick to subjects one already knows something about, because pondering difficult issues without interruption will reduce longevity (*Ishinpō* 23.9a; Stein 1999, 171).

Remaining firmly in the adaptive mode and catering to the needs of learned aristocrats who wish to maintain bodily health, the text only rarely ventures into more technical practices. In the section on *qi* it discusses breathing exercises to enhance vitality, notably one where one holds the breath to the count of 200 or 250, as well as ways of swallowing the saliva, claiming that this will not only increase the potency of essence in the body but also "open the meridians and vitalize the myriad body gods" (1999, 173–74). Another breathing and saliva exercise appears in the section on gymnastics, joined by various methods of stretching and self-massages. For example:

> In the early morning, before you get up, first click your teeth for two sets of seven repetitions. Then close your eyes, make your hands into fists, move your mouth three times as if rinsing to fill it with saliva, then swallow and hold. Hold the breath until you reach your maximum. When you cannot hold it any longer, let it out very, very slowly. Do three repetitions before you stop.
>
> After this, rise to do the wolf crouch and the owl turn, shake yourself to the right and left, and again hold the breath in until you reach your maximum. Do three repetitions, then get off the bed. Make your hands into fists and hold the breath in while stomping the heels three times, then raise one arm and lower the other, and again hold the breath in to your maximum. Do three repetitions.
>
> Next, interlace the fingers behind the head and twist to your right and left, holding the breath each time. Do three repetitions.

> Now, stand up to stretch from both feet, again interlace the fingers, revolve the palms, and press forward. Hold the breath. Repeat three times. Do this entire sequence every morning and evening, completing at least three repetitions, but if can do more, so much the better. (*Yangxing yanming lu* 2.4ab; Stein 1999, 185)

Integrated exercises such as this sequence, which involve holding the breath, swallowing the saliva, massaging oneself, and doing various stretches, from the Tang dynasty onward appear in technical Daoist works as a way to prepare for meditations and advanced immortality practices, leading to the emphasis on physical practices typical for Daoist cultivation today. The exercises are associated with clearing the body of wayward *qi* and making it open and pervasive, so that the *qi* can be made increasingly subtle and transformed into spirit while the spiritual forces of heaven come to reside. The body of the Daoist is transformed into celestial dimensions, and breathing and gymnastics—together with diets, herbs, sexual control, and temporal taboos—pave the way toward this goal. They are not an end in themselves but a stepping stone to a higher level.

The Daoist Perspective

While this Daoist vision is obvious from the Tang onward, the transformative position is dominant among Highest Clarity followers already in the middle ages and, as we have seen, plays a key role in the *Zhuangzi* and the *Liezi*. How, then, did earlier Daoists and more philosophical followers of the transformative position relate to physical practices? What was their perspective on gymnastics, breathing, and the various other longevity methods?

The fourth-century *Baopuzi* provides some interesting insights. Like the *Liezi*, it makes a distinction between a level of existence that extends life through being in harmony with the cosmic processes and the attainment of transcendence which reaches out to the powers of the Dao at the creative center of all. It notes that those who nourish life with herbal remedies, diets, breathing, and gymnastics may deem themselves advanced practitioners, but will never reach the higher levels, for which an alchemical elixir has to be prepared and active communication with the gods be established. The text clearly acknowledges the medical and long life benefits of the practices. It says:

> The ability to writhe like a dragon, stretch like a tiger, waddle like a bear, swallow like a tortoise, fly like a swallow, twist like a snake, dilate like a bird, look heavenward and earthward—all these will prevent the orange colored wax from leaving the Cavern Chamber in the head. When you have climbed like a monkey and jumped like a hare 1,200 times, your hearing will not deteriorate. The deaf may steam their ears with lizard. Or they may form a packet of jujubes, sheep-turd cinnamon, and plumed sparrow cinnamon, and seal their ears with it. All these procedures produce cures. (15.9b; Ware 1966, 257)

But then it notes that while these methods may help health, they will not reach to the higher spheres, and that the truly marvelous alchemical recipes can reach much farther, granting practitioners states of unlimited immortality and oneness with the Dao. The text says:

> Man's death ensues from losses, old age, illnesses, poisons, miasmas, and chills. Today people do gymnastics and breathing exercises, revert their sperm to nourish the brain, follow dietary rules, regulate their activity and rest, take medicines, give thought to their inner gods to maintain their integrity, undergo prohibitions, wear amulets and seals from their belts, and keep at a distance all those who might harm their lives. In this way they may avoid the six baneful things just listed that can cause death.
>
> Physicians today have pills that activate and brighten the kidneys, powders that benefit the circulation, roasted boxhorn for strengthening bone structure, and infusions of yellow hedysarum as a general tonic. . . . Writings also assert that a certain Wu Pu received from Hua Tuo the Five Animals' Frolic as a basic form of gymnastics and managed to live to over a hundred. If such are the effects of the humblest of medicines, just think what can be done by those that are truly marvelous! (5.4a; Ware 1966, 103)

This position radicalizes the attitude in the *Liezi*, where both positions, the adaptive and the transformative, are presented side by side. Here the adaptive position is clearly seen as inferior and the various methods, while effective, are not considered good enough to reach the ultimate goal, complete transcendence in immortality. People who think that by doing calisthenics they can attain the Dao are deceiving themselves, and true Daoists will not waste their time on them, nor will they ever be content with merely adapting to the natural processes and obvious patterns of life.

This view was radicalized further in organized Daoism, where the relationship to the Dao in the form of various heavens and deities superseded all other concerns and health was the direct result of a pure and pious life. Communal Daoists of the Celestial Masters, the earliest school founded in the second century CE, prohibited medical and health treatments in favor of religious cultivation. For them, the world was populated by gods and demons who were eager to possess people and devour their vital *qi*. To combat them, Daoists fortified their houses and bodies with talismans, learned to recognize the demons and call them by their proper names, and visualized themselves as demon-conquering heroes.

If despite such measures someone was attacked by a demon, they would suffer sickness and disease. Moreover, such an attack could occur only because the person had been careless and had a moral failing. As a result, all healing of the Celestial Masters was undertaken through confession, ritual, and magic. First, the sick person was isolated in a so-called quiet chamber, an adaptation of a Han institution for punishing wayward officials involving solitary confinement. There they had to think of their sins going all the way back to their birth to try and find an explanation for the illness. Once certain sins had been identified, a senior master would come to write them down—in triplicate and together with a formal petition for their eradication from the person's divine record. The three copies would then, in a formal ceremony, be transmitted to Heaven (by burning), Earth (by burying), and Water (by casting into a river), whose officials supposedly set the record straight and restored the person's good health. Longevity techniques, such as gymnastics and meditations, were permitted only in the larger context of the supernatural universe and seen mainly as supplementary measures of purification (Kohn 2001).

The same also holds true for the medieval school of Highest Clarity, although its followers were lay-based and thus not prohibited from availing themselves of medical treatments. Still, their universe was dominantly characterized by their relation to otherworldly entities with cultivation practices that involved visualizations of gods, opening of divine palaces within the body, ecstatic excursions to the stars, and highly complex ceremonies of communication, purification, confession, and the exoneration of ancestors. Methods akin to gymnastics and breathing were used mainly as purification measures in the preparation of rituals. Thus, the *Introductory Explanation to the Daode jing* (*Daode zhenjing xujue*), a fifth-century text on devotional observances to Lord Lao discovered among manuscripts found at Dunhuang, instructs followers who wish to recite the *Daode jing* to begin by burning incense and straightening their robes, then bowing to the ten directions. After this, while concentrating their mind and visualizing Laozi together with his main disciples, they should open the sacred text and recite an incantation of invitation and praise to the deity that also places the practitioner into a cosmic context:

> In my room, the seven jewels come together,
> Doors and windows open of themselves.
> Utter in my purity, I strive for deeper truth,
> Riding on bright light, I ascend the purple sky.
> Sun and moon shine to my right and left,
> I go to the immortals and find eternal life.

Following this, adepts are to click their teeth and swallow the saliva thirty-six times, applying long life methods. Then, however, they again move into the more religious spheres and are to see themselves surrounded by the celestial constellations of the four directions: the green dragon to the left, the white tiger to the right, the red bird in front, and the dark warrior behind. Only when placed in such a cosmic environment can they recite the sacred book and establish a direct link to the gods of the Dao.

Conclusion

Starting from a reading of the *Liezi* and examining its understanding of the body, we have found that there are two major positions in the text: the adaptive attitude that proposes complete harmony with the Dao and its earthly manifestations, whether through alignment and resignation or through hedonistic enjoyment of the various bodily states; and the transformative position, which proposes an attainment of the inner potentiality and creative power of the Dao through the systematic transformation of the person, body and mind, into subtler forms of *qi* and eventual pure spirit. Both are attractive to literati readers and connect with the Dark Learning school of Daoist thought, notably the thinking of Guo Xiang, but to a lesser degree also to Xiang Xiu and the Seven Sages of the

Bamboo Grove, whose ecstatic visions were strongly inspired by the transformative views found in the *Zhuangzi* (see Kohn 1992).

These readers and commentators of the *Liezi* were not averse to physical practices either, but belonged to a group of learned aristocrats with the leisure to perform exercises and read the relevant literature, which provided the knowledge of how to modify their food intake, choose proper food combinations, control their sexual urges, and in general modify their lifestyle to the most beneficial for longevity. Daoist followers of Highest Clarity, similarly aristocratic and well educated, adapted the transformative view of the body-mind but also integrated the alchemical experiments of the *fangshi* as documented in the *Baopuzi* as well as the understanding of the celestial spheres and body gods found among the Celestial Masters. They thus moved away from longevity practice, seeing the body mainly as a vehicle for self-transformation whose disposal—often with the help of an alchemical elixir—would eventually be necessary to attain the desired celestial state (see Strickmann 1979). It was not until the Tang dynasty, when Daoist masters who were also physicians and who came to Daoist practice because of illness, such as Sun Simiao (601–693), began to integrate physical practices into the transformative Daoist curriculum, establishing health and a strong body as prerequisites for more advanced levels of practice. The modern vision of the body as key to Daoist realization is thus comparatively recent, but harks back to the practices of Chinese medicine and longevity techniques.

Notes

1. For further details on the Daoist body, see Schipper 1978; 1994; Ishida 1989; Andersen 1994; Kroll 1996; Saso 1997.
2. Numbers in the Daoist canon (abbreviated "DZ") follow Schipper 1975; Komjathy 2002.
3. For more on Guo Xiang's mystical thought, see Kohn 1985a; 1985b; 1992, ch. 3. A list of relevant Japanese studies on the body-mind-fate vision of Guo Xiang is appended to my review of Brook Ziporyn's *The Penumbra Unbound: The Neo-Taoist Philosophy of Guo Xiang* (Albany: State University of New York Press, 2003), found in *Daoist Studies Book Reviews* (http://rels.queensu.ca/dao/reviews).

References

Andersen, Poul. 1994. "The Transformation of the Body in Taoist Ritual." In *Religious Reflections on the Human Body*, ed. Jane Marie Law, 181–202. Bloomington: Indiana University Press.

Barrett, T. H. 1980. "On the Transmission of the *Shen tzu* and of the *Yang-sheng yao-chi*." *Journal of the Royal Asiatic Society* 2 (1980), 168–76.

Campany, Robert F. 2002. *To Live As Long As Heaven and Earth: A Translation and Study of Ge Hong's Traditions of Divine Transcendents*. Berkeley: University of California Press.

Despeux, Catherine. 1989. "Gymnastics: The Ancient Tradition." In *Taoist Meditation and Longevity Techniques*, ed. Livia Kohn, 223–61. Ann Arbor: University of Michigan, Center for Chinese Studies Publications.

Despeaux, Catherine, and Frederic Obringer, eds. 1997. *La maladie dans la Chine medieval: La toux*. Paris: Editions L'Harmattan.

Graham, A. C. 1960. *The Book of Lieh-tzu*. London: A. Murray.

———. 1961. "The Date and Compilation of the Liehtzyy." *Asia Major* 2. ser., 8: 139–98.

Harper, Donald. 1998. *Early Chinese Medical Manuscripts: The Mawangdui Medical Manuscripts*. London: Wellcome Asian Medical Monographs.

Ishida, Hidemi. 1989. "Body and Mind: The Chinese Perspective." In *Taoist Meditation and Longevity Techniques*, ed. Livia Kohn, 41–70. Ann Arbor: University of Michigan, Center for Chinese Studies Publications.

Kaltenmark, Max. 1965. "La mystique taoïste." In *La mystique et le mystiques*, ed. A. Ravier, 649–69. Paris.

Knaul, Livia. 1985a. "Kuo Hsiang and the *Chuang-tzu*." *Journal of Chinese Philosophy* 12: 429–47.

———. 1985b. "The Winged Life: Kuo Hsiang's Mystical Philosophy." *Journal of Chinese Studies* 2, no. 1: 17–41.

Kohn, Livia. 1989. "Taoist Insight Meditation: The Tang Practice of *Neiguan*." In *Taoist Meditation and Longevity Techniques*, ed. Livia Kohn, 191–222. Ann Arbor: University of Michigan, Center for Chinese Studies Publications.

———. 1991. "Taoist Visions of the Body." *Journal of Chinese Philosophy* 18: 227–52.

———. 1992. *Early Chinese Mysticism: Philosophy and Soteriology in the Taoist Tradition*. Princeton: Princeton University Press.

———. 2001. *Daoism and Chinese Culture*. Cambridge, MA: Three Pines Press.

Komjathy, Louis. 2002. *Title Index to Daoist Collections*. Cambridge, MA: Three Pines Press.

Kroll, Paul W. 1996. "Body Gods and Inner Vision: *The Scripture of the Yellow Court*." In *Religions of China in Practice*, ed. Donald S. Lopez Jr., 149–55. Princeton: Princeton University Press.

Mather, Richard . 1976. *A New Account of Tales of the World*. Minneapolis: University of Minnesota Press.

Mitchell, Craig, Feng Ye, and Nigel Wiseman. 1999. *Shang Han Lun: On Cold Damage*. Brookline, MA: Paradigm Publications.

Mugitani Kunio. 1987. "Yōsei enmei roku kunchi." *Report of the Study Group on Traditional Chinese Longevity Techniques*, no. 3. Tokyo: Mombushō.

Robinet, Isabelle. 1983a. "Kouo Siang ou le monde comme absolu." *T'oung Pao* 69: 87–112.

———. 1983b. "Chuang-tzu et le taoïsme religieux." *Journal of Chinese Religions* 11: 59–109.

———. 1989. "Visualization and Ecstatic Flight in Shangqing Taoism." In *Taoist Meditation and Longevity Techniques*, ed. Livia Kohn, 157–90. Ann Arbor: University of Michigan, Center for Chinese Studies Publications.

Sakade Yoshinobu. 1986. "Chō Tan 'Yōsei yōshu' itsubun to sono shisō." *Tōhōshukyō* 68: 1–24.

———. 1989. "Longevity Techniques in Japan: Ancient Sources and Contemporary Studies." In *Taoist Meditation and Longevity Techniques*, ed. Livia Kohn, 1–40. Ann Arbor: University of Michigan, Center for Chinese Studies Publications.

Saso, Michael. 1997. "The Taoist Body and Cosmic Prayer." In *Religion and the Body*, ed. Sarah Coakley, 231–47. Cambridge: Cambridge University Press.

Schipper, Kristofer M. 1975. *Concordance du Tao Tsang: Titres des ouvrages.* Paris: Publications de l'Ecole Française d'Extrême-Orient.

———. 1978. "The Taoist Body." *History of Religions* 17: 355–87.

———. 1994. *The Taoist Body.* Trans. Karen C. Duval. Berkeley: University of California Press.

Stein, Stephan. 1999. *Zwischen Heil und Heilung: Zur frühen Tradition des Yangsheng in China.* Uelzen: Medizinisch-Literarische Verlagsgesellschaft.

Strickmann, Michel. 1979. "On the Alchemy of T'ao Hung-ching." In *Facets of Taoism*, ed. Holmes Welch and Anna Seidel, 123–92. New Haven: Yale University Press.

Switkin, Walter. 1987. *Immortality: A Taoist Text of Macrobiotics.* San Francisco: H. S. Dakin.

Ware, James R. 1966. *Alchemy, Medicine, and Religion in the China of AD 320.* Cambridge: MIT Press.

Watson, Burton. 1968. *The Complete Works of Chuang-tzu.* New York: Columbia University Press.

Zhu Yueli. 1986. "Yangxing yanming lu kao." *Shijie zongjiao yanjiu* 1986/1: 101–15.

列子
I, Robot
Self as Machine in the Liezi

Jeffrey L. Richey

Introduction

Q. I thought you were dead.
A. Technically I was never alive, but thanks for your concern.[1]

The commitment of early Taoist thought to so-called natural values has been much remarked upon, and it is not difficult to understand why this is so. Organic metaphors permeate texts such as *Laozi* 老子 and *Zhuangzi* 莊子. Contrasts between the "artificial" realm of culture (*wen* 文) and the "authentic" realm of the Tao 道 are frequently drawn, and organisms such as fishes and trees are favorite representations of the "perfected person" (*zhenren* 眞人).[2] "Nature," of course, is a semantically slippery term in any language, but it may be said that what early Taoists mean by "nature" is expressed in the term *ziran* 自然: "what is so of itself" or "spontaneity." According to these early texts, that which is so of itself is "natural," while that which alters its original pattern is not.[3]

It may come as a surprise, then, to discover within the *Liezi* 列子 (a fourth-century CE text eponymously titled after the thinker who is supposed by pious Taoists to have lived six or seven hundred years earlier) two tales that celebrate embodiments of artificiality: an uncannily lifelike mechanical man, and an actual man who moves like a "machine" (*xie* 械).[4] In the first episode, King Mu of Zhou 周

穆王 (r. 900s BCE) is first entertained, then scandalized, and finally wonderstruck by a man-made humanoid contraption that performs music and dances for his court. In the second, a quotation from the apocryphal "Book of the Yellow Emperor" (*Huangdi zhi shu* 黃帝之書) describes the "highest man" (*zhiren* 至人) as one "like a machine" (*ruoxie* 若械), whose actions are autonomous and unconscious. Why did the compiler(s) of the *Liezi* choose to tell these stories? What position do these perfectly unnatural figures occupy within the work as a whole? Finally, what can their appearance in the *Liezi* tell us about Taoist thought about the self and embodiment on the cusp between the classical and medieval periods?

Master Yan's Automaton

The performing artificial man (*changzhe*倡者) that appears in chapter 5 ("The Questions of Tang," *Tangwen* 湯問) is described as the work of a craftsman (*gongren* 工人) called Master Yan 偃師, whom King Mu encounters on his way back home from a tour of inspection in the west. In response to the king's query—"What can you do?" (*ruoyou heneng* 若有何能)—Master Yan responds by seeking the opportunity to present "something [he has] made" (*suozao* 所造) to the royal entourage. On the following day, the king receives Master Yan and asks about the man (*ren* 人) who has accompanied him to court, whereupon the craftsman replies, "It is something that I made, which is able to perform" (*chenzhi suozao nengchangzhe* 臣之所造能倡者).

> 穆王驚視之，趣步俯仰，信人也. 巧夫! 鎮其頤，則歌合律. 捧其手，則舞應節. 千變萬化，惟意所適. 王以為實人也.
> The King looked at it in amazement; it was striding quickly looking up and down; undoubtedly it was a man. When the craftsman pushed its cheek it sang in tune; when he clasped its hand it danced in time; it did innumerable tricks, whatever it pleased you to ask. The King thought it really was a man.[5]

The king's amusement turns into fury as the artificial man begins to flirt with his concubines. When threatened with execution, Master Yan disrupts the operation of his creation by cutting it open and revealing its inner workings to the King, demonstrating the exact replication of human physiology in artificial form (*jiawu* 假物). After experimenting with the functional interdependence of its faculties (e.g., speech) and its components (e.g., heart-mind—*xin* 心), the king's wrath subsides and succumbs to marvel: "Is it then possible for human skill to achieve as much as the Creator?" (*renzhiqiao nai keyu zaohuazhe tonggong hu* 人之巧，乃可與造化者同功乎).[6] The episode concludes with the king's confiscation of the reassembled automaton for his collection and the resumption of his journey home.

King Mu is a stock figure in early Chinese wonder lore. The *Mu Tianzi zhuan* 穆天子傳 (*Biography of King Mu*), a text discovered in 281 CE when it was found in a tomb dating to 296 BCE, describes a visit by the king to the Taoist deity Xiwangmu 西王母 (the Queen Mother of the West) in her domain near Mt. Kunlun *Kunlun shan* 崑崙山 in Tibet.[7] In the *Liezi*, the king is returning home from precisely this region as the tale of his encounter with Master Yan begins. Robert F. Campany has pointed out that the early medieval Chinese literary trope of visits to foreign climes "envisions the periphery as the locus of the simple, the natural, and thus by implication the *primordial* condition that has been progressively lost in the Central Kingdom."[8]

By the fourth century CE—at which time the *Liezi* had attained its final form and attracted commentarial attention—King Mu was associated with the emergent Taoist cult of immortals (*xian* 仙).[9] In the third chapter of the *Liezi* (*Zhou Mu Wang* 周穆王, "King Mu of Zhou")—which is generally devoted to the proposition that one's senses may not be the surest guides to the whole of reality—the king's exploits include voyages to another world, which, as Livia Kohn argues, "closely resembles what later Taoist adepts find in their ecstatic explorations."[10] Clearly, by the moment of his entrance into the *Liezi* narrative, King Mu has become a rich symbol of the human encounter with the strange, the fanciful, and the unexpected, strongly charged with Taoist associations.

During the early medieval period, Chinese elites cultivated a taste for narratives concerning the strange and the unusual.[11] Well before this time, mechanical imitations of animals and demons are mentioned in relation to the legendary carpenter Lu Ban 魯班and the famous philosopher Mozi 墨子 (c. 400s BCE).[12] The early medieval chronicle *Sanguo zhi* 三國志 (*Chronicle of the Three Kingdoms*) also describes artificial animals such as oxen and donkeys as well as mechanical servants.[13] Humanoid automata crafted from precious metals and minerals (*baoren* 寶人, "precious materials-people") that beat drums, recite sacred texts, and perform other entertaining feats as part of the operation of a fabulous clock are described by the Buddhist scholar Daoxuan 道宣 (596–667 CE) in his description of the imaginary *Zhishi zhi yuan* 知時之院 (Cloister for Knowing the Time); they also weep upon the occasion of the Buddha Śākyamuni's death.[14] Humanoid automata also appear in the epic traditions associated with the Central Asian culture hero, Gesar of Ling; it is doubtful, however, that these tales influenced the author(s) of the *Liezi*, despite their availability in Chinese during the later medieval period.[15] Finally, there is a tale similar to that of Master Yan in a nearly contemporaneous Buddhist text, the *Shengjing* 聖經 (c. 285 CE), a translation of Indian *jataka* (narratives of the Buddha Śākyamuni's former rebirths) collections into Chinese, which may have served as the inspiration for the narrative in the *Liezi*.[16]

None of these, however, matches the degree of humanoid verisimilitude achieved by Master Yan, and in general, it cannot be said that artificial humans figure prominently in early Chinese literature. Early modern Western European texts, on the other hand, demonstrate an intense interest in the figure of the automaton, which may be defined as:

> a machine that "acts by itself," that is, a machine that has its own engine as part of its machinery . . . .[and] looks like an animal or a human being and acts like one[17]

Charles Barbour has suggested that the fascination of eighteenth-century European elites with automata is related to the emergence of the Enlightenment view of human beings as autonomous and rational subjects.[18] Whether or not this is in fact the case for early modern Europeans is a question that is beyond the scope of this essay. But what might be the meaning of Master Yan's automaton for an early medieval Chinese audience?

King Mu finds Master Yan's automaton indistinguishable from ordinary mortals in every respect—including its ability to provoke rage and violence. Why does he claim it for his collection? There are several possible explanations. He may simply admire Master Yan's ingenuity and wish to acquire a prop for future retellings of his encounter with the craftsman—a conversation piece for the royal court, as it were. He may enjoy the sensation of total control that the automaton affords him. More provocatively, he may be struck by whether humans are distinguishable in any way from other, less seemingly intelligent or autonomous creatures, "natural" or otherwise. Finally, he may be astounded by his inability to distinguish, not only between human and automaton, but also between human creator and divine creator. In either of these latter instances, the problem raised is one that is familiar in both Greco-Roman and Indian thought—namely, the appearance/reality distinction.

Prior to the introduction of Buddhism around the beginning of the Common Era, almost no Chinese thinker regarded distinguishing between appearance and reality as a matter of serious philosophical concern.[19] One way of understanding the "King Mu" chapter in *Liezi* is to interpret it as an early indigenous rebuttal to foreign Buddhist epistemologies that were gaining currency in China during the early medieval period.[20] In this case, however, it appears to be an example of rebuttal through appropriation. Like the "inner chapters" of the *Zhuangzi*, much of the *Liezi* warns of

> the irrelevance of fixed taxonomies, the danger of clear hierarchies of value, the relativity of cultural judgment, and the limitations of language . . . [and demonstrates] delight in the anomalous and the extraordinary as revealing aspects of reality not dreamt of in the received view of things. . . . By the Han, however, this way of thinking about anomalies had gone underground . . . not to resurface until the third and fourth centuries CE in the heady decades of "pure conversation" (*qingtan* 清談) and the writing of the *Liezi*.[21]

Perhaps, the *Liezi* suggests, it is "possible for human skill to achieve as much as the Creator."[22] This remark by King Mu has at least two important implications. For one thing, the comparison between human and divine creative powers may serve as a vehicle for advancing an unconventional view of humanity. On this view, human beings operate according to the kind of mechanical causality that governs all other creatures, without enjoying the kind of unique status as agents afforded them by other, more anthropocentric worldviews. For example, according to both Confucian and Mohist views, only humans are capable of discerning the moral norms of Heaven (*Tian* 天) and choosing to act accordingly.[23] Rather, humans are as blindly responsive to the natural course of events as the automaton is to the King's inquisitive, probing touch: "All that is so without us knowing why is destiny" (*buzhi suoyi ran er ran mingye* 不知所以然而然，命也).[24] This understanding of the automaton as no different from ordinary humans also contrasts with the description of the automaton in the Buddhist original as "superior to a living man."[25] Nor is a living human to be regarded as superior to the automaton. In this episode, as in the *Zhuangzi*, reality is fully apprehended by "making all things equal" (*qiwu* 齊物).[26]

Moreover, the king's parting words may imply that deities are not unique in the sense that they can be imitated by humans. When the king decides to incorporate the automaton into his royal collection, he may be struck by his inability to distinguish, not only between human and automaton, but also between human creator and divine creator. Although the *Liezi* is filled with fanciful references to gods, spirits, and other supernatural beings, the mere presence of such figures in the text need not be seen as evidence of its compilers' piety.[27] Placing the ingenuity of Master Yan on a level equal to that of the Creator's skill is not so much a Promethean way of challenging pious views of deity as it is a way to suggest that, whatever powers deities allegedly enjoy, they are not in principle distinct from the powers available to mere mortals. Just as critics of the Hellenistic philosopher Epicurus (341–270 BCE) saw "no real difference between [Epicurus's] belief in gods who did not care for our world, on the one hand, and out-and-out atheism," an early medieval Chinese reader of the *Liezi* might well object that gods whose creative feats can be matched by human craftsmen are no gods at all.[28] To this objection, the compiler(s) of the text might respond by arguing that it is merely those humans who have failed to cultivate their innate powers who merit unfavorable comparisons with deities—an argument that echoes the concerns of earlier texts, such as the *Neiye* 内業 (c. 300s BCE): "A common theme in the fourth century BC[E] . . . [was] that humans had more direct access to divine powers than was accepted in contemporary ritual practices."[29] On this point of self-cultivation, let us turn to the other narrative at hand.

The Yellow Emperor's Cyborg

In the sixth chapter ("Agency and Fate," *Liming* 力命), the reader is regaled with a series of dialogues. Many take place between human interlocutors, but all echo the themes of the initial conversation of Agency (*Li* 力) and Fate (*Ming* 命) at the outset of the chapter, in which the forces that direct the universe are impersonal and unconscious, causality is deterministic yet spontaneous, and destiny is both unpredictable and unknowable by human agents. At the close of a dialogue between Yang Bu 楊布 and his elder brother, the famous "hedonist" Yang Zhu 楊朱, the apocryphal "Book of the Yellow Emperor" is quoted:[30]

> 至人居若死，動若械。亦不知所以居；亦不知所以不居；亦不知所以動，亦不知所以不動。亦不以眾人之觀，易其情貌；亦不謂眾人之不觀，不易其情貌。獨往獨來，獨出獨入，孰能礙之？
>
> The highest man at rest is as though dead, in movement is like a machine. He knows neither why he is at rest nor why he is not, why he is in movement nor why he is not. He neither changes his feelings and expression because ordinary people are watching, nor fails to change them because ordinary people are not watching. He comes alone and goes alone, comes out alone and goes in alone; what can obstruct him?[31]

What does it mean to connect the apex of human self-cultivation with a machine-like existence? How should one classify the "highest man," who seems to embody both autonomy (*du* 獨) and unconsciousness (*buzhi* 不知), and thus skews the boundary between the human and the mechanical?

One category that springs to mind is the postmodern one of the cyborg—which, as Donna J. Haraway puts it, is "a hybrid of machine and organism, a creature of social reality as well as a creature of fiction."[32] Of course, a simile ("the highest man . . . is like a machine") is not necessarily an equation ("the highest man . . . is a machine"). A cyborg is not like a machine; it *is* a machine, at least in part. Nonetheless, can a human being reconceptualized in such terms—a blend of fact and fiction, nature and culture—still be called human, or should it be regarded as posthuman? To what extent are such contemporary categories faithful to the spirit of early Chinese texts?

Theorists of cyborg nature have subdivided it into several subcategories:

> Cyborg technologies can be *restorative*, in that they restore lost functions and replace lost organs and limbs; they can be *normalizing*, in that they restore some creature to indistinguishable normality; they can be ambiguously *reconfiguring*, creating posthuman creatures equal to but different from humans, like what one is now when interacting with other creatures in cyberspace or,

> in the future, the type of modifications proto-humans will undergo to live in space or under the sea having given up the comforts of terrestrial existence.[33]

Early Chinese thought is famously concerned with theories of human nature. Here, categories created to elucidate cyborg nature can be used to illuminate human nature in early Chinese texts. For example, Confucian discourse about human beings (especially in the *Mengzi* 孟子) can be seen as tending toward a *restorative* goal: restoring lost functions, such as Mencius's "heart-mind that cannot endure the suffering of others" (*buren renzhixin* 不忍人之心), to human beings that, by virtue of their knowledge and agency, often obscure such native endowments.[34] Preferred forms of culture (e.g., devotion to the sagely exemplars and lore of the past) are enlisted in the battle to redeem nature from the pernicious effects of other, nonpreferred forms of culture (e.g., considerations of individual benefit or profit). Similarly, Mohist discourse about human beings might be understood as working in the direction of a *reconfiguring* goal: transforming the clannish self-interest of human beings with the egalitarian spirit of "universal love" (*jianai* 兼愛).[35] An appeal to a personal deity that judges all human beings and bestows punishment and reward according to their treatment of others motivates humanity to recalibrate its moral compass from partiality to universality.

Within the *Liezi*, the most consistent claim made about human beings is that they enjoy no real distinction from other creatures (*wu* 物), with one exception: humans tend to overvalue their knowledge (*zhi* 知,智) and agency (*li* 力) and undervalue the extent to which Heaven (*Tian* 天) or fate (*ming* 命) determines the outcomes of their lives. A chorus sounding this theme builds in intensity as the sixth chapter unfolds:

> 汝之達，非智得也。北宮子之窮，非愚失也。皆天也，非人也.
> Your success is not due to wisdom, nor is his failure due to foolishness. Both are from heaven and not from man.[36]

> 然而生生死死，非物非我，皆命也。智之所無奈何 . . . . 窈然無際，天道自會.
> It is neither other things nor ourselves that give us life when we live and death when we die; both are destined, wisdom can do nothing

> about them . . . .Inscrutably, in endless sequence, they come to pass of themselves by the Way of Heaven.[37]

> 當死不懼，在窮不戚，知命安時也.
> To meet death unafraid, to live in distress without caring, is to know destiny and accept what time brings.[38]

In other words, one should strive to live like all other creatures—those that, unlike humans, are unburdened with self-consciousness—which is to say that humans ought to live perfectly naturally. This is the just the sort of advice one would expect from a Taoist text. The advice is presented through the image of the cyborg, however, and this may be puzzling at first. After all, Haraway's point about the cyborg is that the natural state of human beings now is inaccessible, due to the proliferation of, and dependence upon, technology. This seems quite opposed to the usual Taoist concern to recover naturalness for human beings.[39]

Rhetorically, however, the *Liezi* is drawing a distinction between Confucian and Mohist models of humanhood—which emphasize knowledge and agency as both markers of uniquely human identity and instruments of uniquely human freedom—and its own model, which highlights the generic position of human beings embedded within a web of deterministic creaturehood. In this sense, it is those who artificially set humans apart from other creatures who impose a posthuman identity on them. To reorient its audience's self-consciousness as human beings, the *Liezi* must first disorient it by inverting its customary Confucian or Mohist categories of humanity, which (from a Taoist perspective) really signify posthumanity.

Thus, discourse about human beings in the *Liezi* might be interpreted as advancing a *normalizing* goal: eliminating false self-consciousness on the part of humans so that they might abandon thinking of themselves as somehow distinct from other creatures and resume thinking of themselves as no different from other creatures. To achieve this goal, the text adopts the image of the autonomous, unconscious cyborg as its preferred metaphor for the full realization of human self-cultivation. Rather than "mov[ing] about in random jerks or scuttles, or . . . withdraw[ing] into catatonia," as Peter van Inwagen argues that a non-deliberating person might, his movements are purposeful, although their purpose is unknown to him.[40] The cyborg responds directly to the inscrutable motions of Heaven, does not dwell on its supposed knowledge or agency, and passes calmly through life and death without joy or fear, attraction or aversion. From a Taoist perspective, he is not so much posthuman as he is quintessentially human; yet, from the perspective of Confucian and Mohist culture-worship, he is prehuman.

If this Taoist model of humanhood sounds suspiciously Buddhist, it is probably due to the same reasons that appear to have inspired the borrowing of the *Shengjing*'s automaton tale in chapter 5. As previously mentioned, the *Liezi* is a record of Taoist engagement with competing Buddhist ideas and practices in early medieval China. The impassive quality of the Buddha, identified with *śūnyatā* (emptiness or nonduality) by Mahayanists, is matched by the stoic demeanor of the *Liezi*'s cyborg.[41] It echoes the teaching attributed to Confucius in chapter 4, who urges the reader to identify himself with *wu* 無 (nonbeing or nonduality):

> 無樂無知，是真樂真知.
> Rejoicing in nothing and knowing nothing are the true rejoicing and the true knowledge.[42]

Indeed, the cyborg sounds like nothing so much as a Buddhist *arhat*, as described by the *Nipata Sutta*:

> Free everywhere, at odds with none,
> And well content with this and that;
> Enduring dangers undismayed . . .
> . . . Rid of passion, error, hate,
> The fetters having snapped in twain,
> Fearless whenas life ebbs away,
> . . . lonely as rhinoceros.[43]

The great difference between *Liezi*'s cyborg and his presumed Buddhist rival is that the spiritual goal that each embodies—nondeliberative, nondiscursive tranquility—is here attained without recourse to the complex and forbiddingly foreign philosophical toolkit employed by the Buddhists. No theory of *karma* or twelve-fold chain of codependent origination is needed. Instead, one finds liberation in freedom from deliberation; one gains knowledge by knowing one's fate. Far from being alienated from the realm of nature, the cyborg in fact returns to the normal, natural creaturehood of "dumb animals who are absolutely without anxiety."[44]

Only by imagining oneself in posthuman (or prehuman, depending on one's perspective) terms can one strip away the false identity imposed by culture and resume one's ordinary life.

The Self as Machine

> I can never decide whether this is a tragic or comic vision: the deterministic world unfolds over the eons, eventually producing creatures who gradually grow in rationality and curiosity to the fatal point where they can be caused, inexorably, thanks to their very rationality, to see the futility of their frantic, scheming ways. And so they pass, in a final self-annihilating spasm of ratiocination, into complete stolidity. Perhaps that's what happened to trees! Perhaps in the olden days trees scampered about, preoccupied with their projects, until the terrible day when they saw the light and had to take root and "vegetate"![45]

The Western philosopher makes a joke, but the compiler(s) of the *Liezi* probably would find nothing laughable about the rather Taoist notion of trees retreating from conscious deliberation to unconscious wholeness. The double image of humanhood that emerges from the text—the mechanical as human (automaton), the human as mechanical (cyborg)—paradoxically functions to disable mechanical patterns of thought among its readers. Indeed, Taoist texts such as the *Zhuangzi* and the *Huainanzi* 淮南子 celebrate what Paul Rakita Goldin has called "a thoroughgoing materialism" according to which human beings may, like any other creatures, be made to do anything if their *qi* 氣 (vital substance or force) is stimulated appropriately.[46] Whether visualizing oneself as an automaton (the lifelike but mechanized workings of which are open for display and examination) or as a cyborg (devoid of self-consciousness and its attendant curses), one may use these images to attain the basic goals of early medieval Taoist practice:

> the recovery of oneself as one had been spontaneously in the Tao . . . .The pursuit of primordial purity and a reorganization of life away from desires and emotions and toward the simplicity of the Tao.[47]

In chapter 4, when Confucius urges his followers to "rejoice in nothing, know nothing" (*wule wuzhi* 無樂無知), his disciple

Zigong子貢 responds by "losing himself in vast thusness" (*mangran zishi* 茫然自失) and "meditating deeply for seven days" (*yinsi qiri* 淫思七日). On what did Zigong meditate? The *Liezi* may contain tools for meditation, even though it does not include instructions in their use. The image of the automaton created by Master Yan might serve as a mandala (diagram used as an aid in contemplation) for the practitioner. Meditation on the patterns of causality in physical function and mental deliberation embodied in the disemboweled automaton could trigger the disabling of false processes of consciousness in the devotee, thereby returning his awareness to normal creaturely function, attuned to the Way. The exposure of King Mu's illusion—that he is in control of the automaton, of his subjects, and perhaps of himself—may furnish the conceptual wherewithal to dismantle the reader's own illusion of agency.

Similarly, the mental exercise of imagining oneself as a cyborg, as in chapter 6, might well have the normalizing effect of eliminating deliberative patterns of thought. The early medieval Taoist commentator Guo Xiang 郭象 (d. 312 CE) visualizes his sage in precisely these terms: "He has no deliberate mind of his own . . . He can do so because he acts by taking no [unnatural] action."[48] One thinks of another Confucian disciple, Yan Hui 顏回 and his adventures in meditation as described in the *Zhuangzi*. In the sixth chapter ("Great and Venerable Teacher," *Dazongshi* 大宗師), Yan Hui first startles, then awes Confucius by claiming:

> 回坐忘矣。。。黜聰明，離形去知，同於大通.
> I can sit down and forget everything! . . . I . . . drive out perception and intellect, do away with understanding, and make myself identical with the Great Thoroughfare.[49]

If this sounds unappealing, it probably is because, as Daniel C. Dennett points out,

> We want to be held responsible . . . .What we want when we want free will is the power to decide our courses of action, and to decide them wisely, in the light of our expectations and desires. We want to be in control of ourselves, and not under the control of others. We want to be agents, capable of initiating, and taking responsibility for, projects and deeds.[50]

Nonetheless, the *Liezi* insists that what may seem like the blessings of free will, responsibility, and self-control are actually neither desirable nor real. Self-conscious and clinging to a fictive self-image, one becomes what Confucians and Mohists call "human"; becoming "human," one is alienated from one's true nature. Unconscious and machine-like, one becomes a cyborg; becoming a cyborg, one returns to one's true nature.

In the *Liezi*, Taoism not only responds to its familiar Confucian and Mohist adversaries, but also articulates an answer to the new challenge of Buddhism in early medieval China. In many ways, the Taoists and the Buddhists of this period are asking identical questions:

> Q. What is a human being?
> A. A finite collection of parts, working in concert and under the direction of the universe, that often experiences suffering.
>
> Q. Why do human beings suffer?
> A. Because they engage in mental deliberation about their capacity to influence outcomes through knowledge and action, due to their false self-understanding.
>
> Q. How can suffering be eliminated?
> A. By abandoning discursive thought, accepting one's limited causal power, and identifying oneself with the whole of the universe.

Yet the Taoist answers to these common questions really are not identical to those offered by the Buddhists. Long on epistemology and skepticism but short on logic and psychology, the early medieval Taoist tradition sidesteps questions that absorb its Buddhist counterpart—such as karmic retribution, absolute and relative truth, and codependent causality—and cuts directly to the chase. Quit making trouble for yourselves by imagining yourself as something you are not, it preaches. Let go of the illusion of discursive consciousness and surrender to the embrace of blind belonging to the Way. What better way to free prisoners of artificiality than to shock them by reaching within them and exposing the raw circuitry of discursive thought that powers the process of their suffering?

Notes

I thank Jeff Dippmann and Ronnie Littlejohn for soliciting this contribution to their edited volume, as well as Erica Brindley, E. Bruce Brooks, Eric Henry, Gary C. Johnson, Joseph Murphy, Eric Pearson, Harry Rothschild, Jörg Schumacher, and others who responded to earlier versions of this essay at the 2004 Southeastern Early China Roundtable, the 2005 Southeastern Conference of the Association of Asian Studies Annual Meeting, the 2005 Southeastern Commission for the Study of Religion Annual Meeting, and the 2005 ASIANetwork/Asian Studies Development Program Conference.

1. Human detective Del Spooner to robot Sonny in *I, Robot* (dir. Alex Proyas, 20th Century Fox, 2004).
2. For a selective overview of "natural" themes in early Taoist texts, see Sarah Allan, *The Way of Water and Sprouts of Virtue* (Albany: State University of New York Press, 1997), 136–46.
3. On the importance of *ziran* as a theme in early Taoism, see Liu Xiaogan, "Naturalness (*tzu-jan*), the Core Value in Taoism: Its Ancient Meaning and Its Significance Today," in *Lao-tzu and the Tao-te-ching*, ed. Livia Kohn and Michael LaFargue (Albany: State University of New York Press, 1998), 211–28.
4. On the date of the *Liezi*, see T. H. Barrett, "*Lieh tzu*列子," in *Early Chinese Texts*, ed. Michael Loewe (Berkeley: Society for the Study of Early China and the Institute of East Asian Studies, 1993), 299–301; A. C. Graham, "The Date and Composition of Lieh-Tzŭ 列子," in *Studies in Chinese Philosophy and Philosophical Literature* (Albany: State University of New York Press, 1990), 216–82; Julian F. Pas, "*Lieh-tzu/Liezi*: The Text," in *Historical Dictionary of Taoism* (Lanham, MD, and London: The Scarecrow Press, 1998), 203–204; and Russell Kirkland, *Taoism: The Enduring Tradition* (New York: Routledge, 2004), 177–80.
5. A. C. Graham, *The Book of Lieh-tzŭ: A Classic of Tao* (New York: Columbia University Press, 1990), 110–11. Throughout this essay, translations of extended passages from the text are taken from this source.
6. Ibid.
7. Livia Kohn, *Early Chinese Mysticism: Philosophy and Soteriology in the Taoist Tradition* (Princeton: Princeton University Press, 1992), 92.
8. *Strange Writing: Anomaly Accounts in Early Medieval China* (Albany: State University of New York Press, 1996), 309.
9. Herbert A. Giles, *A Chinese Biographical Dictionary* (Taipei: Ch'eng Wen Publishing Company, 1971), *sub* "1559: Mu Wang 穆王," 594–95.
10. Kohn, 93.
11. See Campany, passim.
12. See Giles, *sub* "1424: Lu Pan 魯班," 548, and Jörg Schumacher, *Über den Begriff des Nützlichen bei Mengzi* (Bern and New York: Peter Lang, 1993), 266.
13. See Eric Henry, "Chu-ko Liang in the Eyes of His Contemporaries," *Harvard Journal of Asiatic Studies* 52, no. 2 (December 1992): 602–603, 610.
14. See Antonino Forte, Mingtang and Buddhist Utopias in the History of the Astronomical Clock: The Tower, Statue, and Armillary Sphere

Constructed by Empress Wu (Rome: Istituto Italiano per il medio de extreme oriente, 1988), 47–48, 259.

15. See Alexandra David-Neel and Lama Yongden, trans., *The Superhuman Life of Gesar of Ling* (Boulder: Prajñ Press, 1981), 170–73; and Robin Kornman, "Gesar of Ling," in *Religions of Tibet in Practice*, ed. Donald S. Lopez Jr. (Princeton: Princeton University Press, 1997), 39–40 and passim.
16 See Édouard Chavannes, *Cinq cents contes et apologues extraits du Tripiṭaka chinois* (Paris: Librairie d'Amérique et d'Orient, 1962), 3:170–72.
17. Paul Metzner, *Crescendo of the Virtuoso: Spectacle, Skill, and Self-Promotion in Paris During the Age of Revolution* (Berkeley: University of California Press, 1998), 160.
18. "Theory Robots," *Canadian Literature* 178 (Autumn 2003): 152.
19. Chung-ying Cheng, "Philosophy of Knowledge," in *Encyclopedia of Chinese Philosophy*, ed. Antonio S. Cua (New York and London: Routledge, 2003), 560. It must be acknowledged that the story of Zhuangzi's skull dream as recounted in the eighteenth chapter of the *Zhuangzi*, entitled *Zhile* 至樂 ("Perfect Happiness"), raises the epistemological question of whether mental formations (e.g., dreams) represent nonmental formations (e.g., waking life), but as Paul Rakita Goldin points out, the *Zhuangzi* does not offer any answer to this question. See Goldin's "A Mind-Body Problem in the *Zhuangzi*?" in *Hiding the World in the World: Uneven Discourses on the* Zhuangzi, ed. Scott Cook (Albany: State University of New York Press, 2003), 226–47.
20. Graham, *The Book of Lieh-tzŭ*, 59–60; Kohn, 92–93.
21. Campany, 125–26.
22. It is difficult to know what the *Liezi*—or the *Zhuangzi*, which also uses the phrase—means by *zao (hua) zhe* 造(化)者 ("the Creator").
23. On Confucian anthropocentrism, see Tu Wei-ming, "The Value of the Human in Classical Confucian Thought," in his *Confucian Thought: Selfhood as Creative Transformation* (Albany: State University of New York Press, 1985), 67–80; on Mohist anthropocentrism, see Benjamin I. Schwartz, *The World of Thought in Ancient China* (Cambridge, MA, and London: The Belknap Press of Harvard University Press, 1985), 141–42.
24. Graham, *The Book of Lieh-tzŭ*, 130.
25. Chavannes, 172.
26. Chapter 2 of the *Zhuangzi* is entitled "Discussion on Making All Things Equal" (*qiwu lun* 齊物論).
27. T. H. Barrett is of the opinion that the whole of the *Liezi* is characterized by a skeptical attitude regarding the kinds of religious claims being made by Taoist sectarian movements in the early medieval period. See Barrett, "Liezi (Lieh Tzu)," in *Encyclopedia of Chinese Philosophy*, ed. Antonio S. Cua, 399 (New York and London: Routledge, 2003).
28. R. W. Sharples, *Stoics, Epicureans, and Sceptics* (London and New York: Routledge, 1996), 57.
29. Michael J. Puett, *To Become a God: Cosmology, Sacrifice, and Self-Divinization in Early China* (Cambridge and London: Harvard University Asia Center, 2002), 123.

30. On Yang Zhu, see Vincent Shen, "Yang Zhu (Yang Chu)" in *The Encyclopedia of Chinese Philosophy*, ed. Antonia S. Cua, 840–42 (New York: Routledge, 2003).
31. Graham, *The Book of Lieh-tzŭ*, 130.
32. Donna J. Haraway, *Simians, Cyborgs, and Women: The Reinvention of Nature* (New York: Routledge, 1991), 149.
33. Chris Hables Gray, Steven Mentor, and Jennifer Figueroa-Sarriera, "Cyborgology: Constructing the Knowledge of Cybernetic Organisms," in *The Cyborg Handbook* (New York: Routledge, 1995), 3.
34. See *Mengzi* 2A6.
35. See *Mozi* chapter 16.
36. Graham, *The Book of Lieh-tzŭ*, 123.
37. Ibid., 127.
38. Ibid., 132.
39. On the early Taoist quest for naturalness as a kind of prelapsarian state, see N. J. Girardot, *Myth and Meaning in Early Taoism: The Theme of Chaos (hun-tun)* (Berkeley and Los Angeles: University of California Press, 1983), 47–76.
40. *An Essay on Free Will* (Oxford: Clarendon Press, 1983), 157.
41. See Kenneth Ch'en, *Buddhism in China: A Historical Survey* (Princeton: Princeton University Press, 1964), 61–65.
42. Graham, *The Book of Lieh-tzŭ*, 76.
43. As translated by E. M. Hare in *Buddhist Scriptures*, ed. Edward Conze (London: Penguin Books, 1959), 79, 82.
44. Søren Kierkegaard, quoted in Daniel C. Dennett, *Elbow Room: The Varieties of Free Will Worth Wanting* (Cambridge: MIT Press, 1984), 101.
45. Dennett, 104.
46. See Paul Rakita Goldin, "A Mind-Body Problem in the *Zhuangzi?*" in *Hiding the World Within the World: Uneven Discourses on the* Zhuangzi, ed. Scott Cook, 234 (Albany: State University of New York Press, 2003).
47. Kohn, 107.
48. As translated by Wing-tsit Chan in his *A Source Book in Chinese Philosophy* (Princeton: Princeton University Press, 1963), 328.
49. As translated by Burton Watson in *The Complete Works of Chuang Tzu* (New York: Columbia University Press, 1968), 90.
50. Dennett, 153, 169.

列子

Dancing with Yinyang

The Art of Emergence

Robin R. Wang

> And we should consider everyday lost on which we have not danced at least once.
>
> And we should call every truth false which was not accompanied by at least one laugh
>
> —Friedrich Nietzsche (1844–1900)

In *Liezi,* an unfolding story allows us to dance with a mystic force of the universe and improvise a justifiable model for thinking. Jiliang was sick but he refused to have any medical treatment.[1] After seven days his situation became serious. His sons stood in a circle and begged him in tears to seek medical attention. In order to teach his sons a lesson about life he agreed to call in three doctors, Qiao, Yu, and Lu, in order to take his pulse and make a diagnosis. Qiao explained that Jiliang's cold and hot temperatures, the invisible and visible forces in his body, were all out of order. So the illness was the result of improper diet, sexual indulgence, and stressful things in his life. It could be cured. Jiliang responded, "This is a *zhongyi* 眾醫 (common doctor), get rid of him now." Next, Yu offered his diagnosis and interpretation: "The current condition started even in your mother's womb. Your mother suffered a deficiency of embryonic *qi* and an excess of breast milk. This illness was not a matter of one day or one night. It has gradually been developing." Jilang responded, "This is a *liangyi* 良醫 (good doctor), serve him a dinner." Lastly, Lu offered his diagnosis and point of view: "The illness is neither from heaven, nor from a human or ghost. Your life was generated and endowed with a form 稟身授形 (*bing shen shou xing*). However it also came with a governor 制者 (*zhizhe*). You should know it. What can all medicine do for you?" Jilang responded: "This is a *shenyi* 神醫 (divine doctor), give him a great gift."

How can we make sense of this metaphorical story? Why is doctor Lu a *shenyi* (divine doctor)? The first *zhongyi's* diagnosis is an accurate description of common human life: dietary indiscretion and life style caused a possible syndrome X. The second *liangyi*'s diagnosis sees the interdependencies in human life. It examines life in a genetic context. In fact, even today, we are told that some distress may be the result of a DNA defect in the human genome. The *shenyi*'s diagnosis points to a "governor" of human life. In other words, Lu means that there is a *shen* 神 (spirit, force, power), a ruling and managing entity in one's life. If one can cultivate this *shen* the illness will be cured without any medications. A commentary claims that "the stupid ones will be perplexed when they hear it but the intelligent ones will be enlightened when they learn it."[2] The cultivation of this *shen* within the human body through persistent efforts and practices later canonized in the Daoist tradition, eventually led to the formation of *neidan* 內丹 (inner alchemy).

What is this *shen* then? The *Yijing (The Book of Changes)* supplies one of many interpretations: "The unpredictability of *yin* and *yang* is called *shen*." In the *Classic of the Yellow Emperor*, "Yao asked Shun: 'In Under-heaven what is most valuable?' Shun replied: 'Life is most valuable.' Yao said: 'How can life be cultivated?' Shun said: 'Investigate *yin* and *yang*'" (*Shiwen*). This chapter will start with the assumption that *yinyang* is the very force of the universe and human life,[3] then proceed to formulate the complexity and diversity of *yinyang* interplay as it is manifested in the teachings of the *Liezi*. Based on this evidence this chapter will argue for the necessity to use a trinary thinking model to grasp Chinese philosophy.

Yinyang as the Emergent Structure in *Liezi*

Like many other Chinese philosophical concepts, the influences of *yinyang* are easy to observe but its conceptual meanings are hard to define. *Yinyang* has been treated as either a simplistic explanation of opposites (Bodde) or a unique example of correlative thinking (Graham). A careful reading of some original texts calls for moving beyond these interpretations. Let's take *Liezi* as a platform to craft a finer architecture upon which to exhibit the interplay of *yinyang* as a sort of dance. Three basic movements can be framed as embodiments of the art of emergence through the analogy of dance.

The Behavior of *Qi*

Liezi offers a detailed account of the cosmos based on the movement of *qi* and the results of this movement:

> Ancient sages govern the heaven and earth through *yinyang*. If the shapes are generated from the shapeless then where do heaven and earth come from? Here is the answer. There was *taiyi*[4] 太易 (primal simplicity); there was *taichu* 太初 (primal commencement); there was *taishi* 太始 (primal beginning); there was *taisu* 太素 (primal materials). At the primal simplicity there is no *qi*. The primal commencement is the initiation of *qi*. The primal beginning is the instigation of shapes. The primal material is the formation of substance. *Qi*, shape, and substance are all completed but they have not yet separated. This is called *hunlun*[5] 渾淪 (undifferentiated or singularity). *Hunlun* refers to the myriad things confounded but not yet separated.[6]

Clearly, the cosmos is progressing through the four stages of *yi* 易, *chu* 初, *shi* 始, and *su* 素. At the beginning *yi* stage, there is a void with no heaven or earth; no *yin* and *yang*; no four seasons or anything; it is vast yet simple. Then at *chu*, *qi* appears and starts to move. This movement generates shape/form and substance at *shi* and *su*. "The clear and light *qi* rose to be heaven and the muddy and heavy *qi* fell to become earth. When these two *qi* interact and attain the stage of *he*, this is a human life."[7] This claim builds on the *Daodejing*'s statement: "Everything is embodied with *yin* and embraced *yang*, through these *qi* they attain harmony (*he*)" (ch.42). These claims reveal a few important beliefs: (1) Everything such as heaven, earth and human being are all made from the same fabric, namely, *qi*; (2) The *qi* is divided into two kinds: *qi* of *yang* and *qi* of *yin*. (3) Only their interactions can generate every existing thing, including human life itself. When *yin* and *yang* dance, the changes of *qi* become manifest and visible and bring forth the whole universe. As the *Zhuangzi* claims:

> *Yin* in its highest form is freezing while *yang* in its highest form is boiling. The chilliness comes from heaven while the warmness from

the earth. The interaction of these two establishes the *he* (harmony) so it gives birth to things. Perhaps this is the law of everything yet there is no form being seen.[8]

Liezi elaborates this vision of the cosmos by identifying the nature of this movement with a property of *zi* 自 (self). The universe is "self-generating 自生 *sheng*, self-transforming 自化 *hua*, self-forming 自形 *xing*, self-coloring 自色 *se*, self-intelligible 自智 *zhi*, self-strengthening 自力 *li*, self-resolving 自消 *xiao*, self-resting 自息 *xi*."[9] These eight states of existence: 生 *sheng*, 化 *hua*, 形 *xing*, 色 *se*, 智 *zhi*, 力 *li*, 消 *xiao*, 息 *xi* are all self-operating. This understanding raises some critical differences from the view of motion typically presupposed in a Western context.

Motion has always been an important issue. Aristotle offers an account of different motions. Galileo Galilei (1564–1642) was driven by the question of what is the underlying nature of motion and this quest led him to discover how objects fall. His observations eventually led to the Newtonian mechanistic laws of nature. However, motion on the earth in many Europeans' minds tends to move in a straight line. With this assumption the linear causality of things is used to explain the universe. By contrast, the motions that *Liezi* observed or was interested in displayed a self-operating circular movement. In this paradigm there is no need for an external force to cause and push the motion. The dynamic *Qi* flows and penetrates in a circle and the only power needed is an internal force to sustain this movement. The function of *yinyang* can put forward an intelligible explanation for this internal force and justify a logically sufficient reason for this vision. The *yinyang* dance activates both attraction and repulsion in an inscrutable and endless sequence. This *yinyang* movement was understood as an oscillation between the *dong* 動 (motion) of *yang* and the *jing* 靜 (rest) of *yin*. Like the alternation of day and night, rest and motion exhibit a rhythm of *yinyang* that is a source of order. In the end *yinyang* is the internal guiding and shaping factor, which is embedded in nature and directs natural processes from within. It is a built-in sustaining force in the universe. The logical consequence emerging from this *yinyang* self-movement is *hua* (transformation). *Liezi* concludes: "Therefore heaven and earth contain *jing* 精 (essence)[10] and through it myriad things are transformed and generated."[11] This transformation 化 (*hua*) is an eternal constancy. The universe is in a state of "constant generation and constant transformation. There is no time not generating and there is no time not transforming. This is the alternation of *yinyang* and the four seasons."[12] Noticeably, *yinyang* interaction is a nonlinear function which contains a product of distinctive variables instead of their sum.

The Patterns of Zhi 質*(Substance)*

In *Liezi*, the important property of *qi* is identified as the harmony of quality and the proportion of quantity. It contains the patterns of *zhi* (substance), such as soft and hard; more and less; clear and turbid. These *zhi* are formed and interact due to the time, position, and place of *yinyang*. When *qi* of *yin* 陰氣 and *qi* of *yang* 陽氣 are integrated in different ways diverse results will be produced. To make a case for the impact of *yinyang* interaction, *Liezi* describes two opposite situations where the *yinyang* is absent and the consequences of each. "At the south corner of the far west . . . there is a country called Gumeng. There the *qi* of *yinyang* does not interact 交 (*jiao*) so there is no distinction between cold and heat. The light of sun and moon does not shine so there is no distinction between day and night. The people there do not eat or wear clothes but sleep all the time."[13] On the other hand, "At the North corner of the far east there is a country called Fu lo. The *qi* of soil is excessive and the light of sun and moon is superfluous. Its soil does not grow the crops and people only eat grass, roots and fruits from trees because they do not know how to cook with fire. The disposition of the people is hard and fierce. People there like to oppress the weak ones and only value victory but not righteousness. They travel all the time and seldom rest; they are always awake and never sleep."[14] These two extremes throw light on what is considered to be the best place in the universe: "the central kingdom of the four seas. It goes South and North across the yellow river and East and West over the mountain Tai, for more than ten thousand miles. The *yin* and *yang* are truly proportioned there so as to produce an alternation of cold and heat. Darkness and light are rightly divided so there is the alternation of day and night. Of its people some are wise and some are foolish. The myriad things flourish and multiply, diversifying in many kinds."[15]

What makes these three places different is the existence, ratio, and proportion of *yinyang* interaction. It is because of the emergence of *yinyang* that there are things such as day and night, sun and moon, cold and heat, motion and rest . . . and so on. These emergent structures are patterns not created by a single event or rule but instead the interactions of each part. The emergent structures are more than the sum of their parts because the emergent order will not arise if the various parts are simply coexisting; the interaction of these parts is central.

Take *Liezi*'s discussion of the human body as another example. The *qi* of full and empty, diminishment and growth are all connected with heaven and earth, corresponding with all the classes and variables of things.[16] "If one's *qi* of *yin* is too strong, one will be frightened by dreaming of walking through great water. If one's *qi* of *yang* is too strong, one will be buried by dreaming of walking through great fire."[17] Likewise, cultivating human dispositions also requires a proportion of different good things. Zixia asks Confucius about his relationship with his four disciples in terms of four different characters:

> Zixia asked Confucius: "What sort of man is Yanhui?"
> Confucius said, "For *ren* 仁 (kindness) character he is a better man than I."
> "What about Zigong?"
> "For *bian* 辯 (eloquence) character he is a better man than I."
> "What about Zilu?"
> "For *yong* 勇 (courage) character he is a better man than I."
> "What about Zizhang?"
> "For *zhuang* 莊 (dignity) character he is better man than I."
> Zixia got up from the mat and asked:
> "Why do these four serve you, then?"
> "Sit down and I'll tell you.
>
> "Yanhui is capable of being *ren* but unable to be *fan* 反 (changing). Zigong is capable of being *bian* but unable to be *na* 納 (bending). Zilu is capable of being *yong* but unable to be *qu* 屈 (cautious). Zizhang is capable of being *zhuang* but unable to be *tong* 同 (compromising). Even if I could have these four characters together I should be unwilling to exchange them for my own."[18]

The commentator explains the deficiency of each character. If one has kindness but he doesn't know how to make a change in responding to a situation, he will not be one with Dao. If one has eloquence but he doesn't know how to bend, he will lack trust and loyalty. If one has courage but he is not capable of being cautious, he will hurt the way of clemency (*shu* 恕). If one can be dignified but he cannot compromise, he will be contrary to the light of harmony (*he*). All of these problems are due to remaining in only one aspect.[19] These discussions call for a balanced character, which emerges through the cultivation of its counterpart. This is the art of *jiao* (interaction, intercourse, and exchange) and the way of heaven and earth: "Being *yin* and being *yang*, soft or hard, short or long, round or square, life or death, warm or cool, floating or sinking, sound the note of *gong* or *shang*, appearing or disappearing, black or yellow, sweet or bitter, foul or fragrant."[20] The *yinyang* interaction creates an external complexity from an internal unity. As the *Huainanzi* describes, "The sage can be *yin* and can be *yang*, can be soft and can be hard. With proper timing one decides to be still or move; one can figure out the end before the beginning stage and can distinguish new things and be able to adjust to the changes. So the sage is never stuck throughout his life time."[21]

The Waves of Gan 感 *(Influence)*

When the *yinyang* interacts it also radiates a wave-like motion in which *yinyang* exhibits the way of *ganying* 感應 (influence and response). This *ganying* radiation is first illustrated in the relationship between human being, heaven, and earth. Like *Zhuangzi*, *Liezi* portrays a special kind of *shenren* 神人 (human of spirit) capable of undertaking a journey of spirit:

> They go into water without drowning, into fire without burning; hack them, flog them, there is no wound nor pain; poke them, scratch them, there is no ache nor itch. They ride space as though walking the solid earth, sleep on the void as though on their beds; clouds and mist do not hinder their sight, thunder does not confuse their hearing, beauty and ugliness do not disturb their hearts, mountains and valleys do not trip their feet—for they make only journeys of the spirit.[22]

All these *shenren*'s abilities are not a matter of skill or technique 術(*shu*) but rather of being with *Dao*. In the physical place where *shenren* dwell, "the *yinyang* are always in tune, the sun and moon always shine, the four seasons are always regular, wind and rain are always timely . . ."[23] Is it because the harmony of heaven and earth produces the *shenren* in that place? Or is it because the *shenren*'s alignment with heaven and earth makes a wonderful universe in that place? These questions seem to have little place in *Liezi*'s account. But the fundamental conviction behind these stories perhaps is the inspiration and aspiration of uniting (becoming one) the virtues of heaven and human being, 天人合德(*tianren hede*).

Heaven, earth, and human being all share the dance of *yinyang*. Through the *yinyang* radiation the universe weaves itself into one. This radiation takes different forms: influence, transmission, and absorption. *Liezi* alleges that "Confucius said, 'The man with perfect *xin* 信 (trust, faith) can *gan*[24] (influence) things. He moves heaven and earth, *gan* the spirits and ghosts, fills in the universe with six directions. There is nothing against his way.'"[25] This *xin* (trust) is different from the Confucian *xin* as a normative virtue or standard. *Liezi* exemplifies the function of this *xin* through the story of a man playing in water. The waterfall is more than two hundred feet high, the whirlpool covers ninety miles; fish and turtles cannot swim there and crocodiles cannot live there. But a man can get in and out of this water. Confucius asks him for his *daoshu* 道術 (his art of dao). The man responds, "I enter by being loyal and trust the water 忠信 (*zhong xin*), and I come out following this loyalty and trust. This loyalty and trust lead me to throw my body to the current and I do not dare to act selfishly."[26] The art of playing in water is to trust the flow of water and follow the flow of water; this is the art of *dao*.

However this trust of flow is neither a mindless floating or mindful fighting but rather is responding 應 (*ying*) in tune with the circumstances. One of the important situations is the *shi* (time or opportunity). One can grasp the time and snatch the opportunities. "Grasping the 時 *shi* will bring things to flourish; losing the *shi* will bring them to perish."[27] Yet, "intelligence cannot know the time to move and the time to stop"[28] due to the complexity of the *yinyang* interplay. It is known by unknowingly, spontaneously following timing.

In the *Huainanzi*, there is a description of what someone who has the *dao* will be like. "With heaven as his canopy there is nothing left uncovered; with earth as his container there is nothing uncarried;

with four seasons as his horse, there is nothing that cannot be used; with *yinyang* as his charioteers there is nothing left unprepared."[29] The person with *dao* is free of worries and can ride the clouds up beyond the sky. He will transform and change and will gallop in the infinitely vast land. It is worth pointing out that here dancing with *yinyang* is imagined on the analogy of a rider on a horse. What does it take to be a good horse rider? Heaven covers, earth holds, four seasons move, and *yinyang* rides. *Liezi* continues this line of thinking and intensifies it by making an interesting connection to the art of charioteering. According to it, there is a *ganying* between what you feel and how you respond, just like one feels in one's feet yet responds with one's heart/mind. "Applying this to charioteering, you must control the bridle from the corners of the lips; decision must come from within your breast and execution from within the palm of your hand."[30] Here it might be the answer for the question why *yinyang* is compared with the rider of a horse. It has to do with the interaction between internal and external. "*Nei* 內 internally, one is centered in heart/mind; *wai* 外 externally, one is untied with the will of the horse. This way one is able to go forward and backward but treading a stretched cord and going around like a compass. One takes the road on a long journey yet one still has strength to spare."[31] This image concentrates on harmonizing the rider's internal mind with the external horse's temper. The *yinyang* operates just like riding a horse, moving with a focal point and adjusting with diversity. It does not passively respond to events, the way a stone would tumble in an earthquake, but rather makes a constructive effort to turn all circumstances to one's advantage. *Liezi* further explains,

> One receives (得*de*, gets) the bit and responds with the bridle, one receives the bridle and responds with the hand, one receives in the hand, and responds in the heart/mind. This way one sees without eyes and urges without a goad; relaxed in heart and straight in posture. Holding six bridles and placing twenty four hooves, he advances, withdraws, and swings around with perfect precision.[32]

One feels here and now, yet can respond there and then. As the Eastern Han intellectual Wang Fu (80–167) claims precisely: "The *dao* of heaven is endowment (施 *shi*); the *dao* of earth is transformation (*hua*); the *dao* of human being is action (為 *wei*). What human actions are all about is to feel and communicate the *yinyang* in order to reach the precious and unique core [of myriad things (*wanwu*)]."[33]

This sense of *ganying* conveys a different meaning than that found in Confucian teaching. In Confucian teaching this is the reciprocal radiation which extends to parents, family, friends, and state.[34] Humans' moral universe and the ruler's orderly kingdom—resonating along the celestial axis—set off good or bad vibrations both in the heaven and on earth. The seed of this thinking is planted in the *Analects*, but it is harvested in the Han thinker Dong Zhongshu and later in Zhuxi.

A Leap from Correlative to Trinary Thinking

The previous discussions of the behaviors of *qi*, the patterns of *zhi*, and the waves of *gan* in *Liezi* reveal a coherent structure emerging through *yinyang* interaction. The conduct of the *yinqi* and *yangqi* generates a transformation (*hua*); the prototype of the *yinrou* 陰柔 (softness of *yin*) and 陽剛 *yanggang* (hardness of *yang*) necessitates an intercourse (*jiao*); the ripple of *waigan* 外感 (external influence) and *neiying* 內應 (internal response) validates a responding (*ying*). Accordingly, the concepts of *hua*, *jiao*, and *ying* can be renovated to develop a deeper and broader understanding of a Chinese thinking model.

The profound and pervasive characteristic way of Chinese thinking has been defined on the model of correlative thinking. This model has been regarded as a "peculiarly Chinese phenomenon," and has dominated "the intellectual life in traditional China more than other civilizations."[35]

> Correlative thought is the most basic ingredient of Chinese cosmology. . . . Correlative thinking in general draws systematic correspondence among aspects of various orders of reality or realms of the cosmos, such as the human body, the body politic, and the heavenly bodies. It assumes that these related orders as a whole are homologous, that they correspond with one another in some basic respect, even in some cases that their identities are contained one within the other. Correlative thought thus differs from analogy, metaphor, and symbol, which seldom refer systematically to larger orders or domains.[36]

The articulation of the correlative thinking model insightfully points out the essential connections among things. It conveys a cosmological system of correspondence between macrocosm and microcosm. This makes a great contribution to any comparison between Chinese philosophy and Western philosophy, especially with Greek philosophy.

> In Greek philosophy, dialectic was understood as the criticism of beliefs in order to discern any possible contradictions. It also often referred to a conversation devoted to the discovery of such contradictions. In tone, these conversations could smack of irony or sophistry, but the fundamental presuppositions were invariably binary: the logical binary relation of contradictory propositions, and the interpersonal binary relation of opponents in the debate.[37]

Correlative thinking shows that for the Chinese the binary structure is not simply just existing in human conceptual work, but is also manifested in all aspects of the universe. There is a unity between heaven, earth, and human being. The focus for correlative thinking is connection, association, and relationship.

However, further study of ancient Chinese texts provides some evidence to make a leap from a correlative model to a trinary one. This trinary thinking model takes some inspiration from contemporary biological and physical models to envisage the following: the *yin* as one, the *yang* as two, and the *yinyang* as three, the result of emergence. It is like an inner art form: silent music, motionless dance, and invisible painting. It claims a subtle pattern or structure beneath the *yinyang* interaction. The focus of this *yinyang*/trinary model will be complexity, diversity, and transformation. It will also have the consequence of achieving the best attainable compromises among conflicting practical, moral, and political interests.

Contemporary biologists tell us of the stunning biological complexity of our world. "Molecules of all varieties join in a metabolic dance to make cells. Cells interact with cells to form organisms; organisms interact to form ecosystems, economies, societies."[38] This biosphere from cell to organism, to ecosystem, contains the self-organization through which order arises naturally and spontaneously as emergent properties. Emergence is the process of complex patterns forming from simpler rules. In the Chinese context, *yin* and *yang* are accepted as simple rules, yet from the course of their interaction emerges multifaceted, complex, and diversified new patterns. This emergence signifies a kind of change, and there are three kinds of emergent changes.

> First, there is chance occurrence, the assertion of a cosmic irregularity, an occurrence about which no law could be stated. Second, there is what we may call a "shift," a change in which one characteristic replaces another, the sort of change traditionally described as an invariable succession and when more refined described as functional relation. Thirdly there is emergence, which is a cumulative change, a change in which certain characteristics supervene upon other characteristics, these characteristics being adequate to explain the occurrence on their level.[39]

The interplay of *yinyang* may be described in this way. First, *yinyang* is a self-organizing process in which internal organization increases automatically without being guided or managed by an outside source. It makes a chance occurrence. In *Liezi*, it is the function of *zi* (self). The *yinyang* dancing of push and pull pumps out the whole universe. Second, *yinyang* interplay is a "shift," where *yin* gets *yang* in one case or *yang* gets *yin* in another case. *Yang* is *dong* (active), moving in the time; *yin* is *jing* (passive), still in the space. In one case, as *yang* fills in *yin* it will receive the form, grounded in the space, or spatialization. This will be the case of *yang* getting *yin*; in the other case, *yin* receiving *yang*, it will have the time, moving in the space, a timelization. Time-*yang* is injected into the space-*yin* or space-*yin* is injected into time-*yang*. *Yin* obtains *yang* and will have novelty and innovation; *yang* obtains *yin* and will have realization and formation. It is a wave property which moves in a wavelike spiral and sustains a steady wave of waxing and waning repeatedly. In *Liezi*, this is the intercourse of *rou* (soft) and *gang* (hard). Third, there is an emergence, a cumulative change. The *yinyang* interplay is a two-way effect and not a one-way or linear causal effect. Combinations of many simple interactions lead to emergent phenomena. Emergent behavior is experienced, for example, in our teaching. Our course, especially in each class, is largely driven by emergent behavior. We teach the same materials many, many times yet the results are different. Because the lesson is driven by emergent behavior, teaching to this particular class might be radically different from another, while the materials are exactly the same. Variations of lessons in a classroom are examples of the *yinyang* emergent play. In *Liezi*, this is the art of *ganying*, the art of riding a horse.

Evidently the *yinyang* interplay involves a scheme with certain properties: (1) there are levels of existences defined through integration; (2) order is emergent as opposed to predetermined; (3) change is constant; (4) the future is unpredictable. These propositions can be captured in the model of trinary thinking. Trinary thinking provides the explanation for apparently unpredictable phenomena in the interplay of their myriad simple components. According to this perspective, all things lack definite position, momentum, and so forth. Things are actually emergent phenomena, being described by a wave function which need not have a single position or momentum. The complex behavior or properties are not a property of any single entity, nor can they easily be predicted or deduced from lower entities. The reason why emergence occurs is the number of *yinyang* interactions. The *yinyang* is the very building block[40] of the Chinese intellectual tradition and the generator of a dynamic thinking process. As *Liezi* clams, when there is *jiao* (intercourse) of *yin* and *yang*, there is a change. Interaction between components increases the combination with the number of components, thus potentially allowing for many new and subtle things to emerge. Both the Chinese and the Greeks considered the circle as a perfect shape. "No matter how much or how little a perfect circle is rotated about its center, it maintains its original appearance: its appearance is constant. It is important to note that perfection is identified with constancy—something that is perfect cannot be improved, so it must remain constant."[41] However, for the Greeks "women, the deadlier of the species, are straight lines, and are therefore able to inflict mortal wounds, just as a thin sharp rapier can. The wisest male, in accordance with the Greek ideal of perfection is, of course, a perfect circle."[42] But for the Chinese a woman is a necessary part of this circle, taking the *yinyang* symbol as an example. Why is this so? Chinese value the *jiao* (interaction, intercourse) and place it as a necessary condition and the very foundation of any existence. This is the rhythm of human life, earth's changes, and heaven's power. The *jiao* is a state of being that has its own structure and meaning. It is also defined as configurative force 神喻 (*shen yu*) or the state of *xuanmiao* 玄妙 (recondite transcendence). It is the continual *yin* and *yang* reconfigurations that bring any potential beings into actuality.

American philosopher Charles Sanders Peirce (1839–1914) has seen the triad in all aspects of human intellectual works and realities. His discussion of thirdness might be useful to probe the *yinyang* trinary thinking model. "The Third is that which is what it is owing to things between which it mediates and which it brings into relation to each other."[43] Thirdness is a mediation between the two that also can link these two together. He calls it a trichotomic. "Trichotomic is the art of making three-fold division. Such a division depends on the conception of 1st, 2nd, 3rd. First is the beginning, that which is fresh, original, spontaneous, free. Second is that which is determined, terminated, ended, correlative, object necessitated, reacting. Third is the medium, becoming, developing, bringing about."[44] The *yinyang* is a thirdness, a dynamical variety. It intercedes between *yin* and *yang* and sustains their interactions. The recognition of this thirdness could avoid some philosophical and practical problems. According to Peirce, "A philosophy which emphasizes the idea of the One, is generally a dualist philosophy in which the conception of Second receives exaggerated attention."[45] On the other hand, the focus on One and Two binary thinking, might lead to a hierarchial relation of things. If one and two only interact then there will be a question of who's in control and who should follow whom. But bringing the conception of Thirdness will ensure that the one and two are understood as interacting without the intention to conquer or control the other. Since Thirdness is in the process of mediation, sometimes one or the other dominates, but Thirdness will make sure this domination is never overdone and will leave room for other integration and cooperation. Identifying Thirdness will allow for a more effective way to grasp the reality. In nature, where things always work their own way out, there is a thirdness in position without noticing.

Correlative thinking and trinary thinking are both processes that acknowledge change and dynamism. However, correlation is the beginning and the trinary is the completion that brings thinking to its fullness. It seeks to comprehend the complexity and diversity of reality with an emphasis on transformation. If correlative thinking proceeds without discernment of its trinary context, it risks falling into abstract polarizations that may diminish one's capacity for the discernment of reality. All the myriad things are in fact trinaries, which can be recognized by decoding their correlative structures and reconstructing the trinary patterns of their emergence.

Let's end by returning to the original example. Within the correlative thinking model, the center of attention will be how Jiliang connected with his environment and his past history. Clearly these will be the diagnosis of *zhongyi* (how Jiliang related with his environment) and *liangyi* (what is Jiliang's past history). Jiliang is not satisfied with these explanations and wants something more than the correlative thinking model can offer. The *shenyi* hunts for the *zhizhe* (a governor) of human body. This governor is an emergence of interplay of different forces in human body. The trinary thinking will be able to capture it. This is perhaps the meaning of Jiliang's experiments with those doctors and a lesson for his sons.

Notes

1. *Liezi jishi* 列子集釋 (Beijing: *Zhonghua Shuju* Press, 1979), 204. The following translations are my own unless otherwise indicated. I have also included the page number from Graham's translation.
2. Ibid., 205.
3. I am currently working on a historical and conceptual analysis of this *yinyang*. But at present, we will just assume the *yinyang* are the basic properties of the universe's structure and function.
4. This word *yi* can also refer to change, as *Yijing*, the *Book of Change*.
5. *Hunlun* is a very special word which first appeared in *Zhuangzi*. In contemporary usage it is used to translate terms such as "black hole" in physics.
6. *Liezi jishi*, 5–6; my translation.
7. *Liezi*, 8.
8. *Zhuangzi*, 5, 42; my translation.
9. *Liezi jishi*, 5; my translation.
10. *Jing* also refers to male sperm and female menstrual blood. So this word indicates the primal force of everything in the universe.
11. *Liezi jishi*, 8.
12. Ibid., 2; Graham trans., 18.
13. Ibid. 104; Graham trans., 67.
14. Ibid., 105; Graham trans., 68.
15. Ibid., 104–105; Graham trans., 67.
16. Ibid., 103; Graham trans., 66.
17. Ibid., 102; Graham trans., 66.
18. Ibid., 122–23; Graham trans., 78.
19. Ibid., 122–23.
20. Ibid., 10; Graham trans., 20.
21. *Huainanzi*, 505; my translation.
22. Graham trans., 34.
23. *Liezi jishi*, 43; Graham trans., 35.
24. Graham translates this as "other things react to him," 41. *Gan* is a more complex word. It refers to move or impact others and also can be transmitted or passed on.
25. *Liezi jishi*, 57; Graham trans., 41.
26. Ibid., 248.
27. Ibid., 246.
28. Ibid., 211; Graham trans., 131.

29. *Huananzi*, ch. 1, 6; my translation.
30. *Liezi*, Graham trans., 114.
31. *Liezi jishi*, 183; Graham, trans., 114.
32. Ibid.
33. This is quoted from Qianfu Lu in *Classical Chinese Dictionary* (Beijing: Xinghua Press, 2000), 448.
34. For detailed discussion see Martin Schonfeld's essay in *Journal of Chinese Philosophy*.
35. John B. Henderson, *The Development and Decline of Chinese Cosmology* (New York: Columbia University Press, 1984), 54.
36. Ibid., 1.
37. Stephen N. Dunning, *Dialectical Readings: Three Types of Interpretation* (University Park: The Pennsylvania State University Press, 1997), 11.
38. Stuart Kauffman, *At Home in the Universe: The Search for Laws of Self-Organization and Complexity* (New York: Oxford University Press, 1995), 1.
39. Stephen C. Pepper, *Journal of Philosophy* 23 (1926): 241–45.
40. According to John H. Holland, "Building blocks are the pervasive, critical foundation of an ability to act with insight in a complex world. Human perception, for example consists primarily in combining well-known, simple components to describe familiar phenomena. . . . A little thought shows that we approach all objects, familiar and unfamiliar, via combinations of familiar building blocks." John H. Holland, "Complex Adaptive System and Spontaneous Emergence," in *Complexity and Industrial Clusters*, ed. Alberto, Quadrio Curzio, and Marco Fortis (Heidelberg: Physica-Verlag 2002), 26.
41. *Seven Ideas that Shook the Universe*, 17.
42. Ibid., 18.
43. "A Guess at the Riddle," in *The Essential Peirce, Selected Philosophical Writings*, Volume 1 (1867–1893) (Indianapolis: Indiana University Press, 1998), 248.
44. "Trichotomic" in ibid., 281.
45. "The Architecture of Theories" in ibid., 297.

列子

How To Fish Like a Daoist

Erin M. Cline

> When I overlook the river holding my rod, there are no distracting thoughts in my mind. I contemplate nothing but the fish. When I cast the line and sink the hook, my hand does not pull too hard nor give too easily, so that nothing can disturb it. When the fish see the bait on my hook, it is like sinking dust or gathered foam, and they swallow it without suspecting.[1]

Introduction

In chapter 5 of the *Liezi*, we meet the fisherman Zhan He, who offers the inquiring King of Chu an account of how to fish like a Daoist.[2] Zhan He's description shows how bringing himself into accord with the Way has resulted in the ability to act without self-conscious reflection or striving. He acts effortlessly and spontaneously. None of this is surprising for a Daoist parable. However, the passage closes with a claim indicating that there is more to this Daoist fishing lesson than first meets the eye. Zhan He says to the king, "This is how I am able to use weak things to control strong ones, light things to bring in heavy ones. If Your Majesty is really able to rule his state in the same way, he can turn the Empire within the span of his hand; what can give you trouble?"[3] In this chapter, I compare the account of *wuwei* ("effortless action") found in the Zhan He passage with two other classical Daoist accounts of the concept: the parable of the butcher in the *Zhuangzi*, and the discussion of *wuwei* and rulership in the *Daodejing*. In the first part of the chapter I describe the basic concept of *wuwei* and examine the way it is illustrated in the parable of Zhan He. In the second section I discuss a number of similarities between the stories of Zhan He and the butcher. In the third part of the chapter I argue that despite these similarities the understanding of *wuwei* presented in the Zhan He passage is closer to the view represented by the *Daodejing*, due to the emphasis on the relationship between *wuwei* and rulership. This is especially surprising considering the close association of the text of the *Liezi* with the *Zhuangzi*, and it draws attention to the fact that the *Liezi* is worthy of careful and sustained study. On this note, I conclude by discussing how a comparative reading of the Zhan He and the butcher parables can be used to highlight the diversity that exists in classical Daoist understandings of *wuwei*.

Wuwei in the *Liezi*

In his introduction to the *Liezi*, A.C. Graham points out that from a Daoist perspective, humans can only live rightly by bringing themselves into accord with the Way. Graham writes, "One characteristic of this accord with the Way is 'spontaneity' (*ziran*, literally 'being so of itself'). . . . Heaven and earth operate without thought or purpose, through processes which are *ziran*, 'so of themselves'. Man follows the same course."[4] The Way moves spontaneously, bringing about various states of affairs in the world, and ethical claims about the human ability to accord with the Way presuppose a particular metaphysical understanding of the world.[5] Although the Way provides our model for how to act, the *Daodejing* cautions that those who actively try to take hold of the Way are not likely to be successful. The key to returning to the Way is found in *wuwei* ("effortless action"): "Those who use it ruin it. Those who grab hold of it lose it. This is why sages practice *wuwei* and so do not ruin; They do not lay hold and so do not lose."[6]

Returning to the Way involves a rigorous process of self-cultivation that is characterized by paring away human distinctions and knowledge. Graham writes that the Daoist delight in the extraordinary is "a recovery of numinous wonder, a reversion to a primitive and child-like vision. Taoism cultivates naivety as it cultivates spontaneity."[7] If one's actions are spontaneous, one must "reflect things like a mirror, respond to them like an echo, without intermediate thought, perfectly concentrated and perfectly relaxed, like the angler or the charioteer whose hand reacts immediately to the give and pull of the line or reins."[8] *Wuwei* is the kind of action that results when humans pare away the distinctions ingrained in them by socialization and return to the spontaneity of the Way. In his recent study of *wuwei* in early China, Edward Slingerland writes that although *wuwei* literally means "in the absence of/without doing exertion," it describes "a state of personal harmony in which actions flow freely and instantly from one's spontaneous inclinations—without the need for extended deliberation or inner struggle—and yet nonetheless accord perfectly with the dictates of the situation at hand."[9]

The *Liezi*'s description of Zhan He's fishing techniques illustrates this dimension of the concept, and its relationship to *ziran* ("spontaneity"). *Wuwei* characterizes Zhan He's actions, but *ziran* characterizes the state of affairs his actions achieve. In his discussion of *wuwei* and *ziran*, Philip J. Ivanhoe writes, "The former offers an ideal for actions according to which what one does simply flows out of one without self-conscious reflection, striving, or effort. The latter describes the ideal for states of affairs according to which each thing or event maintains its natural, unadulterated condition."[10] Zhan He's actions help the world around him to return to its natural, spontaneous state of harmony with the Way. As the *Daodejing* instructs us: "Act, but through nonaction. Be active, but have no activities."[11]

The parable opens by describing how Zhan He constructs his fishing rod and baits his line: "Zhan He made a fishing line from a single thread of silk out of the cocoon, a hook from a beard of wheat, a rod from one of the pygmy bamboos of Chu, and baited it with a split grain of rice."[12] Zhan He's tackle and technique are emblematic of the Daoist belief in according with nature. He resourcefully draws on the natural environment to meet his needs. He uses local resources—pygmy bamboos from Chu—and uses them sparingly, taking only a single thread of silk for his line and a split grain of rice for his bait. Zhan He proceeds methodically, clearly having considered how to best use his materials and having confidence that they will be sufficient to meet his needs.

Next, the parable describes the *results* of his efforts: "He hooked a fish big enough to fill a cart, in the middle of a swift current in waters seven hundred feet deep. The line did not snap, the hook did not straighten out, the rod did not bend, because he let out and drew in the line following the pull and give of the water."[13] According to the story, Zhan He's goal of hooking a fish is not only achieved, but in good measure: he does not just hook an ordinary fish, but a fish "big enough to fill a cart." Further, he hooks the fish under especially difficult circumstances—in a swift current and deep water.

The descriptions of the circumstances that bring about this successful result are especially significant: there is no tension on Zhan He's line, hook, or rod. They show no signs of struggle. This is attributed to the fact that he lets out and draws in his line "following the pull and give of the water." Zhan He works *with* the natural circumstances and rhythms of nature, instead of working against them. While some fishermen see themselves as "fighting" a fish until they finally "land" it, Zhan He applies the criterion of suppleness and flexibility to his handling of the rod and line. This further demonstrates his understanding of the Way and its lack of constancy. By modeling himself, his rod, and his line on the flexibility of the *Dao*, Zhan He exhibits his understanding of the *Dao*. It "undulates and moves like the currents of a river; it wiggles out of your hands like the elusive fish."[14]

A number of particular aspects of the fishing parable give us a sense of the way the authors of the *Liezi* viewed the relationship between humans and their natural environment. The fishing rod, line, and hook, composed of natural materials, are an extension of nature. The fish even swallow the hook as though it were dust or foam in the water. Zhan He's fishing apparatus conforms to the natural order, rather than imposing itself upon the world. Zhan He, in the way he holds and controls the rod and line, further conforms to the natural order. His rod, line, and hook are an extension of nature on the one hand, but Zhan He is a further extension of nature.

This feature of the parable points to a larger cosmological claim, seen in several places in the *Liezi*. Various aspects of nature are considered a part of the same whole, as the following passage reflects: "Guo says, 'I steal birds and animals from the land, fish and turtles from water. . . . Yet I suffer no retribution for robbing heaven.' Master Dong-guo later explains, 'In reality the myriad things of heaven and earth are not separate from each other; and to claim anything as one's own is always wrong-headed. . . . For the man who understands the power of heaven and earth, what is stealing and what is not stealing?' "[15] In these passages we find a distinct approach to the relationship between humans and the natural environment. There are no admonitions against hunting or fishing. Rather, the text focuses on two things: the skill with which one acts—in Zhan He's case, the skill with which he fishes—and the cosmological claim that all creatures are a part of the same whole.

The latter claim implies that all things have value qua being part of the Way. To harm other creatures in certain ways, then—such as ways that destroy ecosystems—would violate the Way.

One way of highlighting some features of the Daoist approach is to contrast the Zhan He passage with *Analects* 7.27: "The Master would fish with a line, but not with a net. He would shoot with a corded line, but would not aim at roosting birds."[16] Both the He Yan and Zhu Xi commentaries on the *Analects* note that fishing with a net meant blocking off a stream, so that one would catch all of the fish that came through, as opposed to catching one fish at a time.[17] According to Zhu Xi, we can conclude from this that Kongzi was *Ren* (humane, benevolent), because "if he treated creatures this way, you can understand how he treated people." There are a number of things to note here. First, the traditional way of doing things—fishing with a line, in this case—is more sparing and more benevolent. This reflects the Confucian view that the traditional way of doing things has something ethically substantial to offer. Practices such as fishing are seen as opportunities for self-cultivation, and they provide unique opportunities to exercise and cultivate certain virtues of character.[18]

Perhaps more importantly, the way individuals conduct themselves when fishing or hunting expresses their attitude toward other things in the world. Zhu Xi interprets this passage as showing that Kongzi behaved in an exemplary manner toward animals, and he maintains that how one treats animals is related to how one treats people. Zhu Xi's view is traceable in part to *Mengzi* 1A7 and the parable concerning King Xuan's compassion for an ox being led to slaughter. Mengzi says to the king, "In the present case your kindness is sufficient to reach birds and beasts, but the benefits do not reach the commoners."[19] According to Mengzi and Zhu Xi, kindness to humans comes more naturally to a person than kindness to animals. Thus, if one is kind to animals, it is a good indicator that they are kind to people. On this view, the Master's behavior when fishing and hunting tells us something about his moral character.

In *Analects* 7.27, we see clearly the Confucian emphasis on practices that both cultivate and express important virtues. The Daoists would agree with some aspects of the Confucian view—like the idea that fishing and hunting are practices that can help one to become a better person—but there are some pervasive differences in the way they view this process. While the Confucian view sees fishing and hunting according to traditional standards as cultivating and expressing certain virtues, Daoists such as Zhan He see fishing and hunting as practices that provide us with the opportunity to shed the artificial postures and patterns society has taught us. Whereas Confucians argue that the world itself cannot be properly ordered until sages put it in order, Daoists argue that the efforts of people like the Confucians is what brings disorder into the world in the first place. From a Daoist standpoint, a solitary fishing trip allows one to tune into the natural patterns of nature, rather than the presumptuous voices of society, and model oneself on those patterns.

Here, the difference between the Confucian and Daoist perspectives is traceable in part to their very different understandings of the Way.[20] As Graham puts it, for the Daoists human beings occupy "the humble position of the tiny figures in Song landscape paintings, and [live] rightly by bringing [themselves] into accord with an inhuman Way which does not favor [their] ambitions, tastes and moral principles."[21] When humans show an appreciation for all living things, they begin to move in time to the Way, and things proceed as they should: naturally and spontaneously.

Zhan He and the Butcher

The *Zhuangzi* is known for compelling stories that bring a range of Daoist ideas to life for readers. One of the most well-known illustrations of *wuwei* in the *Zhuangzi* is the parable of the butcher:

> Wherever his hand touched, wherever his shoulder leaned, wherever his foot stepped, wherever his knee pushed—with a zip! With a whoosh!—he handled his chopper with aplomb, and never skipped a beat. He moved in time, as if to music.[22]

Explaining his actions to Lord Wen Hui, the butcher says:

> When I first began cutting up oxen, I did not see anything but oxen. Three years later, I couldn't see the whole ox. And now, I encounter them with spirit and don't look with my eyes. Sensible knowledge and spiritual desires proceed. I put on the Heavenly patterns, strike in the big gaps, am guided by the large fissures, and follow what is inherently so. I never touch a ligament or tendon, much less do any heavy wrenching! . . . Still, when I get to a hard place, I see the difficulty and take breathless care. My gaze settles! My movements slow! I move the chopper slightly, and in a twinkling it's come apart, crumbling to the ground like a clod of earth![23]

The butcher's story bears a resemblance in structure to the story of Zhan He's fishing lesson. The latter begins with a description of Zhan He's actions, followed by a passage in which he gives an account of his actions to the king, similar to the butcher's accounting to Lord Wen Hui. When the King of Chu hears of Zhan He's success, he summons Zhan and questions him about his fishing techniques. Zhan tells the king,

> I heard my late father speak of Pu Zhuzi's archery with a line attached to the arrow. Using a weak bow and thin line, and shaking the line so that it rode with the winds, he transfixed both of a pair of black cranes on the edge of a dark cloud—because his attention was concentrated and the movement of his hand equalized the give and the pull. I profited by this story, and took it as my model when I learned to fish. It took me five years to learn all that there is to learn about this Way.[24]

Although Zhan He's actions are effortless and spontaneous, it took years of self-cultivation for him to become this way. In his description of Pu Zhuzi's archery, we learn that the effortlessness he describes involves attentiveness. Pu Zhuzi's attention was "concentrated"—he acted deliberately and carefully. Yet, like Zhan He, Pu Zhuzi's actions are characterized by effortlessness. He shook the line so it "rode with the winds." This is reminiscent of Zhan He's practice of drawing the line in and out, following the pull and give of the water. Both Zhan He and Pu Zhuzi move with the natural rhythms of nature.

This picture of *wuwei* is also prominent elsewhere in the *Liezi*. In a discussion of why a swimmer or diver handles a boat better than others, the *Liezi* says, "A good swimmer picks it up quickly, because he forgets the water altogether."[25] Here, the text indicates that good swimmers "forget the water" because they spend a great deal of time in and around water. By virtue of their experiences swimming, they know the way of wakes, currents, and waves. Accomplished swimmers also may be familiar with the particular bodies of water where they swim regularly, so they know where the rocks are, and the places where the bottom is shallow. Perhaps most importantly, though, swimmers are comfortable in and around the water. As a result they are not as self-conscious as others might be when handling a boat, which allows them to "pick it up quickly." This sense of *wuwei* is the same sense of effortlessness that is seen in Zhan He's fishing, and in Pu Zhuzi's archery. One might even say that Zhan He "forgets the line," as the swimmer "forgets the water."

All of this provides an interesting comparison with the butcher's remarks in the *Zhuangzi*: "When I first began cutting up oxen, I did not see anything but oxen. Three years later, I couldn't see the whole ox. And now, I encounter them with spirit and don't look with my eyes."[26] These descriptions—not looking with one's eyes, forgetting the water, and forgetting the line—are all given in an effort to describe the *state of mind* that results from Daoist self-cultivation. They are also consistently given with reference to the Way. Zhan He says, "It took me five years to learn all that there is to learn about this Way," while the butcher prefaces his claim that it took him three years to learn how to cut up oxen by saying, "I value the Way (*Dao*), which goes beyond technique."[27] Here we should recall what the *Daodejing* says: "The Way does nothing yet nothing is left undone."[28] Both Zhan He and the butcher model their actions on the Dao.[29]

Wuwei and Rulership

Although there are a number of important similarities between the stories of Zhan He and the butcher, I would now like to examine some more pervasive points of resonance between the way the Zhan He parable understands the concept of *wuwei* and the understanding of it presented in the *Daodejing*. The first point concerns the use of water as a metaphor for *wuwei*. Zhan He lets out and draws in his line "following the pull and give of the water," and water metaphors abound in the *Daodejing*. Water exemplifies the ideal of *wuwei* by virtue of its suppleness: "In all the world, nothing is more supple or weak than water; Yet nothing can surpass it for attacking what is stiff and strong. And so nothing can take its place."[30] This passage contends that the supple and soft have the greatest capacity to overcome the strong.[31] The idea of water as the highest good due to its suppleness and its corresponding strength is related to the idea of *wuwei*, "effortless action." Those who embody *wuwei* are able to bring about the desired result in a nonaggressive manner, and yet they have a remarkable influence on the world around them. They are supple, yet unsurpassable in strength.

A distinct but related point concerns the fact that Zhan He's materials, like the water in which he fishes, are soft and supple. Zhan He follows the pull and give of water by letting out and drawing in his line, and his rod of bamboo—although it is flexible—does not even bend, let alone break under the weight of the fish.[32] These elements of the story all illustrate the idea that suppleness and flexibility are qualities that lead to success in one's endeavors, serving as a powerful illustration of *wuwei*. Chapter 73 of the *Daodejing* says, "The Way does not contend but is good at victory; Does not speak but is good at responding; Does not call but things come of their own accord; Is not anxious but is good at laying plans. Heaven's net is vast; Its mesh is loose but misses nothing."[33] The image of a net, together with the verses preceding it, references the idea of the supple as strong. Although water flows freely through loose mesh, appearing supple and weak, in reality it "misses nothing." This is an illustration of the Way—"Heaven's net." According to the model of the Way, the least aggressive approach has the greatest strength, just as Zhan He says he uses weak things to control strong ones.

This is one place where we can begin to see a contrast with the story of the butcher. Whereas Zhan He's rod and line are made of supple, flexible materials, the butcher's chopper is hard and sharp. Although his knife glides through the oxen softly without hitting ligaments, tendons, or bones, it is still a contrast with Zhan He's flexible rod and line. Perhaps even more significant is the fact that Zhan He's materials are unrefined natural products. A thread of silk out of the cocoon, a beard of wheat, one of the pygmy bamboos of Chu, and a split grain of rice differ from the butcher's knife in this regard. The latter is a product of human culture and is not modeled on or composed of natural objects. The *Daodejing* notes that "sharp implements" should not be shown or given to the people.[34] And although the butcher causes the oxen to crumble with only the slightest movement of his knife, Zhan He's parable more pervasively emphasizes the metaphor of *wuwei* with the use of supple, natural instruments.[35]

However, the third and most important point of resonance between the Zhan He passage and the *Daodejing* highlights a much more significant departure from one of the views found in the *Zhuangzi*. In his essay, "The Concept of *de* ("Virtue") in the *Laozi*," Philip J. Ivanhoe points out three characteristics of the concept of *de* in the *Daodejing*, including the attractive power of individuals with *de*, and the therapeutic effect they have on others. The third characteristic Ivanhoe discusses is the intimate relationship between *wuwei* and *de* in government. As Ivanhoe puts it, "The ideal Daoist ruler cultivates a still and tenuous state of mind. This generates *de*, which enables him both to attract others and move them to follow the way."[36] The Daoist ruler is able to rule through *wuwei* because his *de* (virtue) “turns people away from those social goods, the ‘goods hard to come by,’ which lead to competition, contention, and strife. It puts people at ease, brings them peace and allows them to settle down where they are.”[37] This view is seen clearly in chapter 32 of the *Daodejing*:

> The Way is forever nameless.
> Unhewn wood is insignificant, yet no one in the world can master it.
> If barons and kings could preserve it, the myriad creatures would all defer to them of their own accord.
> Heaven and Earth would unite and sweet dew would fall;
> The people would be peaceful and just, though no one so decrees.[38]

In contrast, a number of passages in the *Zhuangzi* do not connect *wuwei* with a method of governing. To the contrary, some parables emphasize how those who understand the Way *decline* offers for positions in government.[39] When sage-king Yao offers his empire to a hermit, the hermit replies that he has “no use” for the empire.[40] But one of the most revealing accounts of this view of government is found in the story of an encounter between Zhuangzi and two officials sent by the King of Chu. I wish to focus on this story for two reasons. First, the King of Chu engages Zhan He in conversation about his fishing techniques.[41] Second, and perhaps even more interestingly, the exchange between Zhuangzi and the officials from Chu occurs while Zhuangzi is fishing on the banks of the Pu River:

> Zhuangzi was angling by the Pu River when the king of Chu sent two officers to him, saying, “We would like to trouble you with administering our kingdom.” Without looking up from his pole, Zhuangzi said, “I’ve heard Chu has a sacred turtle. It’s been dead three thousand years and the king keeps it wrapped and boxed and stored up in his ancestral hall. Now, would that turtle rather have its bones treasured in death, or be alive dragging its tail in the mud?”
>
> The two officers said, “It would rather be alive dragging its tail in the mud.” Zhuangzi said, “Go! I’ll keep my tail in the mud, too.”[42]

In this passage, Zhuangzi definitively rejects the idea that those who understand the Way should take positions in government. Unlike the *Daodejing*, these passages from the *Zhuangzi* do not advocate a distinctive conception of rulership. However, the Zhan He passage clearly does, and against the backdrop of Zhuangzi's exchange with the officials from Chu, Zhan He is a mighty contrast.

At the end of the parable, Zhan He's exceptional abilities attract the attention of the King of Chu, similar to the way the butcher attracts the praise of Lord Wen Hui. In both cases, we find ordinary individuals—a fisherman and a butcher—describing how they achieve such success in what they do. However, unlike the butcher and unlike Zhuangzi in his encounter with the officials from Chu, Zhan He offers his counsel to the King of Chu. After describing the way the fish submit to him, Zhan He says to the king, "This is how I am able to use weak things to control strong ones, light things to bring in heavy ones. If Your Majesty is really able to rule his state in the same way, he can turn the Empire within the span of his hand; what can give you trouble?"[43]

Zhan He's remark implies that the king will have no trouble at all if he rules the state through *wuwei*. This statement directly opposes Zhuangzi's response to the officials from Chu, in which he likens rulership to death. In agreement with the *Daodejing*, Zhan He advises the king to rule his state through *wuwei*, and "turn the Empire within the span of his hand," indicating that he will have the greatest strength and effectiveness when he acts effortlessly.

Conclusion

In this chapter, I have shown how Zhan He's fishing parable in the *Liezi* provides an account of *wuwei* that shares some important features with accounts of *wuwei* found in the *Zhuangzi* and in the *Daodejing*. I have argued that the Zhan He passage, although it shares some important structural and substantive features with the parable of the butcher in the *Zhuangzi*, expresses a view that is closer to the account of *wuwei* found in the *Daodejing*. According to this view, *wuwei* is the ideal of rulership. As we see from the Zhan He passage and the *Daodejing*, *wuwei* is not only an ideal to be cultivated by individuals in their various activities, but also by those in positions of leadership within the community and the state.

This view represents a contrast to the understanding of *wuwei* found in the *Zhuangzi*. Although the various classical Daoist texts are sometimes interpreted as offering one single perspective, comparative studies of these texts can help us to better understand the differences between them, and lead us to a more accurate and complete understanding of the diversity of views found in ancient China. A comparison of the parables of Zhan He and the butcher highlights the different ways the parables conclude. Whereas the Zhan He passage closes with Zhan explicitly advising the King of Chu to rule through *wuwei*, the Zhuangzian parable ends when the butcher finishes his description of chopping, and Lord Wen Hui exclaims, "Excellent! I have heard the words of a butcher and learned how to care for life!" In addition, a careful study of the Zhan He passage allows readers of the *Zhuangzi* to recognize the significance of Zhuangzi's exchange with the officials from Chu. Here we find Zhan He and Zhuangzi both on the riverbank fishing, and in dialogue with officials from Chu, but their responses are remarkably different.

Despite these differences, there remains a wide array of shared ideas that unite the texts of classical Daoism. For example, the ethical accounts found in the *Liezi, Zhuangzi,* and *Daodejing* include all of creation in their discussion of how humans should conduct themselves. Learning to move as one's nature commands, in harmony with the rhythms of the Way, leaving nothing undone, is something to be achieved by, and in relation to the natural world as a whole.

Zhan He's fishing lesson contains a fine example of this. He says, "When I cast the line and sink the hook, my hand does not pull too hard nor give too easily, so that nothing can disturb it. When the fish see the bait on my hook, it is like sinking dust or gathered foam, and they swallow it without suspecting."[44] When Zhan He tells us that the bait on his hook "is like sinking dust or gathered foam" to the fish that see it, he indicates that it is part of the natural order. He is not aggressively capturing the fish in a struggle. Rather, by exemplifying *wuwei* in his fishing techniques, he conforms to the natural order, and his actions affect those around him in the same way that the ruler with *de* rules through *wuwei*. The fish swallow the line quickly and without suspecting. His technique reflects suppleness and flexibility, yet nothing surpasses it in strength and effectiveness.[45]

Notes

1. *The Book of Lieh-tzu: A Classic of Tao*, trans. A. C. Graham (New York: Columbia University Press, 1990), 106. In this chapter, I use the pinyin Romanization system. For the sake of continuity, I have converted names from their Wade-Giles Romanization in Graham's translation.
2. Zhan He appears as a character in a number of early Chinese texts. Chapter 8 of the *Liezi* contains a short dialogue between Zhan He and King Zhuang of Chu, who ruled from 613–591 BCE (See *The Book of Lieh-tzu*, trans. Graham, 170–71). In this passage, the king asks Zhan He how to order the state. The *Lushi chunqiu* contains three references to Zhan He. The most extensive of these is found in Book Seventeen, where the King of Chu asks Zhan He how to govern the state (John Knoblock and Jeffrey Riegel, trans., *The Annals of LuBuwei* [Stanford: Stanford University Press, 2000], 17/8.2, 435). Book Eighteen of the *Lushi chunqiu* says that Zhan He, Tian Zifang, and Lao Dan were all sages who "listened to that which is without sound and observed that which is without shape" (18/2.4, 447). In Book Twenty-One, Zhan He advises Prince Mou of Zhongshan, a Warring States prince of Wei (21/4.4, 559). There are also references to Zhan He in the *Huainanzi* (14.466) and the *Hanfeizi*, which says of Zhan He, "Hearing the cry of an ox from within his chamber, he could tell the color of the ox" (Quoted in Knoblock and Riegel, 811). My thanks to Harold D. Roth for bringing these references to my attention.
3. *The Book of Lieh-tzu*, trans. Graham, 106.
4. Ibid., 2–3.
5. There are several important concepts that are a part of this understanding of the world, and I wish to briefly introduce two of them—*dao* (the Way) and *de* (virtue, power). In contrast with the view found in the Confucian *Analects*, in which the Way defines the human order, the Daoists understand the Way as the grand natural order, of which the human order is only a small part. On this view, the Way extends equally to every part of the universe, and it permeates all aspects of reality. Accordingly, the only way that humans can come to appreciate the cosmic pattern of the Way and take their place within it is by abandoning the anthropocentric view of the Way that the Confucians, among others, defend. In the third century BCE the terms *dao* (the Way) and *de* (virtue, power) first became associated, as in the title of the *Daodejing*. For the early Daoists, the term *de* is the inherent quality and efficacy of each thing—a thing's essential nature. The *dao* (Way) is manifested in the individual *de* (virtue, power) of each thing. Unlike the Confucians, who understood *de* as a kind of moral charisma, the Daoists believed that for human beings, *de* was basically the power to relieve living things of anxiety, fear, and delusion. I will return to this idea later in the chapter.
6. *Daodejing*, ch. 64. In this paper, all translations of the *Daodejing* are from *The Daodejing of Laozi*, translation and commentary by Philip J. Ivanhoe (Indianapolis: Hackett, 2002). I have left *wuwei* untranslated in this passage.
7. The *Book of Lieh-tzu*, trans. Graham, 93.
8. Ibid., 3.

9. Edward G. Slingerland, *Effortless Action: Wu-wei as Conceptual Metaphor and Spiritual Ideal in Early China* (New York: Oxford University Press, 2003), 7.
10. Philip J. Ivanhoe, "The Values of Spontaneity," in *Taking Confucian Ethics Seriously: Contemporary Theories and Applications*, ed. Julia Tao, Yu Kam-por, and Philip J. Ivanhoe (ms.). Cf. Ivanhoe, *The Daodejing of Laozi*, xxii.
11. *Daodejing*, trans. Ivanhoe, ch. 63.
12. Graham, 105.
13. Ibid., 105.
14. I am indebted to my student, Sanup Pathak, for this point, which he made in a paper for a Spring 2004 East Asian Philosophy course at Baylor University.
15. Graham, 30–31.
16. Adapted from *Confucius Analects*, trans. Edward Slingerland (Indianapolis: Hackett, 2003), 73.
17. See He Yan, *Lun yu ji jie*, and Zhu Xi, *Lun yu ji zhu*.
18. A modern Western source that shares many of these insights is Aldo Leopold's *A Sand County Almanac* (New York: Ballantine Books, 1970). Leopold writes, "What is the effect of hunting and fishing on character as compared with other outdoor sports? I have already pointed out that the desire lies deeper, that its source is a matter of instinct as well as of competition. . . . But there are two points about hunting that deserve special emphasis. One is that the ethics of sportsmanship is not a fixed code, but must be formulated and practiced by the individual, with no referee but the Almighty. The other is that hunting generally involves the handling of dogs and horses. . . . There is much truth in the old idea that any man ignorant of dogs and horses was not a gentleman" (232). Leopold also shares features of the Daoist view. He argues that we are members of a community that includes the land, and interconnectedness and interdependency define our relationship to the rest of the natural world. Thanks to Philip J. Ivanhoe for bringing Leopold's work to my attention, and for pointing out these features of the Confucian commentarial tradition as well.
19. *Mengzi (Mencius)*, trans. Bryan W. Van Norden, in *Readings in Classical Chinese Philosophy*, ed. Philip J. Ivanhoe and Bryan W. Van Norden (Indianapolis: Hackett, 2001), 114–19.
20 See n. 5.
21. Graham, 2.
22. *Zhuangzi*, trans. Paul Kjellberg, in Ivanhoe and Van Norden, 219. This parable appears in chapter 3 of the *Zhuangzi*.
23. Kjellberg, 220.
24. Graham, 105–106.
25. Ibid., 43.
26. *Zhuangzi*, trans. Kjellberg, in Ivanhoe and Van Norden, 220.
27. Although Zhan He and the butcher both mention multiple years of cultivation, other Daoist parables mention different lengths of time in relation to the skill being described. For example, the *Zhuangzi*'s Woodcarver Qing fasts for seven days before he begins carving. He says, "By that time, the ruler and his court no longer exist for me. My skill is

concentrated and all outside distractions fade away" (Burton Watson, trans., *The Complete Works of Chuang Tzu*, [New York: Columbia University Press, 1968], 126–27). The important point in all of these passages is that the process of cultivating this ideal state of mind consists largely of paring away the distractions that interfere with one's attention. This process takes different forms and different lengths of time for various individuals.

28. *Daodejing*, trans. Ivanhoe, ch. 37.
29. Another similarity between the Zhan He and butcher parables is the use of hyperbole. Certain aspects of each story—a fishing line made of a single thread of silk that does not snap when it hooks a fish "big enough to fill a cart," or a blade that "is still as though fresh from the grindstone" after nineteen years—are obvious exaggerations, perhaps designed to emphasize the fact that Zhan He and the butcher were easily distinguishable from other fishermen and butchers. This underscores the fact that *wuwei* is not simply a state of mind, rather, it is visible in one's actions.
30. *Daodejing,* trans. Ivanhoe, ch. 78.
31. Graham, 53; cf. *Daodejing,* ch. 78.
32. Cf. *Daodejing,* ch. 76: "A tree that is too strong will break."
33. *Daodejing*, ch. 73.
34. See chs. 36 and 67.
35. There is an interesting range of views among classical Confucian philosophers on the issue of cultivation metaphors as well. In the *Analects*, Kongzi tells us to cut and file, chisel and polish, and yet maintains that "Rotten wood cannot be carved, and a wall of dung cannot be beautified" (*The Analects*, trans. Edward G. Slingerland, in Ivanhoe and Van Norden, 1.15, 5.10). Xunzi insists that the artificial (*wei*) defines the normative, evident in his use of harsh self-cultivationist metaphors: "Through steaming and bending, you can make wood straight as a plumb line into a wheel. And after its curve conforms to the compass, even when parched under the sun it will not become straight again, because the steaming and bending have made it a certain way" (*Xunzi*, trans. Eric L. Hutton, in Ivanhoe and Van Norden, 248). Mengzi has a mixed picture, and represents the view closest on the spectrum to the early Daoists. He rails against Gaozi for recommending that we carve up human nature "like making a willow tree into cups and bowls," and instead tries to navigate a middle path with his agricultural metaphors, and his contention that humans have four moral "sprouts" that can be cultivated or left to wither (*Mengzi*, trans. Bryan W. Van Norden, in Ivanhoe and Van Norden, 140, 125–26).
36. Philip J. Ivanhoe, "The Concept of *de* ("Virtue") in the *Laozi*," in *Religious and Philosophical Aspects of the Laozi*, ed. Mark Csikszentmihalyi and Philip J. Ivanhoe, 246–47.
37. Ivanhoe, in *Religious and Philosophical*, 250.
38. Cf. ch. 37.
39. In this essay, I focus on one of several views on governing that can be found in the *Zhuangzi*. I am not claiming that this is the only view that can be found in the text. The important point for the purposes of my study is that there were different positions on this particular issue

among early Daoists. However, it should be noted that the distinction I make in this paper regarding the view of governing found in certain parables in the *Zhuangzi* as opposed to the Zhan He passage and the *Daodejing* concerns a view that *is* represented in several of the "inner chapters," which are regarded by most scholars as the earliest stratum of the text. For more on the various perspectives on government found in the *Zhuangzi*, and their relationship to different strata of the text, see Harold D. Roth, "Redaction Criticism and the Early History of Taoism," in *Early China* 19 (1994), 6–7.

40. *Zhuangzi*, trans. Kjellberg, in Ivanhoe and Van Norden, 206–207.
41. It is uncertain whether the characters of Zhuangzi and Zhan He are dealing with the same King of Chu in these passages. Although the Zhan He passage under study does not specify which King of Chu is being discussed, Book Eight of the *Liezi* specifies that King Zhuang of Chu sought Zhan He's advice on governing (see n. 2). King Zhuang reigned from 613–591 BCE. The *Zhuangzi* does not specify which King of Chu Zhuangzi is speaking with. If the story is set during the time when the historical Zhuangzi is believed to have lived (fl. c. 320 BCE), then it is unlikely that it was King Zhuang of Chu, because Zhuangzi's dates are later. However, it is difficult to be certain about either reference, or a historical Zhan He's dates. There is also the question of whether or not the author(s) of the passages even intended to portray Zhuangzi's and Zhan He's historical dates accurately. The textual history offers little help with these questions, because even if we could date the passages under study, the question of when the stories are set remains. This passage is from Book Seventeen of the *Zhuangzi*, which according to Harold D. Roth contains material "which often imitates the themes and style of the 'Inner' Chapters," and which both Angus Graham and Guan Feng conclude represents the writings of later followers of Zhuangzi. See Harold D. Roth, "Who Compiled the Zhuangzi?" in *Chinese Texts and Philosophical Contexts*, ed. Henry Rosemont Jr. (LaSalle, IL: Open Court, 1991), 81. As readers of this volume are no doubt aware, the date of the *Liezi* is disputed. Scholars such as Waley have argued that the text is from the third century BCE, while others such as Feng Youlan maintain that it belongs to the third and fourth centuries CE. But, as Graham writes, "both parties agree that the book is heterogeneous, that if it is pre-Han it contains later interpolations, and if it is post-Han it utilizes ancient sources." According to Graham, textual evidence favors the latter view. See A. C. Graham, "The Date and Composition of Lieh-Tzu."
42. *Zhuangzi*, trans. Kjellberg, in Ivanhoe and Van Norden, 239–40.
43. Graham, 106.
44. Ibid.
45. My thanks to Philip J. Ivanhoe, Ronnie Littlejohn, Jeffrey Richey, Harold D. Roth, and Michael R. Slater for helpful comments and suggestions on earlier drafts of this essay.

列子

When Butterflies Change into Birds

Life and Death in the Liezi

David Jones

A. C. Graham once remarked, concerning the *Laozi* and the *Zhuangzi* especially but which included the *Liezi* as well, "They do share one basic insight, that while other things move spontaneously on the course proper to them, man has separated himself from the Way by reflecting, posing alternatives, and formulating principles of action. This has generally impressed Westerners as the most remarkable, the most distinctively Chinese, of exportable thoughts of ancient China" (Graham 1989, 172). In the introduction of his translation of the *Liezi*, Graham informs us that, "the *Lieh-tzu* has the merit of being by far the most easily intelligible of the classics of Taoism. For a Westerner it is perhaps the best introduction to this strange and elusive philosophy of life; for however obscure some of it may look, it does not present the infinite possibilities of divergent interpretation and sheer misunderstanding offered by the *Tao-te-ching* itself" (1). Perhaps it is only a matter of historical chance or a consequence of scholarly interests that the West has received the *Daodejing* and *Zhuangzi* as the primary texts for the promulgation of Daoist philosophy, but given the accessibility of the *Liezi*, it is now time to consider its value as a text worth considering. In what follows, I point to some of the more straightforward passages of the *Liezi* that speak to the question of death and death's relation to life, especially in relation to corpses. In addition, it will be suggested that the *Liezi* places the relationship between life and death in the more general context of a universal evolutionary framework. In this regard, the *Liezi* is an even more exceptional Daoist text.

Evolutionary Winds of Complexity

Daoist texts are known for their attention to and appreciation of the natural world; this is so even of the more politically oriented *Laozi*, which is at once a guide for rulership in its deployment of natural metaphors in laying out the best form of governing. The natural way of the world is followed by the "myriad creatures," the *wanwu*, or "everything that is happening." This processual language is intentional and indicative of the Daoist project. Everything in the world, with the exception of the human being that is endowed with discursive thought and thereby enabled to rise in its hubris over other creatures, "moves spontaneously on the course proper to them." Unlike the *Laozi* and *Zhuangzi* where one needs to work a bit to get at this notion of a world of becoming, which is a fundamental starting point for Daoist philosophy, the *Liezi* rather straightforwardly allows its readers to see this starting point in its very first chapter: "Master, you are going away, and have set no time for your return. Your disciples presume to make a request. What are you going to teach us before you go? Did not your master Hu-tzu tell you anything?" "'What did Hu-tzu ever say?' Lieh-tzu answered smiling. 'However, I did once overhear him talking to Po-hum Wu-jen; I will try to tell you what he said. These were his words'":

> There are the born and the Unborn, the changing and the Unchanging. The Unborn can give birth to the born, the Unchanging can change the changing. The born cannot escape birth, the changing cannot escape change; therefore birth and change are the norm. Things for which birth and change are the norm are at all times being born and changing. They simply follow the alterations of the Yin and Yang and the four seasons. (Graham 1960, 17)

If we compare this passage to the opening page, and one of the exemplary passages on change in the *Zhuangzi*, we immediately appreciate the straightforwardness of the *Liezi*:

> In the North Ocean there is a fish, its name is the K'un; the K'un's girth measures who knows how many thousand miles. It changes

> into a bird, its name is P'eng; the P'eng's back measures who knows how many thousand miles. When it puffs out its chest and flies off, its wings are like clouds hanging from the sky. This bird when the seas are heaving has a mind to travel to the South Ocean. In the words of the *Tall stories*, "When the P'eng travels to the South Ocean, the wake it thrashes on the water is three thousand miles long, it mounts spiraling on the whirlwind ninety thousand miles high, and is gone six months before it is out of breath." Is the azure of the sky its true colour? Or is it that the distance into which we are looking is infinite? It never stops flying higher till everything below looks the same as above (heat-hazes, dust storms, the breath which living things blow at each other). (Graham 1981, 43)

In this passage, we are challenged in ways the *Liezi* does not, that is, this passage in the *Zhuangzi* gives rise to the possibility of multiple interpretations. Although such a possibility is a strength of this text, what are we philosophically to make of this change and how do we explain its nature? We must work through the movement from north to south, fish to bird, small to large, and their relation before coming to some sort of conclusion through these presented images. Although this process is agreeable enough, especially if readers are prone to enjoying the literary aspects of texts, the *Liezi* more clearly presents the prevailing position in Daoism with regard to the nature of the world as one of a particular kind of process, that is, the movement and overcoming of the dualistic perspective that leads the discursive brainy biped away from its proper course along the way. The *Liezi* continues:

> The Unborn is by our side yet alone,
> The Unchanging goes forth and returns.
> Going forth and returning, its successions are endless;
> By our side and alone, its Way is boundless.

By "simply follow[ing] the alternations of the Yin and Yang and the four seasons" (18), we can rejoin the other myriad creatures in the world's unfolding of *wanwu*. In other words, we can endlessly participate in the "going forth and returning" of "everything that is happening." This is the Daoist notion of *fan*, where the "particular continues to participate in the 'transformation of things (*wuhua*).'"[1] The *Liezi* immediately presents this idea of *fan* from the outset, which will take the *Laozi* forty chapters to give access to its readers, and when we finally get to it, this is what we encounter:

> "Returning" is how . . . (*dao*) moves,
> And "weakening" is how it functions.
> The events of the world arise from the determinate (*you*)
> And the determinate arises from the indeterminate (*wu*).
> (Ames and Hall, 139)

Although still fairly straightforward, we do encounter the notion of "weakening," which needs development through the metaphor of water found in a number of other passages, and an unpacking of determinacy and indeterminacy.

The *Liezi*, however, contains a wonderful account of universal evolution that begins with a series of particular species transformations:

> Within the seeds of things there are germs. When they find water they develop in successive stages. Reaching water on the edge of land, they become scum. Breeding on the bank, they become plantain. When the plantain reaches dung, it becomes the crowfoot. The root of the crowfoot becomes woodlice, the leaves become butterflies. The butterfly suddenly changes into an insect which breeds under the stove and looks as though it has shed its skin [*ch'ü-to*]. After a thousand days the *ch'ü-to* changes into a bird named the *kan-yü-ku*. The saliva of the *kan-yü-ku* becomes the *ssŭ-mi,* which becomes the vinegar animalcula *yi-lu*, which begets the animalcula *huang-k'uang*, which begets the *chiu-yu*, which begets the gnat, which begets the firefly (Graham 1960, 21)

From a scientific perspective, there are clearly leaps of faith in this passage (e.g., exactly how does the skin of a butterfly transform into a bird after a thousand days?), but this should not deter us from appreciating such a valuable insight into the evolution and mutual influencing of diverse species giving rise to a complex world. If we look even more closely at this passage, we see that it is not just a simple transformation of one species turning into another for it is the skin of the butterfly that changes into a bird, the root of the crowfoot becomes woodlice, not the crowfoot itself, and it is the saliva of the *kan-yü-ku* that becomes the *ssŭ-mi*.

The dying skin is what aids the coming-to-be of something of another (an other) and this other, the bird, returns the favor with its saliva, which in turn aids in the process of yet another species in the unfolding of the evolutionary process.

We can clearly see in this passage the movement of the biological world organizing itself from the bottom up into increasing levels of species complexity without the assistance of any transcendent being or governing principle of the universe. Implicit in the process outlined in the *Liezi* is that life emerged out of simplicity ("within the seeds of things there are germs") and developed intimate relationships across species by building further complex patterns of behavior with each other. These patterns were, of course, too complex to put into words for Liezi, but his insight is both obvious and invaluable. Further, for these complex forms of behavior to develop, there must be a level of intimate relatedness present in the form of some kind of cooperative behavior of the constitutive elements that move the evolutionary process onward. This form of cooperation is presented as moving across the scale of all that is—germs to seeds to scum and so forth. Ultimately, catalysts of amazing precision would need to evolve, weaving their influence within ever more advanced chemical and biochemical manifestations to quicken the pace of cooperation to lead to the development of *Homo sapiens*. The passage ends with, "The *yang-hsi*, combining with an old bamboo which has not put forth shoots, begets the *ch'ing-ning*. This begets the leopard, which begets the horse, which begets man" (22).

The *Liezi* will not, however, allow the species of *Homo sapiens* to be privileged in this process. The human species is part of the evolutionary process and not the progressive purpose of the process. There is no teleology present for "Man in due course returns to the germs" (22) and ultimately "All the myriad things come out of germs and go back to germs" (23). Individuation is nothing more than a momentary lapse in the continuity of evolutionary time that continually returns to itself in innumerable ways. The individuated human self is not exempt from this process and needs to learn that its death is the life of something else.

Such accessible passages let readers get at one of the most fundamental components of Daoist thought, the interrelatedness of all things, and how these things grow from and flourish in relation to each other. This passage also points out in clear terms that human beings are no different from other species, that is, we are not *Homo specialis* and ultimately return to the evolutionary process in which all things participate regardless of our held preconceptions. As the *Liezi* also maintains, "to wish to live forever, and have no more of ending, is to be deluded about our lot" (23). Such an affirmation of our ends is ultimately an affirmation of all life since we return to the very "germs" from which we were constituted and continue to move along with the Way, for "Death is a return to where we set out from when we were born [that is, to the unborn]. So how do I know that when I die here I shall not be born somewhere else? How do I know that life and death are not as good as each other?" (25). This birth elsewhere should not be confused with a theory of reincarnation where a substantial soul inhabits another body for this would render a dualistic view not present in the *Liezi* and would violate the spirit of other Daoist texts. It would further violate the significant quality of returning so clearly presented in the *Liezi*. In this same chapter, it is stated that "[d]ying is the virtue in us going to its destination. The men of old called a dead man 'a man who has gone back'. Saying that the dead have gone back they implied that the living are travellers. The traveller who forgets to go back is a man who mistakes his home" (26). To go home is to go home again. The evolutionary process that extends across all that is and all that has become is the home to which we must return, and this return must be affirmed as a virtuous path for living this life and making it significant. This is the human contribution to the unfolding of *dao*. Clearly this anti-teleological view and the placement of the value of making our lives significant are found throughout other Daoist texts, but hardly are they so explicitly stated.

Living and Dead Bodies

In contradistinction to the Western predilection toward a life beyond the body, the *Liezi* offers an affirmation of the body, a return to the body, and the connection of the body to the physical world from which it has emerged and was engendered. This affirmation of the body is in itself an affirming of the sanctity of the natural world, which avows the human relation to all that is. We only need to look at the relation of lived bodies to that of corpses to realize the unconscious truth of what the *Liezi* brings to our consciousness.

If we look at our *li* (the ritual propriety to which we unconsciously convene meaning) concerning our dead ones or those in the gaze of the public, we can see how we go to great lengths to suspend the process of the body's degradation so we can momentarily enter into the world from which we were born, that is, enter into our world of being unborn and symbolically participate in our own return home. In this world, the body of a loved one is a memento of that person's lived world that we wish to suspend for a moment in evolutionary time, knowing all too well this body will soon be the site of various bacteria and microorganisms throwing a party that will ultimately prevail over any of our attempts at killing them during our lives. These organisms, small and feisty, can often be dispensed with in our lives just by washing them away, but they finally prevail over us as we move toward our return back to whence we came. There is no way to stop them. The inevitability of our deaths is that we are the home for their house party. Our *li* across cultures for proper burials are testaments to the sanctity and interrelatedness of life and death. We seem to have lost this sense in the West, but we once had it as is exemplified by Homer's dismay at Achilles' hubris in dragging Hector's lifeless body behind his chariot and how this action needs correction. Not only did Hector deserve a proper burial, his loved ones and the men he led deserved their moments in evolutionary time not only to mourn for Hector, but to contemplate and affirm the singularity of their own deaths so they may overcome death's *Angst* and will themselves back into the process of life and death, and death and life.

What I wish to suggest here is that we all know of our fate of death, but the real question is how to respond appropriately and authentically to our deaths. The *Liezi* gives us counsel on this question as do other Daoist texts that are unlike and avoid the bad faith of Plato—the person to whom all subsequent Western civilization is nothing but a series of footnotes, as Whitehead declares. The *Liezi* gives us counsel in clear terms not always hidden in anecdotes, parables, and stories prone to "infinite possibilities of divergent interpretation and sheer misunderstanding" but provides us with thought-provoking challenges that force us to see the mutual inclusion of opposites such as unborn and born, life and death. Death in Plato is present only in a peculiar way. As Dennis Schmidt so astutely puts it, "There is an important difference between *how* [the] consciousness of mortality is presented and thought in Plato, and in Homer and Sophocles. In Plato, death never really makes an appearance. What we find is always only the aftermath of death, and then every effort is made to *conceal the dead, to efface the body*"

(Hyland and Manoussakis 2006, 122). Our *li*, however, speak to us in ways otherwise to Plato; our *li* give us another wisdom. They tell us that we must reflect on our dead, look at our dead and accept their silent gaze back at us; we must realize our dead are also the dead of others relating us to those others; our dead are the other to us for their silent bodies speak to us only in the ways the dead can speak to the living, for they remind us that our deaths are no different from theirs. The death of others is the death that is also my death; their death is ultimately not other to me.

Our *li* bespeak the relation to the dead through our mourning of our dead and how this mourning is overcome, worked through, so we may enter, as Herakleitos puts it, the nearness. The *Liezi* speaks to us of that nearness, of the closeness of the human being through its body to the natural processes of returning to the state of being unborn, which is the nothingness of the emptying of the body by the maggots, bacteria, and other multifarious microorganisms that reclaim us so the process may continue once again. Liezi knew this as the Way, and to move along this Way is to ride the wind of universal evolution.

Not only does the *Liezi* offer its readers a rather direct exposition of universal evolution, it also gives us explicit statements on the interdependence of all things and their interdependent arising in relation to other things found in their particular contexts at hand. In the "Heaven's Gifts" chapter, for example, we encounter the following response to Yu Hsiung's comment:

> Turning without end
> Heaven and Earth shift secretly
> Who is aware of it?

The response:

> So the thing which is shrinking there is swelling here, the thing which is maturing here is decaying there. Shrinking and swelling, maturing and decaying, it is being born at the same time that it is dying. The interval between the coming and the going is imperceptible. (27)

The *Liezi* very clearly correlates this macrocosmic pronouncement with the human: "It is the same with a man's progress from birth to old age; his looks, knowledge and bearing differ from one day to the next, his skin and nails and hair are growing at the same time as they are falling away" (27), for ultimately we are nothing, but the ephemeral "breath of heaven and earth which goes to and fro; how can [we] ever possess it?" (30). Not only are our bodies the final destinations for bacteria and microorganisms that usher us into dissolving into the natural world, they are the sites for the coming and going of the cells that are along for the body's ride through life toward its fate of becoming a corpse. If we only look to the concealment of death, to its aftermath of a disembodied deathless life elsewhere, we are destined to miss Liezi's point; we are fated to overlook his, and Daoism's, alternative heaven.

Heaven's Becoming

Tian, or heaven, is not to be seen as a place of perfection or transcendence, for it too is immanent and pervades all that is happening as everything moves along its way cycling eternally through life/death-death/life. The lifeless body—the dead body, the corpse—is dead from only the human perspective, for our decaying bodies are alive at yet another level, a deeper level connected intimately to the double movement of life and death. As our bodies dissolve into the natural world, they begin to decay. Like life, decomposition is a process too and begins immediately when the body dies. If we turn a taphonomic eye to the decaying body we see it produces heat, and this heat gives rise to the production of gases, or vapors, and liquids form caused by the body's own chemicals swelling the body during the putrefaction stage. This process makes the body ripe for a host of scavengers waiting for the party to begin. Maggots (the larvae of flies), flesh flies, blow flies, rodents, and other larger animals aid us in our dissolving back into the natural process. This party at death's moment is the party of life, of more life reconfigured providing an opening for the next stage. Even our "proper burials" cannot alter this process. Even the promise of eternal life and our practice of embalming cannot alter this way of things. Preservation and individuation are the illusion.

The *Liezi* tells us *tian* "is nothing but the accumulated air. There is no place where there is no air. You walk and stand all day inside heaven, stretching and bending, breathing in and breathing out" (28). Even our corpses breathe and flow out as they empty back into the natural world. We can take Liezi as referring to the *qi* that pervades all things, but we should remember that even in our corpses this *qi* is finally released back into the constant returning of things to their source. The self, as an emergent being, is a being that is an event of overlapping vital energizing fields of *qi* that are interdependently related and the individual is nothing more than a focused aggregate experience of those energizing fields of *qi*. In Confucian terms, the prototype for this aggregated field of interdependence is the family, where the family is the sphere of influence for the consensual. In the *Liezi* we are graphically shown to be part of an even greater family for "All the myriad things come out of germs and go back to germs" (23) and "if a thing does not reach its limit it will not revert" (84). To become a sage is to learn how to consent, to agree to and feel together with all things for all things are happening across their scales in this selfsame way. We ultimately are the particular "vital energizing fields" of *qi* emerging from the greater field of our contexts at hand. These contexts have also emerged from a series of ongoing, mutually influencing, and overlapping contexts that lead to future contexts that are either amplified or diminished (if not successfully congruent and reiterative) from the present one. This is the immanent heaven to which the *Liezi* speaks. Although this idea of heaven being immanent is a fundamental feature of all Chinese thought, Liezi awakens us to this point with straightforward clarity.

The "Yellow Emperor" chapter picks up on the important themes suggested so far and the conclusion found at the end of "Heaven's Gifts" adds an important ethical dimension to the discussion: "In reality the myriad things [*wanwu*] of heaven and earth are not separate from each other; and to claim anything as one's own is always wrong-headed" (31). My suggestion is that our bodies, both in their alive and dead forms, are not ultimately even our own, but are hosts for the greater party of life. In this regard, the *Liezi* (like other Daoist texts) is foremost concerned with presenting an ethic for appropriate living. While one needs to work hard through other Daoist texts to achieve some formulation of this ethic, the *Liezi* once again gives its readers an easily accessed model to emulate. After the first fifteen years of living for pleasure, and the second of worry about misgoverning, "the Yellow Emperor breathed a sigh and said: 'Deep is my error! It is an affliction to care for oneself alone, and as great an affliction to govern the myriad things!'" (33). How does one develop compassion for the other myriad things, especially those things that will assist our bodies to dissolve back into the nothingness from which we arose?

To begin to answer this question we can look at our own species, that of the animal. The Western assumption is a necessarily uncomfortable one regarding animals. The human animal's posture toward other animals is from an upright vantage point. This stance views the posture of other animals as slumped and bent over because they are more comfortable walking on all fours. This view gives us a feeling of superiority and this feeling interferes with our atonement with the natural world, or as Henry Rosemont has put it, our "at-one-ment" (Rosemont, 31). In this view, the human being is held as both special and privileged.[2] The *Liezi* addresses this tendency, as does the *Zhuangzi,* but does so in characteristically more explicit fashion.

In the West, the centrality of the human animal—Protagoras's the measure of all things, the rational animal of Aristotle, Descartes' thinking being, and so forth—has become so ingrained in us because we consider ourselves to be *Homo specialis*; we are a special being made in the image of a God that is wholly other to us and we are endowed with the special powers of reasoning, contemplation, creating moralities, and, as Liezi might remind us, we even have the capability of deluding ourselves. Ptolemy placed *Homo specialis* in the center of the universe and this thought still governs us to this day, even though we know better. Even when we were removed from the center of all that is, as in the instance of Copernicus's placing the earth on the universe's periphery, Descartes once again places God's special creature at the center of creation because we are rational and those other animals are rendered as cleverly constructed machines without soul. Although none of us believe this today, it is of little wonder where our attitudes to the animal find their influence. As *Homo specialis*, we are a special breed for we think we can engineer the natural world to meet our ends. On the positive side though, we also possess special abilities to become good stewards to the world we alter. Stewardship, however, presupposes we are of the right mind to act ethically and our dispositions to do so depend largely on the fluctuations of the economies in which we find ourselves. Our relationship to the natural world has become inscrutably an external one. We are so frightened of animals because we have made them other, excluded our species from theirs, and have surrounded ourselves with a universe completely different from what we think is our essential nature. Nature is other to us and we reassert our otherness in ways ranging from embalming bodies to creating perfect worlds called heavens.

The *Liezi*, however, casts things in a much different light and offers a remedy for this maligned condition: "There are ways in which intelligence of beasts and birds is by nature similar to man's. They wish as much as we do to preserve their lives, and do not borrow from man's wisdom to do so. . . . In the most ancient times men and animals lived together and walked side by side" (54). Such a discourse coincides with what we have come to know scientifically in the West, but such understanding still eludes our arrogating presence in what we consider our worldview. The *Liezi* continues, "The divine sages of the most ancient times knew the habits of all the myriad things, and interpreted the cries of all the different species; they called them together for meetings and gave them instructions, as though they were human beings" (55). Although the distinction between humanity and animality is still preserved in this passage, for whom is it preserved? For the animal? Or for the human who has lost his way along the proper coursing of *dao* "by reflecting, posing alternatives, and formulating principles of action" (Graham 1989, 172). Our answer in the *Liezi* is clear, "there are no great differences in mind and intelligence between living species. The divine sages knew this was the case, and therefore in teaching they left out none of them" (55).

The *Liezi* is a neglected Daoist text, but it is one that brings us back to our world without our besotted egos that create such deception for ourselves with the "noble lies" of eternal personal life, superiority over other species, and that there is another place for us in this universe rather than on the earth where we find ourselves. Conversely, the *Liezi* gives us truths and asks us to accept those truths as an affirmation of the maggots, flies, rodents, and other scavengers that usher us along that return to whence we came; for from our shrinking there will be a swelling somewhere else, from our deaths will return life, and that there is nothing to fear for we just return to where we were born. From this nothingness of the where and when of our births are the germs that give rise to the seeds, and when these seeds find water they develop in successive stages. When they reach land they become scum and breed on the banks and become plantain; and when the plantain reaches dung it becomes the crowfoot; the root of the crowfoot becomes woodlice, the leaves become butterflies, the *yang-hsi* combine with old bamboo that begets the *ch'in-ning* that begets the leopard, and then the horse, which begets the human. In due course, the bacteria and microorganisms hear their call to their natural duties that are soon overheard by maggots, flies, rodents, and those other larger scavengers who finalize the process of our return. It's their party now. As the *Liezi* clearly reminds us, by sharing in the grand universal evolutionary scheme of all that is happening is to be interrelated with all that is. Consummating our interrelatedness in this ever changing movement of *yin/yang* and the four seasons is our only authentic alternative for this is just the way of things. To be responsive to this call is to affirm the double movement of life and death; it is the call to let the party begin, over and over again.

Notes

1. D. C. Lau and Roger Ames, eds., *Yuan Dao* (New York: Ballantine Books, 1998), 25.
2. For a discussion of this see my introduction to *Buddha Nature and Animality* (Fremont, CA: Jain, 2007). Most chapters in this book address the issue of human privilege in one way or another from Buddhist perspectives.

References

Ames, Roger, and David Hall. *Dao De Jing: A Philosophical Translation.* New York: Ballantine Books, 2003.

Graham, A. C. *Disputers of the Tao: Philosophical Argument in Ancient China.* La Salle, IL: Open Court, 1989.

———. *The Book of Lieh-tzu: A Classic of Tao.* New York: Columbia University Press, 1960.

———. *Chuang Tzu: The Inner Chapters.* London: George Allen and Unwin, 1981.

Hyland, Drew, and John Panteleimon Manoussakis, eds. *Heidegger and the Greeks: Interpretive Essays.* Bloomington: University of Indiana Press, 2006.

Rosemont, Henry Jr. *Rationality and Religious Experience: The Continuing Relevance of the World's Spiritual Traditions.* La Salle, IL: Open Court, 2001.

Contributors

ROGER T. AMES is professor of philosophy at the University of Hawai'i and editor of *Philosophy East & West*. He is author and editor of more than thirty books, many in Chinese or both Chinese and English, and almost two hundred essays and articles. Among his books and translations related to Daoism are the following: *Daodejing: Making This Life Significant* (with David L. Hall) (New York: Ballantine, 2003); *Tracing* Dao *to its Source* (with D. C. Lau) (New York: Ballantine, 1998); and (ed.) *Wandering at Ease in the* Zhuangzi (Albany: State University of New York Press, 1998). His work has undertaken several projects that entail the intersection of contemporary issues and cultural understanding. His *Democracy of the Dead: Dewey, Confucius, and the Hope for Democracy in China* (with David L. Hall) (1999) is a product of this effort, along with the ongoing translations of his works into Chinese and his involvement in Chinese and East Asian political theory and practice.

TIMOTHY H. (T. H.) BARRETT is professor of East Asian history in the Department of Religion, School of Oriental and African Studies, University of London. His authored works include *The Woman Who Discovered Printing (*London: Yale, 2008); *Poems of Hanshan (*AltaMira, 2003); and *Taoism Under the T'ang: Religion and Empire during the Golden Age of Chinese History (London:* Wellsweep, 1996). With Xun Zhou, he wrote *The Wisdom of the Confucian* (UK: Oneworld, 2001). He has written a number of articles including "Buddhist Precepts in a Lawless World: Some Comments on the Linhuai Ordination Scandal," in *Going Forth. Visions of Buddhist Vinaya* (University of Hawai'i Press, 2005); "Shinto and Taoism in Early Japan," in *Shinto in History: Ways of the Kami* (Richmond: Curzon Press), and the Introduction to *Religion and Biography in China and Tibet* (London: Curzon).

JOHN H. BERTHRONG is the associate dean for academic and administrative affairs and associate professor of comparative theology at the Boston University School of Theology. His most recent books include *Expanding Process: Exploring Philosophical and Theological Transformations in China and the West* Albany: State University of New York Press, 2008); *Confucianism: a Short Introduction* (with Evelyn Nagai Berthrong) (Oneworld Publications, 2000); and *Transformations of the Confucian Way* (Westview Press, 1998). With Mary Evelyn Tucker, he edited *Confucianism and Ecology: The Interrelation of Heaven, Earth, And Humans* (Harvard University Press). He is also author of an extensive list of book chapters and articles.

ERIN M. CLINE is an assistant professor in the theology department, Georgetown University. She specializes in comparative philosophy, Chinese philosophy, and ethics. Her recent publications include "Mirrors, Minds, and Metaphors," in *Philosophy East and West* 58, no. 3 (July 2008); "Two Senses of Justice: Confucianism, Rawls, and Comparative Political Philosophy," in *Dao: A Journal of Comparative Philosophy* 6, no. 4 (Winter 2007); "Two Interpretations of *De* in the *Daodejing*," in *Journal of Chinese Philosophy* 31, no. 2 (June 2004); "The Way, the Right, and the Good," in *Journal of Religious Ethics* 37, no. 1 (2009); and "Nameless Virtues and Restrained Speech in the *Analects*," in *International Philosophical Quarterly* 49, no. 193 (2009).

JEFFREY DIPPMANN is associate professor of philosophy and religious studies and former director of Asia/Pacific studies at Central Washington University. Having earned his doctorate at Northwestern University, he specializes in Daoism and Chinese Buddhism. His publications include "The *Tao* of Textbooks: Taoism in Introductory World Religion Texts," in *Teaching Theology & Religion* 4, no. 1 (2001); "On Being a Civil[ized] Daoist," in

Polishing the Chinese Mirror: Essays in Honor of Henry Rosemont Jr., ed. Marthe Chandler and Ronnie Littlejohn, ACPA Series of Chinese and Comparative Philosophy (2008); and "Vimalakirti's Triumphant Silence: Bridging Indian and East Asian Buddhism," in *Asian Texts—Asian Contexts: The Art of Infusing Asian Philosophies and Religions*, ed David Jones and Ellen Klein (State University of New York Press, 2009). He has served as president of the Pacific Northwest Region of the American Academy of Religion and as a member of the board of directors for AAS' Asian Studies on the Pacific Coast Regional Association.

PHILIP J. IVANHOE has served as associate professor of philosophy and religious studies at Stanford University, as associate professor of philosophy and Asian languages and cultures at the University of Michigan, and as the Findlay Professor of Philosophy at Boston University before moving to City University of Hong Kong in 2007 where he is now reader-professor of philosophy in the department of public and social administration governance in Asia Research Centre (GARC). He specializes in the history of East Asian philosophy and religion and their potential for contemporary ethical, political, and social thought. For a brief biography, see the entry on Philip J. Ivanhoe in *Wikipedia*. Among his publications are: *Working Virtue: Virtue Ethics and Contemporary Moral Problems* (with Rebecca Walker) (Oxford University Press, 2007); *The Sense of Anti Rationalism: Zhuangzi and Kierkegaard's Religious Thought* (with Karen L. Carr) (Seven Bridges Press, 2000); *Ethics in the Confucian Tradition: The Thought of Mencius and Wang Yangming* (Hackett, 2002); *The Laozi or Daodejing*, (Hackett, 2002); and *Readings in Classical Chinese Philosophy* (with Bryan W. Van Norden) (Hackett, 2006).

DAVID JONES is professor of philosophy, editor of *Comparative and Continental Philosophy* (Equinox) and *East-West Connections*, director of the Atlanta Center for Asian Studies, and has been visiting professor of Confucian Classics at Emory. His current books include *The Fractal Self and the Evolution of God* (with John L. Culliney); and *Zhu Xi Now: Contemporary Encounters with the Great Ultimate*) (edited with He Jinli) (State University of New York Press). He is co-editor of *Asian Texts—Asian Contexts: Encountering the Philosophies and Religions of Asia* (State University of

New York Press, 2009); *The Gift of Logos: Essays in Continental Philosophy* (Cambridge Scholars, 2010); editor of *Confucius Now: Contemporary Encounters with the Analects* (Open Court, 2008) and *Buddha Nature and Animality* (Jain, 2007). A past president of the Southeast Regional of the Association of Asian Studies and present president of the Comparative and Continental Philosophy Circle, he was the East-West Center's Distinguished Alumnus in 2004–05.

LIVIA KOHN is a PhD graduate of Bonn University, Germany, and Professor Emerita of religion and East Asian studies at Boston University. A specialist in medieval China, she has spent many years pursuing research on medieval Daoism and Chinese long life practices. She has written and edited more than twenty books and organized numerous conferences and workshops on Daoist practice. Her most recent works include *Introducing Daoism* (Routledge, 2008) and *Daoist Mystical Philosophy* (U. of Hawai'i, 2007). Together with Harold Roth she edited, *Daoist Identity: History, Lineage and Ritual* (U. of Hawai'i, 2002). Her edited works also include the highly recognized two-volume *Daoism Handbook*, and *The Taoist Experience: An Anthology*, as well as *Lao-tzu and the Tao-te-ching*. She is Editor of the *Journal of Daoist Studies.*

RONNIE LITTLEJOHN is chairman of the department and professor of philosophy at Belmont University, where he also is director of Asian studies. He is author of *Daoism: An Introduction* (I. B. Tauris, 2009), and co-editor of *Polishing the Chinese Mirror: Essays in Honor of Henry Rosemont, Jr.* (Global Scholarly Publications, 2008). He is general editor of the forthcoming *The Blackwell Encyclopedia of Asian Religions*, and author of *Confucianism: An Introduction* due for release in May 2010 by I. B. Tauris. Some of his recent articles include, "The Giant Forge and the Great Ironsmith: Revisiting the Wu Xing 五行 Physics of the Zhongyong中庸," in *Dao: A Journal of Comparative Philosophy*. Together with Livia Kohn he is one of the facilitators for the *Journal of Daoist Studies,* and he is a participant in the Southeast Early China Roundtable.

THOMAS MICHAEL graduated from Portland State University with a BA in English literature, French language and literature, and philosophy, and a minor in Chinese language. He received an MA in religious studies from the University of Chicago and a PhD in the history of religions at the University of Chicago, spending a year in Taiwan along the way. He taught at George Washington University in the department of religion and the honors program. He currently teaches in the department of religion at Boston University. His first book, *The Pristine Dao: Metaphysics in Early Daoist Discourse* (SUNY series in Chinese Philosophy and Culture) presents an innovative rethinking of the Daoist tradition, and will be followed by a companion study exploring early Daoist visions of the Sage. He is also currently undertaking a provocative study of shamanism in early China with attention to oracle bones, myth, poetry, song, and official bureaucratic writing.

JEFFREY L. RICHEY is associate professor of religion and director of Asian studies at Berea College. He is editor of *Teaching Confucianism* (Oxford, 2008). His recent essays include "Master and Disciple in the *Analects*," in *Confucius Now: Contemporary Encounters with the Analects* (Chicago: Open Court, 2008); "Teaching Confucianism as a Religious Tradition" (with John H. Berthrong), in *Teaching Confucianism*; "Zhou and Qin Dynasties," in *The World and Its Peoples: Eastern and Southern Asia, Volume 1—China* (New York: Marshall Cavendish, 2007); and "Lost and Found Theories of Law in Early China," in *Journal of the Economic and Social History of the Orient* 49, no. 3 (2006). He is active in the Southeast Early China Roundtable of scholars.

MAY SIM is associate professor of philosophy at the College of the Holy Cross. Her most recent book, *Remastering Morals with Aristotle and Confucius* (Cambridge University Press, 2007), is a comparison of the ethical life in Aristotle and Confucius. Some of her recent essays include "Harmony and the Mean in the *Nicomachean Ethics* and the *Zhongyong*," in *Dao: A Journal of Comparative Philosophy* 3, no. 2 (2004); "Categories and Commensurability in Confucius and Aristotle: A Response to MacIntyre," in *Categories: Historical and Systematic Essays* (Catholic University of America Press, 2004); "A Confucian Approach to Human Rights," in *History of Philosophy Quarterly* 21 (October 2004); "Dewey and Confucius: On Moral Education," in *Journal of Chinese Philosophy: Special Issue on Comparative Developments in Chinese and American Philosophy* (forthcoming); and "Virtue

Oriented Politics: Confucius and Aristotle," in *Aristotle's Politics Today* (State University of New York Press, 2007).

ROBIN R. WANG holds degrees from Peking University, the University of Notre Dame, and the University of Wales. She is associate professor of philosophy at Loyola Marymount University, where she is also director of Asian and Pacific studies. She is co-editor with Livia Kohn of the forthcoming work, *Internal Alchemy: Self, Society and the Quest for Immorality*. She has authored *Chinese Philosophy in an Era of Globalization* (State University of New York Press, 2004) and edited *Images of Women in Chinese Thought and Culture: Writings from the Pre-Qin Period to the Song Dynasty* (Hackett, 2003). Her recent essays include, "Kundao, A Case of Lived Body" (*Journal of Chinese Philosophy* (January 2009); "Zhang Zai's Theory of Qi," in *Companion to Neo-Confucianism*, edited by John Makeham (Springel, 2008); and "Virtue, Talent, and Beauty: Authoring a Full-Fledged Womanhood," in *Lienuzhuan (Biographies of Women) in Authority* in *the Confucian Culture*, ed. Peter Hershock and Roger Ames (State University of New York Press, 2006).

Index

www.ingramcontent.com/pod-product-compliance
Lightning Source LLC
LaVergne TN
LVHW101625040926
847296LV00026B/106